BETTER TO HAVE LOVED

BETTER TO HAVE LOVED | THE LIFE OF JUDITH MERRIL

JUDITH MERRIL AND EMILY POHL-WEARY

BETWEEN THE LINES | TORONTO

First published in Canada in 2002 by

Between the Lines
720 Bathurst Street, Suite 404
Toronto, Ontario M5S 2R4

Earlier versions of chapter 8 were published in the 50th anniversary issue of *Fantasy and Science Fiction* magazine (October/November 1999), and the *New York Review of Science Fiction* (issue 59, July 1993).

Part of chapter 4 was published in the anthology *Women of Other Worlds*, edited by Helen Merrick and Tess Williams, University of Western Austalia Press, 1999.

NATIONAL LIBRARY OF CANADA CATALOGUING IN PUBLICATION DATA

Merril, Judith, 1923–1997.
      Better to have loved : the life of Judith Merril

Includes bibliographical references and index.

ISBN 1-896357-57-1

1. Merril, Judith, 1923–1997. 2. Authors, Canadian (English) — 20th century — Biography. 3. Science fiction, Canadian (English). I. Pohl-Weary, Emily. II. Title.

PS8576.E743Z53 2002   C813'.54   C2002-900110-2
PR9199.3.M44Z464 2002

DESIGN Zab Design & Typography

Printed in Canada by Transcontinental

Between the Lines gratefully acknowledges assistance for its publishing activities from the Canada Council for the Arts, the Ontario Arts Council, and the Government of Canada through the Book Publishing Industry Development Program.

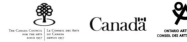

for the extended family
and the universe

Contents

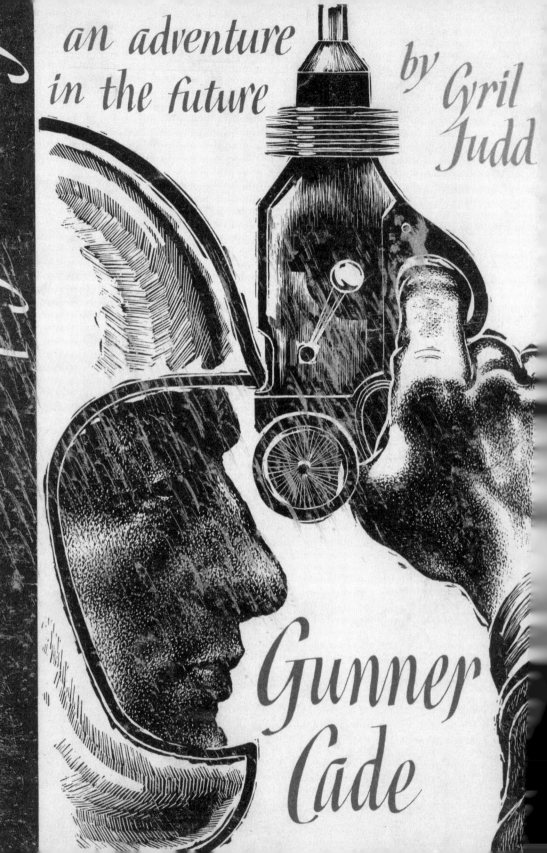

an adventure
in the future

by Cyril Judd

Gunner Cade

Gunner Cade

CYRIL JUDD

SIMON AND SCHUSTER

Acknowledgements

THANKS TO PAUL EPRILE, ROBERT CLARKE, and everyone else at Between the Lines; they have been knowledgeable, professional, and wonderful to work with. My agent, David Johnston of Livingston Cooke, had remarkable faith in the scraps of a manuscript I originally presented to him. The Ontario Arts Council, Canada Council, and Toronto Arts Council all provided financial support either to me or to Judy. Lorraine Filyer at the Ontario Arts Council has been particularly supportive.

Thanks to the Hoity-Toity Writers' Group for editing an early version of the manuscript and ongoing support, especially: Jim Munroe, Paola Poletto, Jessica Westhead, Paul Hong, and Jeff Chapman. Stuart Ross, Allen Weiss, and Ronald Weihs also read versions of the manuscript. For encouragement along the way, thanks to Emily Levitt, Bridget Missabie, Nicole Tremblay, Mary Anne Lacey, Malcolm Rogge, Tanya Battersby, John Hodgins, Gregory Guy, Hal Niedzviecki, and others.

For research, support, help along the way, and ruthlessly picking out errors, thanks to the following members of the science fiction community: Virginia Kidd, Vaughne Lee Hansen, Justine Larbalestier, FEM-SF e-mail list, Barry Wellman, Katie MacLean, Gordon Van Gelder, Nalo Hopkinson, Bryan Cholfin, Elizabeth Cummins, David Hartwell, Lorna Toolis, and others.

Judy owes a lot of thanks to people who kept her writing in the last years of her life, including: Valerie Alia, Maureen Gaulthier, Jim Smith, Judith Sandiford and Ron Weihs, Lorna Toolis, Annette Mocek, Mary Cannings, Sharon Dyer, and all the folks at PAL, and so many others.

My family has given me an inexhaustible supply of love during this lengthy and often emotionally difficult process: Ann Pohl, Walter Weary, Juan Miranda, Maureen Lynn, Julia and Daniel Pohl-Miranda, and Tobias Pohl-Weary. Love also to the people farther away.

And, of course, all my love to Jesse, for being there every day and convincing me to believe in myself.

— Emily Pohl-Weary

Chronology: Important Events in Judith Merril's Life

1923

Judith Josephine Grossman is born on January 21 in Boston to parents Ethel and Samuel (Shlomo) Grossman.

1929

The Great Depression begins; lasts to the end of the 1930s. Her father Shlomo Grossman commits suicide.

1933

Judith, an avid young Zionist, starts sixth grade at the Girls' Latin School.

FALL 1936

Moves with her mother, Ethel, to the Bronx, New York City, when Ethel gets a job at the Bronx House. Starts high school at Morrows High.

1930|38

Goes to Zionist summer camp, reads the Communist Manifesto.

1937|39

Forms an inseparable trio with her best friends Saul and Willy at Morrows High School. Graduates from high school in June 1939.

1939

The Soviet Union makes a pact with the Nazis. Zionism begins to lose its appeal for her.

1940

Meets first husband Dan Zissman at a Trotskyist Fourth of July picnic. They marry on October 26.

1940|41

Judith and Dan live with his parents in Philadelphia. She has several different jobs, ranging from waitress to curtain examiner.

1942 | 43

Gets pregnant with first daughter, Merril, who is born in December 1942. Dan is drafted.

1943 | 44

A camp-following Navy wife and mother, Judith moves seven times to army bases in Chicago, New York, and San Francisco, among others. Merril starts at a nursery school for very young children.

1944

Dan's Trotskyist background catches up with him and the army sends him overseas, into action.

1945

In New York City, Judith meets Johnny Michel, Bob "Doc" Lowndes, and literary agent and editor Virginia Kidd (then Emden), among other literary figures. Shares a railroad flat with Kidd and her daughter Karen, who is the same age as Merril. Judith gets a job as a researcher/ghostwriter.

1945 | 46

Becomes involved as president of Merril's school Parent-Teacher Association. Fights for broad access to public nursery schools. Moves with Dan into an unheated apartment on 19th Street. There is increasing trouble in Judith and Dan's marriage, and they separate. She becomes friends with Jay Stanton and Ted Sturgeon. Takes Merril's name as her pen name.

1945 | 46

Judith is in agent Scott Meredith's stable. She supports herself as a single mother by writing, under pen names, nineteen sports-related short stories for pulp magazines.

1946

Meets Frederik Pohl when he returns from overseas. He moves into her apartment.

1948

In February, divorce from Dan is finalized. In May, Judith's first science fiction story, "That Only a Mother," is published in *Astounding Science Fiction* magazine. She becomes engaged to Fred Pohl, and they marry on November 25.

1949

Writes her first novel, *Shadow on the Hearth*.

1950

The "McCarthy Era" begins in the United States, including widespread sensationalist investigations into suspected U.S. Communists, blacklisting, and political persecution. Judith's first novel, *Shadow on the Hearth*, is published, as well as her first anthology, *Shot in the Dark*. Her second daughter, Ann, is born in September, and she writes her second novel, *Outpost Mars* (originally "Mars Child"), with Cyril Kornbluth, under the pen name Cyril Judd.

1951|52

Her novel *Gunner Cade* (with C.M. Kornbluth, as "Cyril Judd") is serialized in *Astounding Science Fiction*, and then published by Simon and Schuster. She separates from Fred Pohl.

1953

Lives with writer Walter Miller for six months. Divorce from Fred Pohl is finalized.

1954

The Communist Party in the United States is virtually outlawed. *Motorola TV Theatre* (ABC) produces a television dramatization of *Shadow on the Hearth* under the title "Atomic Attack."

1956

Her first *SF: The Year's Greatest* anthology is published.

1956|60

Organizes the first Milford Science Fiction Writers' Conference, with Damon Knight and James Blish. Continues to act as director and board member until 1960.

1960

Pyramid Books in New York publishes her short story collection *Out of Bounds*. Marries merchant mariner and union organizer Dan Sugrue on September 24.

1963

Pyramid publishes her novel *The Tomorrow People*. Separates from Dan Sugrue, but divorce is never finalized.

1965

The United States bombs North Vietnam.

1965|69

Book review editor for *The Magazine of Fantasy & Science Fiction*.

1967

Moves to England for one year. Edits the anthology *England Swings SF*.

1968

Total number of U.S. troops in Vietnam reaches 550,000. Judith attends the Chicago Democratic Convention with her daughter Ann, where Vietnam War opponent Eugene McCarthy runs for the Democratic presidential nomination but loses to Hubert Humphrey.

1968|69

In August Judith immigrates, with daughter Ann, to Canada to become a Resource Person in Writing and Publishing for Rochdale College, Toronto's "Free University."

1969

Doubleday, New York, publishes her short story collection *Daughters of Earth*. Judith helps organize the Committee to Aid Refugees from Militarism (CARM).

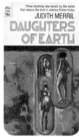

1970

Donates her collection of science fiction literature to the Toronto Public Library system, to found the Spaced Out Library.

1971

Lecturer for science fiction course at University of Toronto. Organizes major international science fiction convention, Secondary Universe Conference, at the Ontario Institute for Studies in Education (OISE), Toronto.

1971 | 83

Writes 25.5 hours of documentaries for CBC-Radio *Ideas*, *Kaleidoscope*, and *Radio International*.

1972

Spends several months in Japan. A collection of her essays on science fiction is published in Japanese.

1972 | 73

Runs a weekly science fiction seminar at SEED alternative high school, Toronto.

1973

Vietnam War ends. The Writers' Union of Canada is founded.

1976

Warner Books publishes a reprint of short stories, *The Best of Judith Merril*. Judith becomes a Canadian citizen.

1977

Kakabeka Pub. Co., Toronto, publishes a short story collection, *Survival Ship and Other Stories*.

1978 | 81

Creates 108 mini-documentaries of three to seven minutes each, to be played following broadcast episodes of *Dr. Who* on TV Ontario.

APPROX. 1983 | 95

Spends winter months in Montego Bay, Jamaica.

1983 | 84

Runs writing workshops at SEED alternative high school.

1985

Founds the Hydra Club North for Canadian science fiction writers. Edits *Tesseracts*, the first-ever anthology of contemporary Canadian science fiction and fantasy. Runs "Out of This World" reading series at the International Authors Festival, Harbourfront Centre, Toronto.

1986

McClelland & Stewart in Toronto republishes a collection of her short stories under the title *Daughters of Earth and Other Stories*.

1991

Toronto Public Library's Spaced Out Library is officially renamed the Merril Collection of Science Fiction, Speculation and Fantasy. Judith has triple-bypass heart surgery.

1992

Moves into the Performing Arts Lodge (PAL) near St. Lawrence Market in downtown Toronto. Tribute to her life held in October at Harbourfront Centre, Toronto, as part of the International Authors' Festival.

1994

Writes "Message to Some Martians" for a CD-ROM, *Visions of Mars*, which is sent by space shuttle to Mars.

1996

Judith attends Wiscon: The Feminist Science Fiction Convention, held in Madison, Wisconsin, as Special Guest of Honor.

1997

Dies from heart failure on September 12.

The second printing of Judith's short story collection *Daughters of Earth*, 1970.

WRITING MY GRANDMOTHER'S AUTOBIOGRAPHY

EMILY POHL-WEARY

Martha begat Joan, and Joan begat Ariadne. Ariadne lived and died at home on Pluto, but her daughter, Emma, took the long trip out to a distant planet of an alien sun.

Emma begat Leah, and Leah begat Carla, who was the first to make her bridal voyage through sub-space, a long journey faster than the speed of light itself.

Six women in direct descent—some brave, some beautiful, some brilliant: smug or simple, wilful or compliant, all different, all daughters of Earth, though half of them never set foot on the Old Planet.
—from the opening of Judith Merril, "Daughters of Earth," 1952

WHEN I WAS SIX YEARS OLD my mother told me she wished she had named me Emma (after the anarchist revolutionary Emma Goldman, I believe). She asked if I would prefer that to Emily, and if I wanted to change my name. I refused, and backed up my refusal with logic by adding, "I'm already used to Emily."

So as an adult, when I reread the introduction to my grandmother Judith's story "Daughters of Earth," I had alternating feelings of shock and dismay. It is

hard to believe that Judy wrote these words in 1952, when she was twenty-nine years old. She was already a Great Science Fiction Writer.

Judy must have been describing our family. She must have been thinking about her mother and her mother's mother. But, in this story, it feels like Judy was also spinning the web of my existence.

This fictional character from her short story "Daughters of Earth," this woman named Emma, speaks deeply to me of a family in which mother influence pervades everyday life. The story, written in 1952, spans six generations of women, making parallels between the lives of grandmothers and their granddaughters. Judy theorizes that if one generation stays close to home, the next one will move far away, and then the cycle repeats.

In my family, as in many families, sometimes it seems like all the women are variations of each other, shaped by known and unknown ancestors as much as through daily experience. This condition fascinated Judy. Many of the stories she wrote were concerned with the kind of change that happens throughout successive generations of women.

My grandmother was not a particularly prolific fiction writer. The importance of her contribution to the literary world rests in the subjects she broached. In the early years of science fiction, when she was the "only smart woman she knew," she wrote with clarity and strength about "female" issues: sex, love, pregnancy, motherhood. She also tackled political issues, including the sensationalist terror of the time—nuclear holocaust—as well as McCarthy-era repression and the House Unamerican Activities Committee. She wrote about the increased fear of difference and of other races (through the concept of alien), especially as experienced during wartime, and about the stifling norms of female sexuality. Although the male-dominated genre might not at first seem like a logical choice for a woman with feminist and left-wing political views, Judy felt at home in the New York City world of science and space-inspired futurist writers of the 1940s. But she couldn't really predict the future, could she?

"Daughters of Earth" continues:

This story could have started anywhere. It began with unspoken prayer, before there were words, when an unnamed man and woman looked upward to a point of distant light, and wondered. Started again with a pointing pyramid; once more with the naming of a constellation; and once again with the casting of a horoscope.

One of its beginnings was in the squalid centuries of churchly darkness, when Brahe and Bruno, Kepler, Copernicus, and Galileo ripped off the veils of godly ignorance so men could see the stars again. Then in another age of madness, a scant two centuries ago, it began with the pioneer cranks, Goddard and Tsiolkovsky, and the compulsive evangelism of Ley and Gernsback and Clarke. It is beginning again now, here on Uller. but in this narrative, it starts with Martha.

☞

Martha was born on Earth, in the worst of the black decades of the 20th century, in the year 1941. She lived out her time, and died of miserable old age at less than eighty years at home on Earth. Once in her life, she went to the Moon.

She had two children. Her son, Richard, was a good and dutiful young man, a loving son, and a sober husband when he married. He watched his mother age and weaken with worry and fear after the Pluto expedition left, and could never bring himself to hurt her again as his sister had done.

Joan was the one who got away.

Judy swore, "When I was about fifteen, it dawned on me that my mother meant for me to be a writer, and I stopped writing completely. I didn't start again until after I had a baby and I was in San Francisco and my mother was in New York."

Despite the late start, she wrote two novels, co-authored two, and wrote almost fifty short stories. Most of them fall into the science fiction genre, and I believe she chose this medium because it allowed her wider scope than any other genre. Later in life (1956 to 1968) she mutated from a writer to an editor to produce her legendary annual series of best of the year anthologies, under various titles beginning with *SF: The Year's Greatest Science Fiction and Fantasy* and ending with *SF 12*. In 1968 she moved to Toronto to join an experimental college called Rochdale and then became a successful "documentarist" for CBC Radio. For much of her life Judy did not stay long in one place.

In the early 1990s, fellow SF writer Spider Robinson said of Judy:

She is far more than merely a national treasure. She is a planetary treasure. The one common writer's ailment she has apparently never suffered is carpal tunnel vision. So long as she is loose in the world with a typewriter and a telephone, no bullshit anywhere is safe. And her typewriter has recently been upgraded with seats and an airbag.

Without Judith Merril, neither science fiction nor Canadian science fiction nor Canadian literature nor the world at large would exist in their present form. Whatever we may make in future of the start she gave us, we who care about Canadian fantasy and science fiction may take some small comfort in being able to say that it is, at least to an extent, all her fault.

After Judy died in September 1997 I found myself rereading stories like "Daughters," trying to better understand myself, my grandmother, and my family. I listened to dozens of taped interviews with her and eventually started to complete her autobiography.

Judy had begun work on her memoirs in the early 1990s but had experienced great difficulties in pulling things together. She found it nearly impossible to conceptualize finishing her autobiography, because once she was finished, what could she possibly do next? Together we tried to capture as many of her stories as possible. We even recorded two tapes filled with descriptions of all the sections of "the book" that she wanted to include. I promised her that if, someday, she was unable to finish, I would take on the job.

Many people who knew Judy will understand that the fire-like intensity of her love and interest in people did not always dampen into strong and lasting friendships. Some people were loved briefly and discarded as no longer interesting, while others, like Fritz Leiber and Walter Miller, were never far from her mind. At times it seemed Judy loved to burn bridges. I often wonder whether I too might have been brushed aside if she didn't need me as constant caregiver. I suppose she found me interesting as well; I was her source of information about the outside world. For Judy, the world was separated into two unequal parts: things that interested her, and mundane details. While at times her distinctions between the two categories seemed arbitrary to me, anything that got relegated to the latter category was quite simply ignored.

In the meantime, unfortunately, Judy didn't sit down nearly enough to write, or even talk, about many of the people who were most important to her. She did the interview about Walter Miller (on which chapter 12, "Walter Miller and the Custody Battles," is based) only five days before she died. I didn't do that interview; it was carried out by Ronald Weihs, of Toronto's Artword Theatre. She had been holding out as long as possible on telling the story on tape because it was heart-wrenching every time the memories came flooding back. Several times, late at night when we were looking through her boxes of yellowing photographs, or when we were sitting together over dinner, she would tell me pieces of the story. The hardest part for her was knowing that Walt had died a couple of years earlier, without trying to get in touch with her.

Walter Miller was not the only one she found it hard to think about. She loved many people with an intensity and a strength that seemed larger than life. The actual process of telling her stories was painful for her, and the end of her life was characterized by a tremendous sadness: her lifelong friends, the people she affectionately called "the Crazies," were dying. Each time one of the Crazies passed away, she lost a chunk of herself. She was so alone. We never even got to talk about the people she loved and lost in the later stages of her life—the feelings were still too fresh.

In the end she left me with a very incomplete manuscript and thorough instructions about everything she wanted included in the final book of memoirs. By the time of her death she had only completed sections on her early childhood and career ("In the Beginning," "A (Real?) Writer: Homage to Ted Sturgeon," and "Getting Started as a Writer"), as well as parts of the sections on feminism, the 1968 Democratic National Convention, and coming to Toronto's free university, Rochdale College. She wrote the introductory essay "Transformations" partly in an attempt to figure out why she was writing this book, and also as part of her applications for grants from the Ontario Arts Council and the Canada Council. Everything else I pieced together from interviews, correspondence, essays she had written earlier in life, and my own memories. Her relationship with Marian Engel and Gwendolyn MacEwen, for instance, was completely pieced together from correspondence. The section on Fritz Leiber (who died four or five years before Judy) also had to be pasted together by scrounging through files and old interviews. Judy had begun her memoirs by writing in a first-person narrative, and so I decided to maintain her personal voice in the pieces I added.

One complicated problem reared its head when I realized that we hadn't captured anything on tape about Judy's everyday life. These things were perhaps too obvious to talk about formally. Because of this, I have had to leave out detailed information about her involvement with the Merril Collection of Science Fiction, Speculation and Fantasy, the Performing Arts Lodge, her dear friends Maureen Gaulthier and Valerie Alia, her attempts to reconcile with her oldest daughter, Merril, and the remaining awful rifts between herself and people who were once close friends. I was also not able to include much about her life in Canada, including great stories about founding the Writers' Union and subsequent battles with Joyce Marshall and others against the "evils of bureaucracy." I got little on her stays in Jamaica or her love of jazz music, except a folder of fading photographs, some flyers and posters for concerts, a dozen tourist knick-knacks, and the short piece "Jamaica: A View from the Beach" (chapter 21).

Due to my lack of information and planning prior to her death, I was forced to leave out entire sections on people she loved, respected, and sparred with during

The fourth birthday party of Judith's granddaughter Julia Pohl-Miranda, April 1989, Toronto. From left: Judith, Adriana Rapetti, Emily, Tobias Pohl-Weary, Daniel Pohl-Miranda, Julia Pohl-Miranda, Ann Pohl, Tashi Moscovitch. *Juan Miranda*

the last decades of her life—such as the people at the Merril Collection and PAL, John Robert Colombo, Jon Lomberg, Ron Weihs and Judith Sandiford, Stafford Beer, Barry Wellman, Candas Dorsey, Élisabeth Vonarburg, David Hartwell, and Phyllis Gotlieb, along with earlier loves such as J.G. Ballard, Forest Ackerman, and Ted Cogswell. I am sure there's another book (or two) to be written here. In the meantime, I decided that the best way to paint a picture of Judy's later years was to reprint a selection of letters to her best loved and not-yet-lost friends; thus the letters in chapter 24 to Kate MacLean, Virginia Kidd, and Valeria Alia—and beginning with some open letters that Judy wrote about once a year to update family and friends.

In the interests of consistency and clarity we have made minor editorial changes and corrections in Judith's unpublished writings and letters, and in the letters of others included here. In some cases, where the material either seemed irrelevant or obscure, we have made cuts in the letters (indicated by [...]). We have also imposed a standard style or format on the dates and addresses given in the letters.

For me, putting the book together has been a learning experience (which is what we call everything that isn't exactly "fun" but is nevertheless a good thing to do). To be fair, some of that experience was beautiful. My family's legacy of intense and strong women is now much easier to comprehend and accept gracefully. I can see clearly how the patterns repeat themselves and bind with individual spirits; and how they mutate. But much of the experience was difficult. There was the section on her future predictions, for instance. It was so depressing, I put it off as long as I could. I chopped it up and rearranged it, and then set it straight again. I didn't agree with what she was saying and felt like her words greatly reflected the loneliness of her last years. Still, when I came across her 1973 essay "Toronto Tulips Traffic and Grass: The Love Token of a Token Immigrant," I was dumbstruck by the way in which her political and moral viewpoints had so thoroughly succeeded in bouncing down through my mother's generation into mine. It was as if she were writing my own reactions to the violent June 15, 2001, Ontario Coalition Against Poverty protest at the Queen's Park provincial legislature building. I called my mother up immediately and commented on that fact. Her response was interesting: she said that Judy's mother had a similar socio-political analysis, and that no one could ever accuse Judy of softening in her old age. It's true. My grandmother fought injustice until the day her heart gave out.

After more than three years of struggling through the interviews and voluminous correspondence files, and picking out pieces to add to the already existing material, I found the book was finally taking shape, culminating in a series of stories about the people and places Judy was connected to, and the projects she engaged in—through (as she says in "Transformations") "almost seventy-five years of a life in which almost all relationships and objectives combined literary, political, and personal intensities, inextricably interwoven."

❧

When I think of Judy, I see stars. She was a person so singular, and possessed of such strength of spirit, that she burned brightly. Of course, those who knew her will remember that she never wore outfits with less than five contrasting colours, that she always left her silver-white hair ghost-wild, that she burped and swore freely and yelled and made mischief—just for the hell of it.

Emily's sixteenth birthday party, November 1989, Toronto. From left: Martin Miranda, Julia Pohl-Miranda, Judith, Emily. *Juan Miranda*

Judy loved so intensely that at times she seemed to me merely the sum of all the people and places that had entered her heart during three-quarters of a century. Her passion was not by any means extended only to people. Her microwave was lavished with the tenderness one might bestow on a favoured pet. The electronic cart she used in her later years was decorated with plastic shopping bags, and treasured for the increase in mobility it brought her.

She wasn't exactly the kind of grandmother every granddaughter dreams of. She never baked, had little interest in my boyfriends, didn't care if I had the flu, and would rather argue than utter warm encouragements any day. She smoked pot. She even bought me my own microwave—I believe because she was tired of feeding me whenever I visited.

Anyway, the raw truth is that I miss Judy dearly. And so, part of the difficulty in putting this book together came in the freshness of the stories, and her extravagance as a storyteller. Judy did not leave out details. She told stories about the people she loved, exactly the way she remembered them. (I found out later that many people remembered them differently.) While she was alive, we were close, and, later, listening to her voice on tape was like having her in the same room with me.

Working on someone else's autobiography—even if it was about my grandmother —was problematic, especially because sometimes I just didn't agree with her. Contrary to the predictions she made in "Daughters of Earth," we never were exactly the same people, and so I frequently found myself cringing while I, nevertheless, continued to type.

She was, at times, rather ornery, and extremely stubborn. After she died I found myself making tough choices about whether to censor her stories, however slightly, for the sake of people I love and respect dearly. At a certain point I realized that Judy's ghost would not strike me dead, and I chose to walk the diplomatic line of middle ground.

If I have left anything or anyone out, and I know already that I have, please forgive me.

PRELUDE

'Tis better to have loved and lost
than never to have loved at all.
—Alfred, Lord Tennyson

SADLY, RICHLY, LOVE OUTLIVES THE LOVER. People change, or don't change, just go different, go away. In the end, one of every pair must die first. If you live long enough, the only sure thing is that, one by one, your lovers leave. Is it hardest when they die or when they stay in place, no longer loving?

Every way to lose a lover is unbearable. But any way to lose a lover does not end the loving. Grief is not knowing where to give the love that does not stop.

TRANSFORMATIONS

I don't read introductions myself: not ahead of time. Anything the author, or his friend or admirer, has to say about it may interest me after I have read the book. Occasionally, I go back to a preface partway through the book, hoping for some sort of background to place unfamiliar or difficult material in context; but that's rare, and there really ought to be a different label for that kind of introduction…

I understand that the basic function of the introduction is advertising. I am supposed to tell you how good the book is and make you want to read (buy) it. Quickly then—this is a good book.

— *from Judith Merril, "Introduction,"* SF: The Best of the Best, *1967*

AT THE TIME I SIT DOWN to write this introduction, *Better to Have Loved* is a collection of memoirs and mementos I have been working at, erratically and unevenly, for almost six years. It is filled with remembrances and reflections of people, places, events, and ideas I have loved and lost during almost seventy-five years of a life in which almost all relationships and objectives have combined literary, political, and personal intensities, inextricably interwoven.

Judith sitting in her favourite chair next to the stereo, in the Performing Arts Lodge apartment, Toronto, 1997. This photo was taken about four months before her death.
Imageries

This book has been taking shape, slowly, through many transformations, from the first hint of an idea twenty years ago. I had been asked to write an "Appreciation" for a posthumous collection of Mark Clifton's stories, and I was reading my way through a fat correspondence file I had not opened for many years. (At the time such deaths had not yet become a commonplace of my old age.) I had met Mark personally only once, briefly, but for five years, in the 1950s, we had been fluent correspondents, friends, confidantes, fellow-thinkers, and critics of each other's work.

I was surprised both by the readability of the letters and by the freshness of much of the content (then twenty-five to thirty years old). I wrote the appreciation as an annotated selection of excerpts from his letters. That file led me to others, and I began to feel that some of the best writing I had ever done was in personal letters, rather than the carefully crafted prose of my public work. So the first idea of this book was that of a very slightly annotated "selected letters."

Then some of my (male) friends and compeers began publishing politely laundered autobiographies of their successes and I was snow-blinded by the bleach in the detergent. Here were lists of stories sold, banquets attended, speeches given, editors lunched, even wives married and divorced, with never a shriek or tear or tremor or orgasm, and hardly a belly laugh anywhere. My memory (notoriously bad for facts and figures, but usually good for character and dialogue) insists that in those down and dirty days of ghetto science fiction most of us were young, passionate, frail, tough, loving, quarrelling, horny human beings, testing ourselves against each other and the world. Somebody, I thought, should tell it like it was.

Some bodies were in fact beginning to do so, most notably Samuel R. Delany in his *Heavenly Breakfast* and Fritz Leiber in his autobiographical columns in an SF magazine. But neither of these writers had been involved in the science fiction community I entered in New York in the early forties; that "literary ghetto" spanning the thirties to the fifties, with its brilliant and intricately interactive population and its clear/mad insights into both human and technological evolution (before the possibilities of wealth and mundane prestige brought in less intense practitioners), which constituted a "movement" (literary and sociological, as in "Bloomsbury") of serious potential scholarly interest.

In January 1990 I had a last long visit with Fritz in San Francisco, during which we were videotaped in a memoir-esque discussion of extraordinary candour. That same month in New York I talked at length with "Chip" Delany about his experiences with autobiographical work, and on the same trip I went to the first birthday party of my (then) youngest relative, great-granddaughter Kelli MacDonald. When I came home I was planning, rather than just thinking about, memoirs. A year later, recovering unsatisfactorily from a heart attack, I got to work on the materials I had been uncovering. Heart surgery the following August left me with a born-again conviction that it was then or never.

Of course, the shape of the thing was changing again. I was living now on borrowed time, and looking back to less cautious and more energetic days. I kept rediscovering what a rich life my own (usually dirt-scratching, single-parent, underpaid-writer experience) had been. The book that had been meant to be about the worlds and people I passed through was becoming more about my joy in passage.

I was once a writer of science fiction; that means my practice has always been to make the environment as important as the characters in a story. So at one level the book that has been finding its shape since then is a bundle of oldie-but-goodie gossip for SF fans and also, of course, for lit-crits and academics. Now that the field is yielding up doctoral dissertations, people want to know stuff that Fred Pohl and Isaac Asimov, etc., never told them about how we lived, dressed, ate, argued, dated, mimeoed our manifestos, and (in some cases) learned step by slow step how to write our stories, and (in even fewer cases) how to make sure we got paid for them.

But some things do change, even in writers' habits. When I was a writer of fiction, nobody ever saw the work until I was completely finished. Now I found myself taking every opportunity to read bits and pieces to audiences and to show the work-in-progress to willing readers. And I learned some things I wasn't expecting.

For one thing, there are a lot of younger people out there trying to figure out, before it's entirely too late, where the hell we are going and (maybe) where we might like to go instead. Some of them realize that the ideas we were playing with back in our dirty little ghetto were often serious under the frequently Bat Masterson-variety of silliness. The basic fact is that an audience likes to have a native guide.

Then again, many young women (and a few young men) with little or no interest in the SF part of it really want to know just how far we have come, baby: what was it like for a "gender-bender" forty or fifty years ago, and particularly for one who is perceived as having "made it" in "a man's world"?

The interest does not limit itself to the gender issues. My life has been a history of significant alternative/subversive "movements." I was born into the early Zionist movement and moved myself as a teenager into the Trotskyism of the thirties and forties (the only political stance that was both anti-U.S.-imperialism and anti-Soviet-Communism). From there I moved on to emergent science fiction;

Judith with her grandson,
Tobias Pohl-Weary, Emily's brother,
St. Catherines, Ontario, 1977.
Walter Weary

then to anti-Vietnam protest and Canadian support of war resisters; which led to the Free University movement, hippie/yippie entanglements, tuning-in and turning-on; all of this accompanied (until they started yelling at us, "Honky, go home!") by involvements with Black issues.

A NOTE TO THE READER: Editors are paid (however poorly) to deal with writers' obsessions. Readers must pay for this privilege. I do not wish to drive my readers mad (or away). I feel I must, however, warn readers right off that those who feel the need to know what-happened-next? might find it uncomfortable to follow my obsessive path.

This is not an autobiography; these are memoirs of my loves, and my most ardent loves have almost always been intertwined with the excitement of ideas. I can only move through my life following my own (however idiosyncratic) trail of memory, thought, and speculation.

I include, from time to time, chronological updates, fleeting mentions of date and place, and at the beginning of the book is a brief chronology of events that occurred during my life.

Judith Merril (1997)

ONE | IN THE BEGINNING

I BELIEVE I HAVE BEEN one of the world's luckiest people.

I feel this way in the face of broken marriages, chronic poverty, some cataclysmic love affairs, and the frequently expressed opinions of many people (who do not know me very well) that I have lived "a hard life." Among the varied reasons for this book is an effort to understand the nature of the magic, the charm, that lasted so long and now—now when they would say my life is "easier"—feels to be fading. Is it a magic fed only by hungers? A charm that fails in the face of repletion—grown daughters, grandchildren, rewards and honours?

I have had a fair, more than fair, number of friends and lovers: mostly men at first, but later mostly women. With all of them I was able to share, to an extraordinary degree, ideas, viewpoints, empathies, ecstasies, hopes, grim humour and grim humours, through written, oral, actional, and subliminal communication.

Most of these people were also writers (most of the rest were musicians), and some of them were also discerning and helpful readers. Some were not people at all, but places, books, music, activities, sensations, or, sometimes dearest of all, ideas. One is tempted to intone an honour roll. But literary logistics demand that my loves enter the narrative one at a time as they did in life—though not necessarily in the same sequence.

In the beginning, I was born to be a writer, and my identity has for so many years been defined, both by the outside world and by my inner consciousness, as a "science fiction writer." Though I have not written new fiction seriously for many years now, I feel I must establish what that odd label means to me. So I begin with the man who was "my editor," because it was he who supplied me with a working definition.

I think most successful writers (and other artists as well?) are so in part because they have found one special person—one ear, one eye—to whom at some vital level all their work is addressed; the mysterious partner who can always perceive what one meant to say, and so can tell whether one has succeeded in saying it.

My editor was a man named Anthony Boucher. That wasn't his birth name. Like me, he had different names at different times in different spaces. In the world of speculative fiction he was Tony Boucher, author, critic, editor, and co-founder of *The Magazine of Fantasy & Science Fiction*, the first—and for many years the only—literary magazine in the field. His other enthusiasms included detective fiction, opera, religion, mathematics, martinis, and logical debate. He was the only person I ever knew who made me wonder—briefly, but seriously—if the Christian concepts of the soul and survival in Heaven might possibly contain some validity, simply because I had never known him to be wrong in an argument. He was one of the first true loves to leave me by dying—almost twenty-five years ago—and because he did somehow manage to believe in Heaven, I can still occasionally imagine I am addressing him when I write.

Tony liked to describe science fiction as "the literature of the disciplined imagination."

Shortly after his death in 1968, in a keynote address to the first Secondary Universe Conference, I described myself, in keeping with his concept, as a "romantic realist." I think this not-quite-oxymoron is central to the psychic profile of any good science fiction writer; if so, I was born to the trade because I had two grandfathers. I knew only one of them: Barney Hurwitch, my mother's father, who was a master tailor in Boston.

My father's father, Joseph Grossman, was a legend. He was the Great Rabbi of Philadelphia. Possibly he was only a great rabbi: perhaps the Jewish community of that city was strong enough in the early years of the century to have had more than one Great Rabbi. If so, Rabbi Grossman would surely have had an edge for legendary status, because all the members of his large family seem to have been either spiritually or artistically prominent. The Grossmans, when not rabbis, were writers, radical intellectuals, symphony musicians, or, at a minimum, teachers.

Rabbi Grossman died shortly before my birth, and I was, officially, named after him: my birth certificate says "Josephine." But the ink was hardly dry—or so the legend goes—when the telegram arrived from my grandmother: "If it's a girl, don't name her after him." My parents heaved a sigh of relief and took advantage of a provision of the laws of the State of New York (designed for Catholics, who take an additional saint's name at confirmation) to call me Judith.

"Judith J." it says on all the school records. For half a century, roughly, I carried Joseph around encysted in my legal identity (until my Canadian citizenship papers made the pen name, by which I was generally known, my legal name).

In the early "Judith J." years, this grandfather seemed more trouble than he was worth. We moved a lot when I was a kid; I once figured out I was in nine different schools by Grade 6. Only one of those was in New York. In Boston

Judith as a young girl, about eight years old. circa 1931. *Courtesy of the Merril estate*

and Philadelphia, every time my records arrived at a new school we had to prove again that Judith was indeed Josephine. Most of the bureaucratic hassles were fielded by my mother, but in Grade 4 I was somehow left to plead my own case. When I said, sensibly and respectfully (I thought), "But can't you see I was born?" I was slapped for my impertinence.

I did not love my unknown grandfather.

Later I heard bits of legend, such as surround all famous rabbis, and I am sorry now I never knew him. But as a child, I liked to keep my legends at a distance: Babylon, Greece, Camelot, Robin Hood; The Virginian (whom I otherwise loved) was a bit too recent. I was having problems enough with Shlomo's legend.

My father, Samuel Solomon Grossman—Shlomo—was adored. He was the youngest of a family of thirteen, all of whom adored him. My mother adored him. I adored him. The Jewish community within which he worked adored him. Oddly, I have yet to hear anything to indicate he didn't deserve all this love and admiration, although it is possible his dad, the Great Rabbi, might have had a different view. Shlomo was meant to carry on the family business, but halfway through Seminary he decided he did not actually have a calling and went to live in "bohemian" Greenwich Village and be a writer.

He abandoned the orthodoxy of his family, but not his Jewishness; he worked for the newly formed Bureau of Jewish Education, writing children's songs and plays; he worked for the Yiddish newspaper, the *Forvarts*, as a columnist and drama critic; he was one of the founders of the Yiddish Art Theater; he translated

Simcha, Judith's brother, who died at the age of three, circa 1924.
Courtesy of the Merril estate

the work of Sholem Aleichem, whose stories of Jewish life in Russia in the late nineteenth century were later loosely adapted for the musical *Fiddler on the Roof.*

At the education bureau Shlomo met Ethel Hurwitch, from Boston. They married and had a baby boy, named Simcha—Hebrew for "joy." For three years all went well; then, in the epidemic that followed World War I, Shlomo contracted encephalitis. He was in hospital when I was born, and from that time on the legend spiralled downward: Ethel was laid low with rheumatism; Simcha was hit by a car and killed; the quick wit and fluent phrases that had made Shlomo the white-haired boy of the Jewish cultural community dimmed in the aftermath of his disease. Broke, and broken, they went to live with Ethel's family. When I was six, Shlomo jumped out of a window. In 1929 window-jumping was the way to go.

Fifteen years later, when I had a daughter of my own, I wrote a very short story about that day. Rereading it now, I do not remember the events—but I remember remembering every word and gesture at the time I wrote it. Words are strong magic: when I have written something out, I no longer have to carry it in my head; conversely, I am never sure what I think about a new idea until I have written it out. Here is what I wrote, when I was twenty-one, before I had decided to be a writer.

PICTURE OF GRACE

She couldn't go out and play because Daddy would be back very soon, and he had promised to bring her a wonderful surprise if he got the job, so Grace sat in the big chair with Mummy, and watched the other children playing in the backyard under the window.

When she got tired of that, she started asking Mummy what Daddy would bring. Would it be a picture book? And how big? And what kind of pictures?

After a while she realized Mummy was getting nervous again and she knew she better stop talking about the picture book. She was just trying to think of something else to do when the bell rang.

Grace practically rolled off the chair onto the floor, and scrambled to keep up with Mummy hurrying to the door. But Mummy got there first, and Grace heard her quick gasp and the loud sound of the breathless words before she could see that it was Grampa and Uncle William, and not Daddy at all.

"It's Mike! Something's happened."

Grampa and Uncle William pushed the door shut, and Mummy backed away before them until she was sitting on the couch, and they were standing over her, looking bigger than they really were. Somebody had motioned Grace over to the love seat in the corner of the room, where she knew she wasn't supposed to be able to hear them.

She sat there very quietly and heard Grampa say it.

"He's dead, Elsie. It was an accident."

He said it just like that, and Grace knew she had known all along that was what he had been going to say. The big tears started rolling very slowly down Mummy's cheeks, and Grace just sat there taking up space. She wanted to tell Grampa that he was wrong, and go over and tell Mummy it was all right. She thought she would do it in just a minute, but she didn't.

She just sat there and pretended she hadn't heard. She knew they hadn't meant her to hear, and she knew if she had she ought to be crying. She remembered how she had cried for hours and hours when Gramma died, and now it was her own Daddy, and nothing was happening.

She sat there in desperation, on the love seat in the far corner of the room, wondering what she would do when they told her, wondering why she didn't cry.

Then Mummy called from the sofa, with the big tears still coming down her cheeks though she wasn't crying out loud.

"Grace, honey, did you hear?"

"No," she lied, and it was quite easy, except that her voice sounded very loud, and she was sure Grampa knew she was lying.

"Come here, dear."

Obediently she got up and crossed the room. She stood very close to her mother, and heard her say the words.

"Daddy's dead, Grace. He got hit by a car."

Then Mummy's face got all twisted up, and her whole body was shaking with sobs. Uncle William was pulling out a very large white handkerchief and Grace tried to pat Mummy's hair. She was beginning to understand now. Daddy was dead. There would be no picture book. No surprise. No new job, and no wonderful smile and hug when he got home.

She sat down and put her arm around her mother. She found it is really very easy to cry when you try.

We had been living in Boston with my grandfather Barney and my spinster aunt Nan for a year, more or less, when this happened. I was not allowed to go to the funeral, and nobody told me the truth. They said he'd fallen down some stairs and hit his head, but I knew better. I knew the "accident" was because my father wasn't making any money. So he had made a dummy and thrown it down the stairs so he could go away on his own and earn a lot of money and come back. I put myself to sleep with that every night for a year before I gave up on it. (I was eighteen before I found out again what it was I had agreed not to hear.)

My private fantasy faded, but the public legend didn't. All the time I was growing up, at holiday gatherings, and Zionist events, and summer camp and Hebrew School, sooner or later someone would come over and pat my head or tilt up my chin, and say—once more with feeling—"So this is Shlomo Grossman's daughter!?"

❧

My Zaidy Barney was the antidote. Nobody adored Barney, and he didn't adore anybody. He was a tailor, and all the men in his family had been tailors, back in Babroisk, in Lithuania.

His oldest brother, William, came over to Boston first, opened his tailor shop, and, one by one, brought the other brothers over to work for him. Barney was the master tailor; with his designs and cutting, William eventually opened a women's wear specialty shop on Beacon Street. William got rich; Barney worked for him. Barney was highly skilled and decently paid, and both he and my Aunt Nan worked right through the whole Depression, but Barney was just too irreverent to get rich.

We could talk to each other. When he was sick for a long time, I was his favourite company because I wasn't unduly respectful and we found the same things funny. He was practical, iconoclastic—probably secretly atheist—and endlessly inventive. When I asked him how his hair got so white, he said it used to be blond but he washed it too much. When I asked how come a Jew had blond hair and blue eyes, he said, "There must have been a Cossack in the woodpile."

All the others of his generation talked an inflected Yiddishized English, but Grampa spoke colloquially. When he first came over, he told all the girl machine operators in William's shop to slap him every time he said something wrong. He sat up there cross-legged on the master tailor's table and got giggling slaps till he could speak Boston English.

I remember only one real clash. My mother and father had both imbued me with Zionism; after Shlomo's death we were always about to go to Palestine (not yet Israel) and live in a kibbutz, and I was a dead-serious Hebrew student. One year I realized that Grampa Barney was skipping whole sections of the readings when he presided at the Seder, the ritual Passover feast, and I called him on it. I guess the only thing Joseph and Barney shared was a passion for language, but even there they were at opposite poles.

My favourite Rabbi Grossman story was one I heard from my first mother-in-law, Sara, who grew up in Philadelphia. Sara had a brother named Ben who was very pious as a child, and who in fact grew up to be a rabbi. One day when Ben was nine years old, his mother sent him to the butcher on Friday morning to buy the chicken for the Erev Shabbos dinner. They were very poor, and Friday night was the only time they had meat. On the way home Ben started to worry; that chicken had not looked just right to him. He took it back to the butcher: "I don't think this chicken is kosher." The butcher told him to get out and go home. He started off again, worried some more, and went instead to the neighbourhood rabbi, showed the chicken, and was told it had not been properly killed.

Ben was desperate. He knew there was no more money for another chicken; he was afraid to go back to the butcher; he could not go home and knowingly expose the whole family to sin. He decided this was a job for Rabbi Grossman.

It was about six miles to the rabbi's home. Ben walked all the way, carrying the chicken. When he got there, the rebbitsin, Mrs. Grossman, answered the door and told him crossly that the rabbi couldn't be disturbed, he was preparing for Erev Shabbos.

Ben burst into tears. She relented. The rabbi appeared, heard the story, looked at the chicken, nodded, and went into a back room. He came out with a giant volume of *The Law*, opened it, put on his prayer shawl, and read at high speed for ten minutes. He slammed the book shut, wrapped up the chicken, and said, "There. It's kosher."

I got the iconoclasm from Barney, and the love of ritual from Joseph; the need to communicate clearly from one and the razzle-dazzle from the other; hands-on practicality here, love of abstruse theory there; I was pre-programmed to be a romantic realist and write stories of the disciplined imagination.

TWO | A MEMBER OF THE UNIVERSE

A MAN WHO LOVED ME ONCE described his inner image of me: a little girl with her nose pressed against the outside of the bakery window, feasting on all the inaccessible delights inside.

The image felt like a fit: more than that, it felt good. It is indeed where I am most at home, where I feel—uncomfortably—most myself: out there looking in at heaven.

☙

Dorchester, in Boston, 1934: I was eleven. Once again, my mother and I were living with my grandfather Barney and my Aunt Nan.

Our house was at the top of a crescent that rose from the main street and curved back down: a two-family house owned by a large Italian family who made wine and baked bread every week and raised vegetables and fruit and chickens in the backyard.

I had just been to the Saturday movie matinee to see *The Little Minister*, a 1934 film starring Katharine Hepburn and based on the James M. Barrie story about a Scottish pastor falling in love. It was a big reading year for me, and I had just recently devoured all of Sir James Barrie, most famous for his "Peter Pan" character.

To walk home from the movie house along the streets was half a mile or so, but I took the shortcut across two backyards. It was dusk, just—perhaps late fall or early spring?—a magical light. I stood on the top rail of the fence separating the sandy yard behind me and our chicken-and-garden-filled yard, and my eyes were full of tears, my throat was all lumped up. The tears were terrible sadness and exultant joy and everything, and I joined the universe.

That wasn't the only time. If you're going to be a member of the universe you have to keep joining. You never know when it will happen— Ornette Coleman's "Lonely Woman" in the Vanguard in New York ... mist in the mountains of central Japan ... certain rare secret moments of lovemaking ... parts of Beethoven's "Seventh" ... a meteor shower at midnight by the side of the highway in the Texas panhandle ... first sunlight at dawn on the waters of Montego Bay ... Duke Ellington's "Diminuendo" and "Crescendo in Blue" ... sometimes city lights coming on at twilight, in New York, San Francisco, Toronto ... the home-birth of my youngest grandson ... LSD with a beloved friend in an orange grove in Florida ... a clear soprano voice, a cappella, singing "L'cha Dodee"—"Come, O Sabbath Queen"—from the last row of wooden seats under the great tree where we had Saturday morning services at Camp Tabor—most often outdoors or with music or both, but where- and however, a thrill races along all your nerves and a smile explodes from your very centre onto your face.

The Little Minister/back-fence time was not really the first, but it was the first time I knew that I was joining the universe.

I have a thick folder of fragments in my files. One of them is from my first try at writing about this; no date, but it must have been 1969 or 1970, shortly after I moved out of Rochdale College in Toronto.

I have never been able to feel quite at home in any of the restricted-membership clubs. That's a tautology of course, because all clubs are membership-restricted: that's what they're all about. So what I mean is, anything less than the universe seems like too damn less. Once, twice, three times, I found clubs that felt as if they included all I knew of the universe. They had people in them with some of that tear-shimmering vision, and each of them let me feel comfortable and at-home inside for a while—a place a little smaller than the whole starry-skied cosmos to settle in—a place, say, to look out the window from. But the thing

Judith's head cut and pasted against an image of the Milky Way, circa 1958. She appears to be about thirty-five years old.
Unknown origins, courtesy of the Merril estate

about a window is, it's in a wall. All clubs are restricted. After a while you either settle for some part of the universe, a corner somewhere with perhaps some gorgeous or instructive views—or else you find out little by little, and with a terrible acceptance of loneliness, that all the walls you can really stand to live with are already built into your skin.

Any corner is only a corner.

We had the top floor and attic in that house on the crescent, and there was a little square cupola on top—what they used to call a "Widow's Walk" in New England. It was my place. The only way to get in was a trap door at the top of a ladder and none of the adults could—or would?—go up there. It had windows around all four sides, and the house was on a bit of a rise; no matter which way I turned, I could see what seemed to be all the world, except for one small arc where high hills cut off the horizon. At age eleven I found that it was enough to look out at, and looking down felt good in those days too. (Now I prefer to look up.)

Eleven was a big year, in several different ways. I fell in love for the first time, with Errol Flynn as Captain Blood. (I was reading my way straight through the Rafael Sabatini shelf in the library.) Then I read myself out of the children's section, and my mother went down and intimidated the librarian, so I could take out adult books. I read my first Thorne Smith novel, *Skin and Bones*, and my first Aldous Huxley, *Brave New World*. (The librarian did question that one, but I assured her it was on my school reading list; I thought I was taking out *The Good Earth*.)

I started smoking. My mother never noticed while I was stealing her cigarettes, but when I bought a pack of my own and she found them in my old doll carriage in the attic, she blew up.

I got my first bra, after some boys in the schoolyard yelled something about "sandbags." With it came, of course, in those days, the first girdle—something called a "pouf." I got my first period, and a stern talk about not letting boys "touch" me now, because I could get pregnant. And I got my first boyfriend: Cyril Hirsch Brown (!!! Where did that come from? I can't remember the names of people I met last week!!!), who took me to Open House Day at M.I.T.

I got an astronomy book. It wasn't from the library; somebody gave it to me; it was my own. It was beautiful, with unusually glossy pages and glittering star photographs. I think it was a book for young people by Sir James Jeans, but I may be confusing it with any number of star and cosmology books from later years, because the whole thing was traumatic. I loved it until I got to the Infinite Universe in Chapter 7. Infinity, the book said, was beyond measurement. I did not understand.

There were a few adults in my life who had sometimes given me usable answers to difficult questions. I asked each of them, and they all said the same thing: the universe was indeed infinite, and "infinite" meant "beyond counting."

Before I tangled with Chapter 7 I had almost decided not to be either a lawyer or an architect, but an astronomer. I gave it up. I never finished the book. (Did I throw it away or give it away?) I was troubled and confused, but more than anything else I was angry.

Astronomy clearly was a clever and cruel hoax. How was one to live in a universe that was beyond perception, beyond numeration, beyond conceptualization? Beyond even definition, because nobody could tell me what infinity was, only what it wasn't. And that answer was simply absurd: you can always keep counting—just add one more, indefinitely—infinitely, if you have (as in an infinite universe) infinite time to keep counting!

I had neither the information nor the will to contradict all these authorities. I was, quite simply, terrified. So I devised my own cosmography.

I constructed a mental model of the universe composed of two infinities cancelling each other out: the scientific and the theological. I did not believe in the mystic/anthropomorphic biblical God; no more than did any intelligent adult I knew. Now I disbelieved equally in their mystic/"scientific" cosmology. The universe is "infinite"? "Infinite" means more than we can count or measure? Fine! Outside that infinitude is a Great Big Box—much too big and remote for us to perceive or count or measure it; and on the Box sits God, in a rocking chair, white-bearded, stern, kindly, rocking.

I remember the relish with which I used to describe my little model, and the silences that ordinarily followed my scientific heresy. They never were quite sure it was a joke.

After a while I was able to keep on joining the universe.

THREE | HIGH SCHOOL

ONE OF MY MANY childhood moves was from Boston to New York just before my sophomore year of high school, because my mother had been offered a job running a place called the Bronx House, which was a settlement home for young offenders. It was the first job she had been offered that was not as a dietitian.

I loved returning to New York. I didn't like the settlement house so much. My mother had a room there, and initially I shared it with her. We had already been through several live-in job situations where I had been uncomfortable as her daughter, and to my mind this one was even more awful. Living in a settlement house meant I had to deal with a lot of potential delinquents.

Eventually I complained so much that she found me a place to live a couple of blocks away from her with a woman who was, in fact, the writer Jack London's widow. She was a real thrill: European, ultra-clean, ultra-severe in her approach to everything. There was no conceivable way I could live there and satisfy her. I was always too dirty, too messy. Inevitably, I ended up back at the settlement house with my mother.

I did not love the Bronx House. But high school I loved from the beginning. The Bronx neighbourhood was a new and different world for me—I was a sponge soaking up the ambience, not a cultural connoisseur. I don't know how to describe it exactly; there's nowhere else like the Bronx, and it was nothing like it is now.

Mainly, of course, I was concerned with what was going on at school. I learned to fit in quickly, but still I felt very much like an outsider. When I first came to New York, I had a Boston accent, which sounds affected to people in the Bronx. The first semester I was in high school, my way of speaking was being influenced by living in the Bronx—bit by bit my accent was changing. I was anxious to sound like the rest of the kids.

I remember one particularly humiliating day when I was reciting in geometry class. In the same sentence I said half with a Boston accent and then half with a Bronx accent. The entire class broke up in five minutes of hilarity. The laughter seemed to go on and on and on.

The other kids were convulsing because they had just discovered that, as they suspected, my accent was fake and phoney. All because I had slipped this once. As a teenager, you don't make mistakes about that kind of laughter. When it happens, you know what it's about. It's about hating and fearing smart ones. I knew it even then.

In retrospect, I owe a lot to that moment because I stood up there in front of the class while everybody else was laughing hysterically, and the teacher just looked around bewildered (he was a little old man with chalk dust all over his jacket), and I swore to myself, "I am going to learn to speak in such a way that no one will ever know where I'm from."

And I did.

Judith around the age of sixteen, circa 1939.
Courtesy of the Merril estate

❧

In Boston, where I was living before the Bronx, there was a school, the Boston Public Latin School, which had a long and honourable history. It was the first secondary school in the colonies, and had always been a college prep school.

A companion school, called the Girls' Latin School, was opened. To get in you had to have a high average from grade school. It was located downtown and drew the best students from the entire city. For my mother, it was an honour and an achievement that I got selected to go to that school. I don't know if she was impressed, exactly, but she was pleased.

No boys for me, then. It was all very academic. The best part of Girls' Latin, to be honest, was the gym classes. It was the only time I ever went to a school where the phys ed was for girls, instead of imitation boys. We didn't play baseball. We had tennis, swimming, fencing, archery, and dance. It was extraordinary to finally be doing things I wasn't naturally bad at. I could never catch or throw a ball, I could never run well, I was always the last one chosen for any team. While I was at Girls' Latin, I found out I was a good swimmer, and good at water sports.

I also found it interesting that everyone at the school was a good student—you were expected to be good—so we didn't have a lot of drag in the classes. It was an all-girls' school, and we were expected to be able to achieve.

I don't remember any of the teachers from the girls' school. There was one teacher who read poetry marvellously, but I don't remember her name or recall her doing anything else that was interesting. I don't think I learned much there honestly.

It was great going to a girls' school for those two years. But it was much greater going to Morrows High School afterwards.

☙

Throughout my two years at Morrows, I had some memorable teachers. (I had some bad teachers too, but that's to be expected. In comparison to the bad, the good teachers were even more of a surprise and delight.)

Geometry came to me like water. There was the teacher who was totally in love with math but couldn't teach for shit. Fortunately, I didn't need anyone to teach me geometry, so we were really on each other's wavelength. According to the rest of the class (and this is probably the best example I can give of how everybody really does hate the smart girl) I was too smart in geometry. I made them look bad. I couldn't be bothered memorizing everything. We were supposed to memorize both the axioms and the theorems and then work out problems. The axioms were fairly obvious, but I never learned all the theorems. I just worked everything out each time by starting with the axiom and working my way through. After a while I would have my hand up for every question, but the teacher wouldn't call on me until he was sure no one else could do it.

The Latin teacher, Mr. Coyle, was Irish, close to retirement, and a dedicated classicist. Morrows High did not offer Greek, but Mr. Coyle volunteered to give private classes. Anytime there were at least four students who wanted to learn Greek, they could just come to his office and have a private class there. Mr. Coyle's heart broke when I wouldn't take the Quenelle exams. I had had two years of Latin at the Girls' Latin School, and then two more years at Morrows High. At the end of the second year at Morrows, I took a regional mid-term exam that was really supposed to be taken after three years. I got 96 per cent. Mr. Coyle talked me into repeating the class so that I could take the exam again the following year and get 100 per cent, because the average got sent out for consideration for state scholarships. Mr. Coyle was also active in the student government, so he was really my advisor, my guidance director, and everything else. I disappointed him bitterly when I went to City College. That wasn't what he wanted for me. He wanted me to become a person who studied languages, or an academic. I had never the faintest inclination to become an academic, but he was a wonderful man.

Another person who left a great impression on me was my economics teacher. He was young, maybe in his first or second year of teaching. It was only a one-semester course. When we got onto the subject of yellow journalism, he said, "Now there is one publisher in this country, whose name I will not mention, but whose initials spell R.A.T." And the whole class started yelling, "Hearst! Hearst! Hearst!" We were referring to the head of the *New York Journal*, William Randolph Hearst.

Then there was the history teacher who knocked my self-esteem down a bit. When his class started, I found the textbook incredibly fascinating and read the whole thing in one week. He quickly realized that I had read the entire book, and knew all the material. He required us to keep a notebook, with notes on each week's assignment of so many pages of reading, but he excused me from this, since I had already done the work. He said to me, "Judith, just be sure you review before class. Glance through the relevant pages and see what the lesson is going to be about."

Of course I never reviewed any of it. Then, when we were up to the French revolution, he asked a couple of people to tell him about the fall of the Bastille. Nobody seemed to know anything about it. After a time he turned to me and said, "Now Judith, will you please tell us in your most dramatic and literary terms about the fall of the Bastille?"

I remembered nothing of that section of the book. I did remember riffling through a copy of *Life* magazine from Bastille Day the previous summer, and I remembered a lot of the pictures, so I told them all this fascinating story about the mobs in cars storming the Bastille and tearing it down stone by stone and freeing all the prisoners.

At the end of my story, the teacher said, "Very interesting story, Judith, I wonder where it happened."

My high-school boyfriend was a guy named Willy, who was a year ahead of me. He was an artist who grew up to be an economist. He was already quite involved in economics while we were still in high school. His parents were from Czechoslovakia or Poland, but he had grown up in the United States. His home life was European intellectual. His mother was into all kinds of health foods, and Willy and I were given a great deal of freedom: he was supposedly painting, so nobody would interrupt us.

We did a lot of petting and making out but I remember us having this entirely serious conversation on a park bench. We had been debating whether we should go all the way. Finally we both agreed that although he, being a boy, needed some release I, being a girl, was better off postponing anything like that. Ultimately we decided he should go find sex somewhere else.

It was agreed upon between us, but I think it was probably my idea. It was a painful decision, but it seemed to make the most sense. I would have been fifteen or sixteen when we came to this conclusion. (When I was seventeen I met Danny Zissman and we didn't actually screw until after we decided to get married.) It had nothing to do with him being respectful. It had to do with what we thought was appropriate and proper in the entire context of the politics of physiology.

Willy got me involved in student government. He was school president in his last year there and I was also involved. I don't remember what rank I attained, but I wasn't that interested in being a power figure. Willy was—he went to City College initially, but he wound up at Princeton as a really hot-shot economist in the Institute for Advanced Studies.

☙

I had a tumultuous and lonely adolescence, and I do not confess that easily. I didn't know I was good-looking, and therefore nobody around me knew I was good-looking. Some guys were specifically interested in my mind, but when they told me that I was good-looking, I knew they were either lying or else inflamed with passion, so I never got any satisfaction out of it.

I hear that lots of girls languish their way through high school without a boyfriend. But I didn't seem to know any. Everybody else had a boyfriend. It was the Depression, you understand, there was nothing else to do.

I didn't "date" any of the guys I knew in high school. Willy and I didn't really go out on dates. We just hung out together. We spent most of our spare time at his house, or my house, or in parks. We didn't go out on real dates, and for me, at the time, real dates were where it was at.

The first real date I ever had was with a guy named Charlie Starr. He was a couple of years ahead of me in high school, and he invited me to his high-school prom. Charlie had a big crush on me. He was an oaf, basically—a nice agreeable oaf, but an oaf nonetheless.

We went to the prom with two other couples. Every year the high-school prom was held at the Astor Hotel, so before it started we took the bus down from the Bronx to Jack Dempsey's, which was a bar on 49th Street, and ordered three cocktails. We passed them around so that everybody got a taste. Then the boys filled their pockets with peanuts and we went off to the prom by taxi, even though it was only seven blocks away, so that everyone would see us arrive in a cab.

That trip was Charlie's first time out of the Bronx. I used to go downtown once in a while to buy tickets for standing room at a theatre. I also used to go downtown to the museums. I knew how to behave. Charlie had never been out of, probably, a thirty-block circuit around the Bronx, and he didn't find this at all odd. He was a Jewish boy from the Bronx who was going to grow up to be a more contemporary version of my Uncle Al, who had a factory and was a patriarch. Why he got fixated on me I will never know.

But that was my first experience of dating. I had been to the movies with a few guys, but always in the afternoon after school, never as an evening date. After that I had a couple more dates with Charlie, but nothing as memorable as the trip we made to Jack Dempsey's and the Astor.

It was the Depression, so nobody had any money, and dates cost money. There were four or five girls in my home-room class who dated regularly. These were the queens of the class. For some reason, the fact that I had no real dates was significant and, indeed, torturous for me.

Willy and I used to ride the 5th Avenue open-top buses all the way downtown. The route flowed near where I lived. There were two variations of this route. One took you down to Washington Square and back, giving you about three or four hours all together of necking on top of the bus. The other route took you down to Times Square.

To put things in context a bit, the 5th Avenue bus was a pretty expensive "date" because it was a ten-cent fare to go down to Washington Square and back. All the other bus fares were only five cents. The great thing about the bus (and what made us take it again and again and again) was that on 42nd Street, in between the burlesque houses, there was a hot dog stand where you could get a hot dog and a malted for a nickel. (Also, in New York at that time, the only place you could neck, other than the movies, was on the top of the 5th Avenue bus.) So for thirty cents Willy and I could pay the 5th Avenue bus fare, spend ten cents on food, and have an entire glorious evening of pleasure.

However, I could never tell my friends, "I have a date for Saturday night. I'm going to dress up for my date. We're going to such-and-such a place." It was more like Willy and I would already be hanging out, doing whatever we normally did, and we would figure out whether we had enough money to ride the bus. We always pooled our money, if we had any, and the person with money was more often me than him.

There is one other important high-school guy who was much more significant to me than any of my boyfriends, although he was never technically one himself. The name I knew him by was Joe Smith. Joe was the ranking young communist at Morrows High. He was the organizer for the American Student Union, the front organization for the Young Communist League.

At that point I had not yet encountered the Trotskyists, so I was still a

Camp Tabor: Judith's Zionist girls' summer camp, circa 1938. She is fourth from the right in the third row up.
Courtesy of the Merril estate

socialist. Joe and I spent most of our time together arguing politics. It was the time of the Moscow trials, and I used to describe myself as the only kid at Morrows High who went directly from socialist to Trotskyist without passing through communist. This was because nothing in this world would have seduced me into the Stalinists—not just because of the Moscow trials, but because the tyranny in the Soviet Union was obvious to all those of us who cared to see it. I knew even then that Stalin's regime was the opposite of everything my socialist principles were concerned with.

That said, Joe and I enjoyed each other's company without any element of sexuality being involved. We were straight politics, all the way. We went to see *Snow White* when it came out, and even though we were both absolutely gripped by the movie, when it was over we sat down and hashed out a whole political analysis of it.

Later, after high school, Joe told me that he had been assigned by the Young Communists to go to Morrows High. He also told me that the name he was using was a false one he had created to use while organizing.

It is important to remember that the entire context of my high-school time was a political one—fully half of the students in that school were confounders of welfare. The strongest single group in the school was indeed the American Student Union.

☙

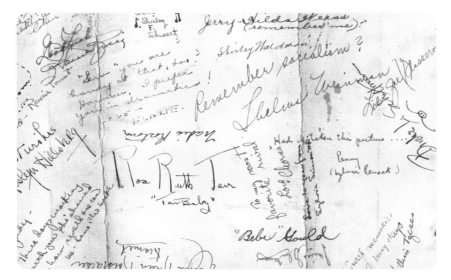

There is one example from back in my early high-school days where a guy didn't initially run from me. At my girls' summer camp we had Saturday morning Shabbat services, and all the boys from a camp across the lake would come to join us because they didn't have any services over there. Occasionally we also had dances with these boys. At the dances I was a complete wallflower. Nobody ever danced with me, except one of the boys' counsellors named Bob, who seemed dedicated to teaching me some of the flirting skills I didn't know anything about. He was the sweetest guy in the world. He tried to show me that I knew how to dance, and he did mock-gallant things such as offering me a flower down on his knees.

Meanwhile I had become friends with one boy who was quite nerdish, because we were both left out most of the time. It seemed to me that he was not totally stupid, so one day when he came over to services I lent him my copy of *Das Kapital*. I think this might be what piqued Bob the counsellor's interest in me.

However, a couple of weeks later two other boys brought the book back to me with the message that my so-called friend didn't want to talk to me any more. I think it was because a counsellor (not Bob) had seen him reading the book and told him to return it immediately to whoever gave it to him.

The funny part is that these other two boys who had to bring the book back to me were visibly curious, and wondering, "What is this stuff? What kind of girl can this be?" They weren't analyzing anything on a political level, they just had a kind of extreme curiosity.

FOUR | WHAT KIND OF FEMINIST AM I?
(A SHORT HISTORY OF SEX)

MY MOTHER RAISED ME to be a man. I don't mean she dressed me in boys' clothes, or fought to get me onto boys' teams. Quite otherwise. She scorned athletics. And being a tailor's daughter herself, she made over good-fabric hand-me-downs for me and made them beautiful. (But not me; I wasn't beautiful.)

My mother came to Boston from Russia with her parents when she was five. Soon she was assistant mother to six younger siblings. She was a reader, but for the eldest daughter of hard-working immigrant parents, post-secondary education was a romantic dream. She did manage to take a couple of extension courses at Harvard with philosopher and psychologist William James after she started working in the family dress shop. She was a bluestocking, a suffragette, and one of the founders of Hadassah. I have to feel back for memories through the years when I did not want to hear anything she said. I would guess she had little use for other women, and no use at all for being one. Although she was beautiful in the style of the day, she remained a spinster till the advanced age of thirty.

She never trained me to hide my light. I was encouraged to argue analytically, to assert my opinions, to demonstrate in every possible way how smart I was. Mom kept telling me it was too bad I was so plain, too bad I had no talent for music or art, too bad I was no good at sewing or cooking—but then I didn't need any of those things, did I? I was smart, and I could write.

I didn't know I was supposed to need a man's protection, because I never had it. I wanted to have "dates" like other girls, but the few times I actually went out on them I felt stiff and awkward—and usually bored. I wasn't lonely; there were always boys around, almost all my friends were boys. I did send away for free makeup samples, but I never let my mother know, and I hardly used them, because I had nobody to try them out on.

I didn't want anything my mother wanted. When I was fifteen I realized she meant for me to be a writer, and I even stopped doing any serious writing. I didn't start again until much later, when I was a mother myself and living far away from my mother.

Ethel and Samuel (Shlomo) Grossman, Judith's parents, circa 1920.
Courtesy of the Merril estate

My mother was always righteous, perhaps even puritanically so, about giving me full sex information when I was small. But she warned me not to share my information too freely, since many parents did not tell their kiddies these things. (I was utterly astonished, in conversations with schoolmates, to discover this was true: even in the third and fourth grades there were kids who didn't know where babies came from.) I felt privileged.

Most of her information was clinically correct, but as she (presumably) observed me approaching menarche, she began to get a little skittish. Though now that I think about it, the bits of misinformation she fed me were probably more honest errors than actual evasions. She took pains to create occasions where I would see her in the bathroom during her period, and to make sure I observed the use of belt-and-pad. We don't know exactly why the bleeding occurs, she said, but it has something to do with "washing out poisons." She intimated that I might be starting to get "unwell" (does anyone still use that once-common term?) myself, and warned me that I must now become very careful not to let boys touch me, because I would soon be able to get pregnant.

And wouldn't you know? Just weeks after that impressive warning, my cousin Danny (thirteen to my eleven, a man of the world, whose father owned an electric-stuff factory—very glamorous to me, I guess my first true love)—relayed a request from his friend, Dwight, who wanted to know if I would fuck? I was saved from having to ask what the word meant. I knew at least it involved "touching," so I said with sincere apology that Mummy had told me I mustn't let boys touch me any more because I might have a baby. I felt bad about it on two counts: I hated refusing Danny anything, and I really wanted to find out what fucking was—but I had promised.

Of course, I knew all about intercourse. I just mean that I still hadn't figured out how a penis got into a vagina, and I certainly didn't know about fucking.

Judith with her first husband,
Dan Zissman, circa 1941.
Courtesy of the Merril estate

In high school I had three friends, all boys, two of them at different times in the role of "boyfriend." I knew they were attracted to me because of my mind. It had to be that, because I didn't have a pretty face or a cute figure or cute clothes. I saw the tricks and wiles girls and boys were practising on each other and despised them. In retrospect, when I have looked at old snapshots, it is clear I had it inside out. I wasn't "cute" (a very important word in those days), and I didn't play by girls' rules, but I was somewhere between good-looking and beautiful, and I had a sexy body. It wasn't that those three boys liked me for my mind. It was that they were the only three who were not terrified by my mind, and could therefore enjoy (or try to enjoy) my body.

I met my first husband at a Trotskyist Youth Fourth of July picnic in Central Park. His name was Danny Zissman, and he was tall and blond and witty and handsome and we fell instantly, madly, moon-July in love. At the time we met there was a war coming. By the end of summer we were determined to be married. Both families were nervous, for identical/opposite reasons: they knew how we had met and neither of us looked Jewish. But when the Zissmans found out I was Rabbi Grossman's granddaughter, I could do no wrong. I was seventeen, and a virgin. He was twenty-one and likewise. We didn't hardly even think about Doing It until we had decided to get married. It turned out to be a lot of fun.

Sex, I mean, not marriage. I have been married three times, and almost married one other time. The first marriage lasted seven years, the second one three, and the almost-marriage and then the third marriage just one year apiece. They were, I'm pleased to say, four quite different men, so that wasn't the problem. By the third time I was married, I knew what at least part of the problem was, and I watched it starting to happen on the way back from the Justice of the Peace.

There are no quick fixes for this problem, nothing slogans or laws or sister-hoods can command. The only solution is generations. Every one of us has at least one Role Model, or maybe Rule Model says it better. For some of us, from big happy families, for instance, it is complex, involves much more than one role/rule, and is almost unbreakable. For those of us like myself, from "dysfunc-tional" families, the number of roles is reduced, and sometimes the possibilities for remodelling are greater. But for most people there are clear unquestioned images of Father, Mother, Husband, and Wife, and when we assume those roles as we mature, we step, unquestioning, into the model.

In some societies, marriages are put together by specialists—arrangers—who examine the models in the two families, and pair young men and women who will recognize and conform to each other's role or desired image. In our way of doing things, two people may live together for a dozen years, and only after they formalize the arrangement do they discover that their meanings for Wife and Husband are, so to speak, in different languages. Or two people who managed that first shift quite nicely may find when they add a baby that Mother and Father have no relationship to each other.

Although I desperately wanted to be a boy when I was younger, now I am not at all sure I would prefer to have the restraints that are put on men over those that people have attempted to put on me as a woman. Bear in mind, of course, that I am speaking from a middle-class perspective, and that this is not necessarily true for a working-class woman.

❧

For years, many of the sexual experiences I wound up having were the result of meeting someone with whom there was an enormous amount to exchange; a great deal to be learned on both sides. In most cases, we almost needed to get rid of the sexual tension in order to free up all the rest of the stuff and be able to just talk. Sometimes it was exactly that calculated, but most of the time we just shared the feeling that everything we were exchanging was good. There was no sense of having to plan for the future. We did not ask each other questions like, is this love? Is this going somewhere? Do we want to make a commitment?

It's just that I truly believe one of the best places to talk is in bed. With the exception of three or four relationships in my life, almost every one was a mixture of these things: the sex wouldn't have been as good if the intellectual part wasn't happening; and the intellectual element wouldn't have been as enriching if the sex didn't free it up.

I find it really hard to present this opinion today. In the present gender-political scene, as long as it's heterosexual, it's almost heresy to say that it can be a valuable experience to be involved intellectually or professionally with someone you're sleeping with. There's an expectation that it must always be exploitative on one end or the other.

It was easier to present it in the forties and fifties, when the thought of a woman going to bed with whomever she wanted was already so outrageous that the idea she might be learning something was ameliorating rather than intensifying.

Now, if you suggest it's a good way to get an education, all kinds of ugly undertones crawl into it.

❧

At a tribute to my life that was held a few years ago in Toronto, science fiction writer Spider Robinson was one of the speakers. He started out his speech by

Science fiction authors Spider
Robinson and Samuel Delany
at the tribute to Judith's life
at the International Authors'
Festival, Harbourfront Centre,
Toronto, 1992.
Albert S. Frank

saying that after he was invited to come, he began to pull his thoughts together by finding older fans whenever he went to a science fiction convention and asking them for anecdotes about me. He found that almost all the anecdotes from the early years were in one way or another naughty-minded, like, "Well, she slept with everybody …"

I found this sort of interesting, because I was unaware of it at the time. There is only one man who ever said it to my face, and made me stop to think. His implication was that the only reason I was selling my fiction was that I was sleeping with the editors.

At the time, I did a little check-off list, and discovered that there were four men who happened to be editors that I had slept with. Three of them were guys who didn't buy stories from me anyway. (I'm sure that had nothing to do with sleeping with them!) One of them was someone I slept with often, and kept selling stuff to.

Spider said that when he asked for little humorous stories, he thought he would get anecdotes about some of my viewpoints with which other people really disagreed. He was stunned that all the stories he was getting revolved around sleeping around, so he started analyzing each story as if the telling itself was terrible behaviour. That's when he realized that the stories were basically about things everybody does nowadays—the main thing seemed to be that I was doing them too soon.

I didn't do that much sleeping around, so I find myself reacting defensively, much the way I would have if I had known what people were saying at the time. But now my defensiveness is for a different reason: I feel defensive in the face of women who are convinced that all heterosexual gender politics are exploitative.

I suppose, in my life, there have been times when my partner and I were exploiting each other consensually, but that's called a trade. Certainly, I feel I came out of every relationship richer intellectually and creatively than when I entered it. I am still struggling with how to present this fact without either sounding like a naive know-nothing to whom any man could say anything and make me feel like I've gained something, or seeming to apologize for being heterosexual (which I am perfectly willing to apologize for—I think everybody should be bisexual).

Often physical acts of love make other kinds of communication between men and women easier. This is only true when love-making is distinguished from those relationships that involve prospective and future expectations or possession, because those things make acts of love all much more difficult.

I believe there is an inequality between the sexes, but that a lot of the inequality is in the minds of women, who have been raised and trained and conditioned to believe that men have more power and will always be sexually exploitative. I don't mean that it's only in the minds of women, but that part of the problem is that women are prepared to accept unacceptable behaviour. If women expect that they must behave in certain ways, then they often put themselves in the position of having to behave in these ways, even if the man they are with is not trying to set up such a situation.

Basically, I think there are three main ways in which men are oppressed in our society: they are taught not to have emotions; to separate their bodies from their intellects; and to be competitive and aggressive.

Part of what has made my view different from that of most feminists is that I was not given the same conditioning when I grew up. My mother was already a feminist from the first wave, and I didn't have a father. There was no male protecting me and telling me I was beautiful.

☉

Science fiction writer Fritz Leiber once wrote a story called "The Nice Girl with Five Husbands" for an amateur press publication he mimeographed in 1952. It was a very short mood piece about an Earth guy who drifts accidentally into a future world.

He's only there for a few minutes, but while he is, he meets a little girl playing a bouncing ball game with a chant. The kickoff of the story was that the child was chanting Einstein's field theory for combining gravitational and electro-magnetic forces. At the end of story, the equation was set out.

The guy starts talking to the girl and discovers that she comes from a happy, idyllic family where her mother has five husbands. I don't remember now whether it was made explicit that the husbands also had five wives. It was clearly a utopian society.

There was a period in my life, which lasted about three years, where I thought of myself rather fondly as The Nice Girl with Five Husbands. I was living in the small town of Milford, Pennsylvania, and was involved in a long, drawn-out custody battle over my daughter Merril, and potentially over Ann. (It was all the rotten things that custody battles can be—with stupid witnesses and leering lawyers. A truly horrible experience.) My daily life was severely restricted because we were constantly being watched. The house had to be absolutely clean, and the children had to be absolutely good. We had to be the model American family, except that we didn't have a father on the premises.

It was a very small town—it was nothing like living in a big city, where you have a lot of intellectual and social contacts. My whole range of social behaviour was restricted. Opportunities for sexual activities, in particular, had to be carefully planned, and they could never happen at home. Except for the week during the annual Milford Science Fiction Writers' Convention, the only people I could talk to about things that interested me were writers Virginia Kidd and Damon Knight. Not Virginia's husband Jim Blish (another writer), because he and I never got along well. The convention was held in Milford because we started it and lived there.

As a result of the situation, most of my social life was carried out almost entirely by correspondence. Another equally real life was taking place in that small town with my children. On rare occasions, some kind of sexual life was mixed into all this, but it had to be completely hidden. It was still, after all, the 1950s.

An intense intellectual/social/sexual relationship became the standard in my life. Whether it was in correspondence or when we met at a conference, my relationships all had their own level of real interest and pleasure—but only when convenient. Convenience, for me, meant that neither of us happened to be attached to somebody else, and circumstances were such that I wasn't going to get into custody trouble.

The husbands would change names occasionally—as one friendship would get deeper, another would drift away—but none of them were actual husbands in the sense in which we normally use the word. They could, however, have been husbands in the sense that applies to the girl's mother in Fritz Leiber's story, where the whole element of possessiveness was not there.

I am quite convinced that most of the worst features of both masculine and feminine gender-related behaviour have to do with this possessiveness factor.

Clearly, I am a feminist. But I am often reluctant to call myself one, because there are a number of ways in which my ideas about gender relations and sexual politics differ from what I will call the "official feminist camps." One such difference is that I believe women are not so much oppressed by men as that men and women are oppressed by the society in which we live. The strict set of rules that apply to gender behaviour is equally oppressive for both sexes.

I have never been willing, or able, to accept the most common gender roles for women, particularly those that applied to my young adulthood. Actually, I shouldn't say never because there have been one or two times in my life when I tried the stereotypes out. I decided each time that they didn't work for me, and at a certain point just stopped bothering with them at all.

I never saw much reason why I should concern myself with pleasing the tastes or ego of someone who wasn't concerning himself with mine; and I don't see why my choice of occupations or public behaviour should be determined by the fact that I have breasts and a vagina.

However, I do see many reasons why there is a natural division of labour in many societies. In a society where an increase in fruitfulness is essential for survival, a good example is the biological imperative—a woman's main job will necessarily be to have children. Men, in these societies, are adjuncts—they are there to keep the women and children safe.

In industrially advanced societies there are few physical dangers. There is no longer any reason why one gender should be keeping the other safe, and multiple births are not particularly desirable.

It is also important to look at who is controlling the actual economic power. More and more this is divided in our society, but it's still not equally divided. For example, if a married woman who works in the home wants to get a bank loan, she has to get her husband's signature. This lays a philosophic base for the economic power structure.

For the same reason, a man in our society usually has no reason to fear that if he beats his wife, she's going to run away from him. This is because he's controlling the money. She doesn't see how she could possibly manage if she had to leave the house with five dollars in her pocket and no regular income. In relationships where this is the case, the men are exercising the most power and control.

I think the same is true for the relative quality of life of the men and women in those kinds of relationships as it is for prison guards and inmates. The guards have to live in the same kind of high-tension situation as the prisoners. They work in the same physical facility, eat the same terrible food. The only difference is that the guards can go home when their shifts are over. But when the guard is present on the scene, is there a difference in the quality of life experienced by the guards and the prisoners? If one assumes that being in control of another person makes a difference, then the guards have it better.

As between men and women, I don't believe everything is that simple. In most cases, control is mixed. Certain aspects of power (such as who controls the money) fall to the man, others (such as who is going to have a headache tonight) fall to the woman. Aside from control, there are behaviours that society demands of one or the other gender. Women are to be nurturing, concerned with other people's feelings, and generally obedient. Men must be totally competitive and ready to fight. Women are emotional. Men must favour intellect over emotion—big boys don't cry, etc.

Which set of demands gives a better quality of life? It depends on how quality is defined. When I was a kid, I wanted desperately to be a boy, because boys could do things people were always telling me I couldn't. Not that I had any sense of men or boys being in control of women. I wanted to be a boy because they had more freedom. I went through incredible psychic turmoil because an aunt told me if I could kiss my elbow, I would turn into a boy.

This desire to change my sex continued for quite some time—until adolescence, when I began to discover some of the advantages of being female. I never felt I had to be a prisoner of somebody else, but up until that time I did have less freedom than boys and men to do what I wanted to do, and go where I wanted to go. Eventually I began to realize that I could take advantage of many of these same freedoms. I think these days many adolescent girls have taken the freedoms, but some are still timid and timorous.

As I grew older I began to feel that, in many ways, women have the better of it. We are not required to lie to ourselves to the same extent as men. We are required to do a lot of lying to other people, but if I feel happy or loving or sad, there is no one to tell me I should not express these feelings. If I feel angry, no one says I shouldn't feel that way, but there are a whole bunch of rules about how I'm allowed to express the anger.

Men don't have any of these privileges. They are allowed to feel a certain amount of all these things, but if they are indeed following the conservative rules of society, they are not permitted to show them. They're required to keep a straight face. If a man twists his ankle, he's not even supposed to say "Ouch Ouch Ouch" with each step. A woman can do that.

When I was involved in the custody battles over my children, there were definitely ways in which it was harder for me because I am a woman. For example, I was watched carefully to see if I was misbehaving sexually—much more so than a man would have been. There were also certain ways in which it was easier. For instance, as long as I managed to feed my daughters, and keep a roof over their heads (however absolutely poor I might have been) I was admired for this. A man, if he had custody of his children, and didn't support them in middle-class comfort, would have been in constant danger of having them removed.

None of what I have just said is meant to suggest that women should accept indignity or depravation. I only mean that we should recognize that in our society, men and women are both constantly subject to indignities and depravations. Neither sex is exempt. The theory that men are on top, and we are on bottom, does not always make our lot worse than theirs.

FIVE | (SOME KIND OF) WRITING: SCIENCE FICTION AND THE FUTURIANS

I WAS SLOW.

I cannot remember a time when I did not write. My first publication was not until I was seven—a poem in a mimeoed summer camp newspaper—but I have a ghost of a memory of a rare quarrel with my father much earlier. I must have been four, had just learned to read, and was demanding half his desk space because I was a writer too—or thought I was.

Then at fifteen I discovered that my mother intended me to be a writer, had been raising me specifically to be a writer—a writer like my father. So I quit—or thought I did.

I kept on writing for the high-school paper, and edited the yearbook. During my single year at university, my main activity was working on the school paper; I was also writing for the Trotskyist Challenge of Youth, but that was all journalism and politics, not what I thought of as Writing. When I was twenty-one and a mother myself, and had the width of a continent between me and my own mother, I started writing seriously again.

Almost all writers—almost all artists—are, to some degree, rebels. Some (non-realist) romantics like to talk about the role of poverty and "suffering" in the making of an artist. The truth is that both poverty and agonizing frustration are close to inevitable in any apprenticeship to any of the arts, in any culture, at any time. Rebelliousness—the reckless rejection of society's manners and morals, of authority, tradition, and, above all, security—is basic to survival during the life-in-a-garret phase.

Some people, and I am one, also believe that art is by nature revolutionary: that a vital function of the artist is to produce and publish "virtual realities" of social change. Certainly the inverse is true: no radical change can ever occur until a believable and seductive new vision is made public. Professors and politicians may seduce, but only artists can create belief in the new vision—the new myth. (Bear in mind: artists—well, artistes—include great orators, and demagogues.)

So: is rebellion inherent in the artist? Is the artist an essential element of revolution? Is a rebellious nature simply a useful defence against the scurvy treatment visited on student-artists in every society? Why quibble? By any and all reckonings, rebellion is part of the job description.

"Authority" expected me to become a writer. So I was slow.

&

It was my first husband Danny who got me completely zonked on science fiction. Then, not too much later, in 1942, he had the bad sense to get drafted. Before that, in 1940–41, we had lived with Danny's parents in Philadelphia. I helped make ends meet (barely) by taking different jobs ranging from waitress to curtain examiner. The same year that Danny was drafted I got pregnant, and our daughter Merril was born in December. From 1943 to 1944 we moved seven times to army bases in Chicago, New York, San Francisco, and other places.

So, by 1944, when I started "writing" again, I was a camp-following Navy wife and mother in San Francisco. Danny, my comrade/husband, was in a radar-technician training course on Treasure Island. That summer the records of Dan's political activities (most especially his union-activism while working in a defence plant) caught up with his Navy files, and he was pulled abruptly out of radar school to be shipped overseas. He avoided assignment to the suicidal Pacific beachhead landings by volunteering for the submarine service. He went to Pearl Harbor and I went back to New York with our almost-two-year-old baby girl, Merril.

There I was, twenty-one, living the life of a young mother in a little apartment in the West Village in New York City, and passionately devoted to SF. I found part-time work with a distant cousin as a research assistant, and I did a bit of ghostwriting. (That didn't count as being a Writer.) Then I met the Futurians, a group of determinedly rebellious, mostly left-wing, science fiction fans just in the process of becoming professionals. There was a woman living nearby named Edith, a close friend of Danny's from back in Philadelphia, who was now living with the writer Paul Goodman. I never actually met Goodman, but she was the one who introduced me to a number of her friends who were members of the Futurian Society of New York (FSNY).

The Futurians were extraordinary people. They were a group of young writers who were set to start history, not to repeat it. They each had their own visions about the future; it was coming, and they were thinking about it better than anybody else. They were all gifted and talented in one way or another. Most were without academic discipline; drop-outs, either from high school or after a short period in university. All of them had the weird, erotic erudition typical of teenagers immersed in reading science fiction. Like me, they were in flight from their families. Some of them were nice and some of them were nasty, but they were all very smart. I had been brought up to feel that smart was the most important thing in the world.

Most of the original members were a few years older than me. Many of them were old friends—they had gotten to know each other through the columns in science fiction magazines about ten years earlier. The best-known Futurians, perhaps, are the writers Isaac Asimov, Frederik Pohl, and the literary figure Donald A. Wollheim (DAW Books). Other members I quickly ran into included Virginia Kidd, James Blish, and Damon Knight. Damon eventually wrote a book called *The Futurians*, which has all the details about how the group started.

Judith with first husband, Dan Zissman, the year they married, circa 1940. She was about seventeen years old.
Courtesy of the Merril estate

Like every other social and professional grouping, the FSNY had been fragmented by the war. In the three or four years before the United States entered World War II and the men were dispersed, members had established one or more shared apartments in downtown New York. One of the most renowned was called the Slan Shack. I got the sense that at any one time between six and nine people were living there together. These apartments were essentially communes, long before we talked about people living in communes.

At the time I met the group, several of the members, including Asimov, Pohl, Cyril Kornbluth, and Dick Wilson, were not on the scene because of the war. In fact, the members still in the States were a minority of the Society that existed prior to my joining. Wilson and Pohl were somewhere overseas, and Asimov was doing something for the Navy. A few service-reject Futurians, though, were still in the city, clustered loosely around three central figures: Johnny Michel, Bob "Doc" Lowndes, and Donald Wollheim. Johnny and I became very close friends immediately.

The only women in the group besides myself were Virginia Kidd and Donald Wollheim's wife Elsie, who wrote a little and was nominally called a Futurian. Elsie was the bookkeeper and secretary for her father's jewellery business, and I worked there for a couple of months in the period just before I got an editing job at Bantam Books. Virginia Kidd was a writer, editor, and (later) literary agent. The instant we met, Virginia and I became close friends—and she remained my close friend and literary editor for the rest of my life.

All of us had a tremendous amount in common, because we were living, eating, and breathing science fiction. Most of the Futurians had published at least one or two stories by the time I met them, and a couple were editors of pulp magazines. Johnny Michel was, by Futurian consensus, the brilliant young writer of the group. Wollheim and Lowndes had already achieved their first, shabby, editorial jobs.

At the time I met him, Johnny Michel shared an apartment with his friend Larry Shaw in the middle of the Village. There was a running spar with him, and in part with Donald Wollheim (whom I seldom saw, but often heard quoted from Johnny), because although I had already left the Trotskyists, Johnny and Donald could tell that I was still one in my heart. My thinking was still inherently Trotskyist. In fact, I was a Trotskyist's Trotskyist, because I left the organization when I realized that it was Stalinist, not because I had disagreed with its ideology. I found their authoritarian organizational tactics unbearable. I eventually ran into serious ideological problems and battles with several of the Futurians because they were Communists and I was a Trotskyist. From their point of view, this was a pretty rotten sin.

It rankled Johnny and Donald that I should be so misled, and they frequently took occasion to remind me of this. The situation was particularly difficult for Johnny because of his close friendship with me. He was getting a great deal of trouble from Donald. Predictably, they didn't try to argue politics with me. The argument I got most often from them was a Stalinist one, which would never, ever reach me: "What's the sense in being a Trotskyist? You've got no organization, you've got no numbers … Why don't you fall in with people who have some kind of a party behind them?"

For his part, Doc Lowndes was a shoestring editor at a chain of particularly low-paying pulp magazines, mostly westerns and detectives. One he worked on, though, was called *Super Science*. It lasted partway into the war, surrendered to paper shortage, and then resumed again afterwards. Lowndes was chubby, extremely erudite, affected, and slightly dapper—kind of Oscar Wilde-ish, although to my knowledge (which is not necessarily complete) not homosexual, because he was on the prowl for women all the time.

One of my research jobs was on the history of the Old West, and Doc started buying short filler articles from me. Then he and Johnny both began pointing out that I could make much more money out of the same material by turning some of the anecdotes into stories.

I had never written fiction. I told them I didn't know how to write a story. They said, write one and we'll tell you what's wrong with it. I said I didn't want to write westerns. They said, okay, try a detective. I did. They tore it apart. I rewrote. They suggested a few more changes. I did them and Doc bought it for *Crack Detective Magazine*. Ecstatically, I wrote to Dan:

Feb. 19, 1945
Monday morning, W-Day plus one

Sir:
Hereafter in addressing your wife, you will kindly restrain yourself to the use of the official title, "Oh most revered, high and worshipful Professional Hack Writer."

DOC BOUGHT MY STORY LAST NIGHT—beyond dispute or further question, finished, as is, and to undergo no more than the customary amount of editorial revision.

DOC BOUGHT MY STORY LAST NIGHT. It remains now only for him to catch hold of the publisher long enough to get a check signed. 3200 words—I stand to gain exactly 32 bux …

I still wasn't sure about becoming a Real Writer, but this was only hack stuff after all: a demonstrably learnable skill, writing "formula" for a cheap commercial market. And, with my new semi-pro status, I was voted into the FSNY.

What was it about science fiction that attracted the Futurians? I think I can answer that best by quoting something said to me many years later. I was at the Milford Science Fiction Writers' Conference, an annual event that I co-founded and used to go to every year. A young writer named Thomas Disch came to the conference for the first time. When we met, he said something that foreshadowed a sense of satisfaction on my part. "I wanted you to know, Judy, that when I was thirteen years old, I picked up an anthology of yours in a little town in North Dakota where I was living, and for the first time I knew that things could be different."

For many people, discovering science fiction is discovering that one can, to some extent, invent what kind of different things will be.

Certainly, for the Futurians, the idea that things could be different was not just a fantasy. When it was formed, the Futurian Society was a group of talented fans who were all, to one degree or another, left of centre. Some of them

The first page of the Futurians'
original *Gholy Ghible*, written in
1942 by Johnny Michel and
Donald Wollheim.
Courtesy of the Merril estate

were mild socialists and a couple were card-carrying Communists, but every single one of them engaged in major intellectual and ideological battles with fans who were not leftist—as well as with Trotskyists like myself.

Virtually everyone in the Futurian Society thought of themselves as budding great artists, political figures, or both. None of us were ordinary human beings. We were loyal buddies. The science fiction world was a tight literary ghetto at the time. There was a song that came out of one of the early conventions, where the Futurians had come into conflict with some more right-wing fans. It was a parody of "In 36 the sky was red/ and lightning threatened over head …" It had to do with the fact that one fan in particular, named Will Sykora, had committed political treachery, and caused harm to the Futurians.

Everybody who was involved in science fiction read everything—it didn't matter whether the writers were people you agreed with ideologically. In those days the fans were also much more participatory than in other literary genres, and writers were much closer to the fans. There was less inherent hierarchy.

The existence of a semi-organized body of people who were determined to help each other certainly made good luck for fledgling authors happen a lot easier than it would have otherwise occurred. I think this kind of thing manifests itself in classical terms when one is selected to go to Iowa or Breadlove or one of the more traditional writers' workshops where you start to meet older writers who are determined to be helpful.

Whereas in other literary fields you wouldn't dare take an idea from another writer and use it, because that would be considered plagiarism, science fiction people loved to build on each other's stories. The business of giving away ideas and promoting other people's work was a part of the community at large.

The Futurians did this to an amazing extent. For example, every Futurian had a pen name that included the family name Conway. A good number of the stories that appeared in science fiction magazines at that time were written by someone or other Conway. Very few stories were even published under real names.

Among established writers, there was a long tradition in the 1930s, 1940s, and into the 1950s of borrowing from each other's work in an approved fashion. If somebody came up with an invention you liked, and you could see a better or different angle, you added to this person's invention. It was considered perfectly normal and ethical, and so was sharing ideas while you were in the midst of writing.

We shared something of an international scientist's ethic. One of the most fascinating illustrations of this is the series of back covers on the magazine *Amazing Stories*. As early as 1938, and certainly into the 1950s, *Amazing* used to have illustrations out of the future. By the time the actual space program got underway, scientists were producing space suits that looked exactly like the ones from *Amazing*. The fact that a lot of the atomic and space scientists had grown up reading science fiction probably influenced the design. But to a great extent the designs were inevitable, because they were things that would actually work; they had already been analyzed in twenty or thirty science fiction stories. In each new story, the design had been refined: this gasket was added, or that joint was improved. After all the thought that had been put into it, the logical space suit already existed; all it needed was the money to make it.

The first page of the Futurians' *Book of Ghu Ghu*, in which Donald Wollheim is named as Ghu Ghu himself, with Johnny Michel as his high priest. It was written circa 1942 by Johnny Michel and Donald Wollheim. *Courtesy of the Merril estate*

❧

In the years before I met up with the Futurian Society, the original members had created a religion called "Ghughuism." They had even written thirty or forty humorous pages of a "Gholy Ghible." Some of it was quite clever.

Ghughuism was always spelled with gh-, and all the changed words (Gholy, Ghible, etc.) became diffused into science fiction. I think the references have probably disappeared by now, but for a great long time, they appeared in the writing of people who had never seen the Gholy Ghible, and knew nothing about it except that this was something people had done. It eventually became part of science fiction fan mythology without most people even knowing the origins.

Around this same time a number of us started something called the Vanguard Amateur Press Association (VAPA), which was happening parallel to a gradual dissolution of the Futurian Society. A lot of people were publishing fanzines or zines of various kinds. There were two or three different Amateur Press Associations functioning in the New York science fiction community at the time, but the Vanguard was an elitist one. It was not open to just anybody, and had a relatively high literary level. My own VAPA publication was called *TEMPER!* Every now and then I would change the title slightly, the most distinctive one being an issue called *DISTEMPER!*, which was entirely poetry, and criticism of poetry.

There were magnificent arguments carried on between one small press publication and another. One of them was about whether SF was your whole

The young author at work,
circa 1949.
Courtesy of the Merril estate

life or just something you did as a hobby. There was a definite sneer aimed at people who did it for kicks.

Science fiction fandom evolved out of the letter columns in the science fiction pulp magazines. People began writing there, and then they began to write to and visit each other. The first SF conventions were held around the middle of the thirties, and they were very small. I believe the first Worldcon was towards the end of the 1930s. During that early decade, literate fans got to know each other at these small conventions. The conventions quickly got larger and larger, drawing fans from right across the United States. Damon Knight, for instance, was initially living in Oregon. He came to New York and met the Futurians when he was a teenager by way of attending a convention in Chicago at which several of them were also present.

There was a fair amount of larger-world politics and conflicts about those politics involved in the conventions. However, they were mainly organized to discuss the world of the future, and were primarily attended by people who wanted to become serious science fiction writers. The significant thing about science fiction fandom, up until perhaps the early 1970s, was that it was almost entirely made up of people who truly thought of themselves as upcoming writers. So these conventions were intensely participatory. Unlike fan groups in most other areas, these were not admirers. They were people who were quite literally on their way to becoming part of the community, or already were part of it.

Inevitably what happened was that the "fans" began creating their own mimeographed magazines because they needed somewhere to publish (and read) their own and their friends' work. At the beginning of the 1940s, when I became part of the community, fanzines were already a well-established means of communication and personal identification. Later, when people settled into either the role of fan or the role writer, and stopped thinking of themselves as moving anywhere, there tended to be distinctions made regarding the kind of fanzine a person published. One was a personal zine, in which you were primarily talking about your own life. The other zine was about science fiction concepts, publishing, and issues of that sort.

BOB LOWNDES WAS Virginia's particular friend, and one day I bumped into her at Doc's apartment. At the time Virginia was living in some "square" part of the city—square compared to where I was, in the West Village. She had a baby about a year younger than mine, and her husband was also away in the service.

Virginia had started her writerly life in Baltimore, but when I met her, she had recently come to New York City in order to become a "famous writer." In contrast, I started in New York, and was still resisting the idea that I wanted to be a famous writer.

Jan. 30, 1945
342 East 46th, New York 17, N.Y.

Dear Judy—
You may or may not remember me. You met me one night at Doc's—in October, I think.

I know very little about you, beyond the facts that you are also a pro tem Futurian, and a member of the Vanguard APA. [...]

Would you like to come up some afternoon? I should love to have you. Alone, I mean. I hope to see more of you later, and the circumstances then will make little difference—but this first time I should like to talk to you alone. That sounds like Secrets, doesn't it? Not though. Bring your off-spring, of course. I have enough toys here, I think, to keep him or her happy. (My infant is still a babe in arms, and /on account of a bad leg/ I'm afraid to navigate with her. I hope it will be an easier matter for you, because I really do want you to come up. I don't see how else we can get together.)

Any afternoon next week except Monday will be entirely convenient for me. Will you stay for dinner, too?

Most cordially,

Kidd

(formally Virginia K. Emden)

Wednesday, Jan. 31, 1945

Dear Kidd,

Yes, I do remember meeting you—and, if I'd been so inclined, wouldn't have had a chance to forget. I've been hearing about you from Doc and Johnny both—and have been anxious for quite a while to see you again.

I suspect Lowndes of being seriously remiss—I have commissioned him several times with invitations to you. Of course, it never occurred to me to write.

Yes, I have a child—a daughter—slightly over two years old. At present she's in nursery school, but how much longer the family finances will stand for that, I don't know. Anyhow, I'd like to talk over your brainstorms—have had a few myself at various times, but never tried to do anything much about them.

Instead of trying to make a date this way—you will be at Donald and Elsie's Sunday afternoon, won't you? I'll see you there, and we can either arrange then to see each other again during the week, or, if you can stay out Sunday evening (I can't this week), and haven't made any other plans—then come home with me. We can have dinner here, and talk all the Secrets we like.

I'll see you Sunday then—and I'm already beginning to feel a tickling temptation to confuse and confound Futuria by greeting with something sweet and feminine like, "Darling, did the baby get over that colic you wrote me about? I hope you didn't use that awful Barton's Babybloom Business your mother-in-law told you to, because I did once, and—"

You get the idea—uh-uh, I promise I won't. Anticipatorily,
Judy

Judith with Virginia Kidd (then Virginia Emden) and daughter Karen, New York, circa 1945. *Courtesy of the Merril estate*

We both had young babies and husbands overseas. It didn't take us long to decide that we should be living together and combining our efforts, which would give us both more opportunity to write.

More than anything else, Virginia was the first smart woman I knew. (Aside from my mother, whom I was not yet prepared to admit was smart.) This common intellectual respect formed the basis of our friendship. Virginia was every bit as intelligent, every bit as well-read, every bit as inventive as I was. And we found, bit by bit, that there were many, many other things we had in common.

I went for dinner with my baby Merril, and stayed for two days. After that we started looking for an apartment we could share.

Friday, Feb. 2, 1945

Dear Kidd—
Your letter delighted me, and I could fill sheets and sheets right now with ideas and modifications and ramifications of your idea—one that I have held for some time now, but never activated, largely because there seemed to be a distinct shortage of roommates who did 'speak the language'. [...]

Only one thing I feel I must warn you about, before you start building dreamhouses (as I confess I am already prone to do)—I am THE laziest, and probably THE sloppiest and filthiest young mother on record. If you think you can stand it, we can probably work out something pretty good.

I like the sound of you, V.K.E.

With which pronunciamento I retire, blushing.
Try to make it Sunday—
Judy

Wednesday morning, Feb. 7, 1945

Kidd—
I owe you an apology. Of course the understanding was in the air that Thursday was replacing Wednesday [for a Futurian meeting]—but I am unaccustomed to people able to pluck their understanding from the air—

and (cautious good sense again, OK) have gotten into so damned many difficulties of late by making assumptions that this time I decided 'twas better to put it as though it were all my idea.

WHY do you have to write the kind of letters that make me start answering them before the coffee is even ready? I'll return, more lucid, in a moment.

Nothing premature about you. We're all making plans—and I do mean all—the latest being that Damon and Larry, 'tseems, are already working on convincing Chester to move here—to my apartment—after you and I have found another. Everyone is very approving about the whole affair, and I begin to have an idea we'd better plan on an extra room as a sort of Futurian Clubhouse—because Lowndes, Michel, Shaw, et al., could not possibly be quite SO delighted unless they saw something very good indeed in it for themselves. [...]

By the way, I have a big laundry basket Merry slept in her first few months. Unless Karen is the overgrown variety, she'd probably fit, and we might even be able to stow her away for part of the evening. And while I'm at it—better bring the milk after all. Sheffield's seems to be an unknown quality hereabouts.

And it might be a good idea if I got Merry to school on time this morning.
Foggily,
Judy

Feb. 14, 1945

Dear Kidd:
There is something awry in Hangover House, because this IS Monday morning, and I am feeling perfectly fine. I suspect it has something to do with the state of the weather, which I find incredible—but nice, if true—and there is probably a connection somewhere with the unhappy fact that I was in bed at eleven on Saturday night, and twelve last night.

What is still more unhappy, I have not looked upon the vine—red, white or in between—since the last time—when we all looked together and found it good. This is through no choice of my own, but simply because the opportunity has not arisen, and neither has the state of my finances. (There is a rumor about that finances should have another n in it—but don't believe a word of it.) [...]

Now, some thoughts on *Futurian Home Journal*. I am already fond of it, and would like to see it issued weekly, in more finished form than the first.

One sheet is sufficient, and it COULD be good. I believe there is enough matter of interest specifically to Futuria to maintain such a sheet. For the next copy, suggested, an article outlining specific plans for future Thursdays (I'll go into that later in the letter); an hilarious accounting of the doings of last Thursday, up to seven A.M.; just a thought—if we included news of the doings and happenings in the lives of Futurians—mimeod the thing, say once a month (four issues together), and we will be able, until then, to fill in with detailed accounts of the progress of the apartment-hunt....

Let's have some thoughts on it—and you might put pen to work on "An Hilarious Accounting"—I have an idea you could do a better job than I.

As to this planned Thursday's business, here's my outline:

1. Meals to be as cheap as possible.
2. Wine or beer, as suits the donor, to be contributed each week by a different individual. (Avoid the unpleasantness of last week with Damon.)
3. All those planning to attend for supper to notify HH by Tuesday—or even Wednesday, but at least a day ahead.
4. Work schedule to be posted, and different jobs assigned to each person from week to week.
5. Dinner to be served by 7:30—means the cooking squad should be on hand no later than 6:30. Dinner to be over, and cleaned away, by nine, so as to leave time for other activity during the evening.
6. Such "other activity" to include music, poker, conversation, and anything else the group desires. We might even occasionally work our way up to a mass migration uptown to a play or something. It might be possible occasionally to prevail on Doc to bring over some records—any number of such things.
7. Final suggestion—that is if nobody has anything special planned for that night, Friday would mean more of us could sleep later the next morning. Thursday was originally chosen because I understood Doc went to see you Fridays, and did not know to what extent I could attempt to tamper with that arrangement.

Judy

Two members of the Futurian Society: Johnny Michel and Larry Shaw (front), New York, circa 1947. *Courtesy of the Merril estate*

The dinners would be followed by long, long, debates that went on throughout the night. I suppose we did what most people who have been to university think of as student talk, except that almost all of us were dropouts. It was very rare for one of us to have a university degree. I had taken some university courses, as had some of the others, but almost all of us now found ourselves unsuited to classroom learning.

We also used to hang up what we called a wall newspaper —which was usually filled with stories that were sheer hilarious invention. One person would come and type out a single-page newspaper, which we would cut and paste up onto the wall for dinner. Then we would mimeograph and distribute it to our friends. Sometimes it would contain scandalous gossipy things about what one or another of us had done during the week. But here and there we added some truth; if someone got a story published, there would be an announcement for them.

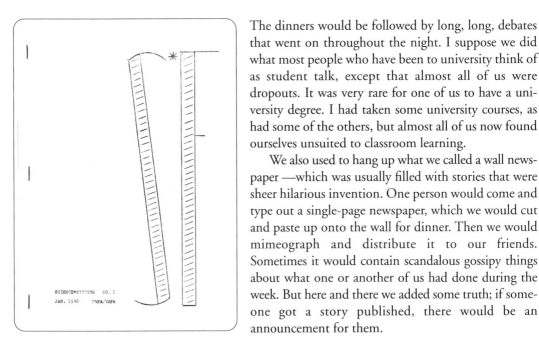

SCIENCE*FICTION NO. 1
JAN. 1946   VAPA/VAPA

The January 1946 issue of the Vanguard Amateur Press Association's zine, Science Fiction. Courtesy of the Merril estate

Feb. 19, 1945

Dear Zissman-let
Oh God—I wish I hadn't done it. But it's too late now. This is my last piece of bond paper, and I am determined to honor (?) you with it. […]

So far you have done all the work on FHJ [*Futurian Home Journal*] while the ass editor has just tagged along. Full of plaudits, but not visibly contributing anything … If I don't die before Thursday, I will have An Hilarious Accounting ready—only I think we ought to run an account of the month's evenings in the last Thursday of each month's issue. […]

My little squib is going to look pretty silly … Oh, good sentence, Kidd! Oh, what a wonder-par is the liquorary compilation … Besides it would take care of one issue per month—no scrambling for material and I said I'm lazy …
Toujours sleepy (wrote Willie tonight)
Kidd

Tuesday, Feb. 20, 1945

> My liddie kidder;
> Zissman-let! Hmph!
> "Nobody," he said
> As he guzzled up the house red,
> "Nobody," he said "Could call me a snobbish Slan!
> But I only love Futurians with liquoracy!"
> (liquoraracy?)

WHAT did happen to the meter?

SO—you're too damn lazy to put out an ish of FHJ all by yourself—well, sister, it's your baby for this week. AND THE NEWS OF THE WEEK—listen, lady, if you don't think Doc buying my story is the most important thing that happened to ANY Futurian this week—then you underestimate my capacity for 1) joy-unbounded 2) expressions of same 3) grabbing the limelight! […]

Had my first "fan-letter" today. I quote: "Dear Judy, Will be on hand Thursday, I think. Gives food? # Sold a couple of fact articles to Tilden this morning. I eat for another week & a half. Why don't you try some fact stuff? Easy to look up, if you know where to go, and easier than fiction for a beginner to sell. # Been giving some thought to your detective opus. I didn't like it, as you probably gathered, but I think it shows considerable promise.

"That framework is an extremely difficult one to build a good story on, no matter how good you are. A much more rewarding angle on the murder plot is why rather than how. # (Time out for a discussion with Chester about fruits.) # Anyway, the main thing about your story is that it's well-written. Your mistakes were ones of construction, not of style. You can handle words, and that's half the battle. # Now can I get in for half-price? # yours, Damon."

I find myself strangely delighted. Ah vanity, thy name …
'Bye now—gotta go wash clothes, and impress Sara [Dan's mother] with how clean I've become.
ghugowithyou
Judy
———————————— A hangoverhouse EFFUSION

The contents page of the January 1946 issue of *Science Fiction* shows a range of SF-themed fiction, poetry, reviews, and non-fiction articles by Judith and Dan Zissman, James Blish, Larry Shaw, Johnny Michel, and other writers using humorous pseudonyms (including Arthur Lloyd Merlin).
Courtesy of the Merril estate

Feb. 20, 1945

Judy—
CONGRATULATIONS!!!!!!!

But I'm not surprised. I knew it was a sale when I read your first rewrite. But I'm so damn glad. Hope Dan is more thrilled than Jack [her husand Major Jacob "Jack" Emden] was. Someday I'll show you that letter …

But I expect he will be. Dan seems to be in complete sympathy with your aims.

The hint has been duly recorded and will be acted on. Have fun—
Love Kidd

We found a place together in a really old tenement building on the extreme west side of New York. We were on Washington Street, west of the whole area that's usually called the Village, near the railroad tracks. Virginia and I rented two adjoining four-room flats. They were something like thirteen dollars a month each, because this was the bottom level of New York rent.

These apartments were usually known as cold-water flats, because originally they only had cold water and no heat. Ours were not, in fact, just cold water, and most of the apartments in the building had heat. But a lot of them still had only one toilet out in the hall for all the occupants of the four apartments on each floor. They were best described as "railroad flats," because they were in the undesirable lots located right nearby the railway tracks, and also because of their architecture. The apartments had no hallways at all. You entered into the kitchen, and from that room you entered the next room, then the next room, and then the last room. There were no private rooms with doors whatsoever; you had to walk through each room to get to the next one.

The largest room in each of our apartments, which was also the last room you came to, had a triangular closet. Those closets shared the wall in between our two apartments. We decided to remove the wall inside the closets, thus ending up with an eight-room apartment that wrapped around the entire floor in an enormous U-shape.

Living with Virginia was lots of fun against the backdrop of great intellectual stimulation, caring for children, coping with relationships, buying groceries, and all those things that are part of everyday life as a single working mother. It's hard to describe how much fun those things became, all these years distant. We lived a marvellous Parisian existence in our apartment on Washington Street next to the railway tracks. Our apartment became known as the Parallax, the central place for meetings of those Futurians who were not in service and had remained in New York. We lived there together for two or three years. Virginia stayed for quite some time after I left.

Once a week everyone came over for a communal dinner. Virginia and I would do the shopping and the cooking, then we would proportion the cost of the meal to everyone who ate. Usually the others had some sort of rota to do the after-dinner cleanup.

☙

I must give motherhood a societal context in these strange times. During the war, there was a marvellous, total change on the part of society with regards to women working. In New York City, for the first time, something called the Mayor's Committee on Nursery Schools was established. This organization ensured that in every neighbourhood there was a really good nursery school available for working mothers.

My older daughter Merril had already started nursery school in San Francisco when I was Dan's Navy wife and therefore had priority. She was in nursery school before she was two years old, and she loved it.

There were times when I had odd jobs, and there were times when I was just writing stuff for Bob Lowndes to buy, and then there were other times when I was working for my cousin doing research. I absolutely needed to earn an income beyond the meagre Navy allotment—so at that time I was mainly writing to make money.

This posed some difficulty because being a real writer also meant that my home was my office. Merril was two and a half at the time when Virginia and I moved in together. She was fascinated by my typewriter. She would come over to where I was sitting and put her sweet little fingers on the keys and start typing along with me.

After a while I decided something had to be done about this. I bought a two-dollar old typewriter in a second-hand store and gave it to her. That solved the problem for a while.

Later I had another child, Ann, and as she got older the same problem manifested in similar ways. I told myself that the child's desire to have all of the mother all of the time is not a reasonable one. No system on earth has ever made this possible except the affluent European-North American society of today, where women can afford to do nothing except raise children. This has never ever been possible before: women had to till fields, scrub houses, and work outside the home.

Virginia not only understood but shared with me all the dilemmas posed by our commitment to both being good mothers and great writers. We were both doing serious work as writers and struggling with the conflict between writing and mothering. Sometimes the child couldn't win. I don't think that this was necessarily bad for my children, but of course I must believe that, or I couldn't have made the decisions I have during my life.

Maybe mothers who wish only to be mothers should be totally excused from doing any other work. Certainly, at our society's current technological level, and since we don't really need all the labour force we've got, this is feasible.

I think it is often as damaging to the small child to be the total focus of a mother's attention as it is to have too little of a mother's attention. And I, of course, achieved the perfect proportion!

Not at all. But I think it is in the nature of human relationships that there be conflicts of this sort, and I don't know how to avoid them. I like to think that because of the choices I made, I was a greater resource for my children and a far more interesting mother.

☙

Back in the day to day, Virginia began seeing a lot of my arch-nemesis James Blish, and eventually divorced her husband when he came home from overseas so that she could marry Jim. Because of their relationship, my friendship with Virginia suffered. Jim liked to refer to himself as a "book fascist," making clear that his model was Mussolini fascism, futurism, and so forth, rather than German-scum stuff. Of course, he was not fascist, anti-Semitic, or any of those terrible things, but every time he used the phrase, I saw red.

For some time, the main feature of our Thursday-night (once Wednesday) Futurian dinners was the political arguments between Jim and myself. I was a much better debater than Jim, and what's more, I had right on my side. I thought the whole book-fascist thing was sophomoric intellectual shit, so, week after week, I would grind Jim into the dirt. And week after week, he would come back with the answer he hadn't thought of the week before. Eventually, Jim and I got to be quite unfriendly.

As for my friendship for Virginia, despite my arguments with Jim it was settled that we were the kind of friends who stay friends in one incarnation or another for an entire lifetime, friends who were always able to get past the inevitable ups and downs.

[n.d., around December 1946]

Dear Judy.

It's three a.m. and I'm stalking the Muse with my 'ead tooked oonderneath my arm. Also partly I'm not writing, and partly I'm waiting for the coffee to heat.

It seems to me that there is some quality in you—not of equitableness. I know you're hot tempered well enough! ... But of untouchableness ... I've watched you tell slander and abuse and rudeness—and some of it from me (and I'm not taking it back by this letter—when I spoke straight from the shoulder to you about HES ["Wonderful Henry"] I meant it and still think it true)—the hearing of which would have left me with murder in my heart, had I been the object … I don't see how you take it, or at least I didn't until just now when I was thinking about it.

Pause for coffee. (Y)

You're a rare specimen, Jude.

I meant to write the first page, tell you how very much I enjoyed having you here for dinner the other night, wish you a very Merry Christmas and a good year, and quit—
Love Kidd

P.S. Wish I had some money—but I don't, not to spare, so no presents this year. My love to Sol [a high school friend]. I hope he drops around. Likewise to Maggie.

[n.d., probably 1947]
Staten Island

Dear Judy—
Hi and ok. It's probably what I wanted to hear, anyhow.
    I may be able to work it out, commuting, or I may not do it at all. The little heart will not break, either way.
    Karen started in nursery last Monday, and there hasn't been a moment's difficulty. There were the usual exclamations about her not crying for her mother, and so on—but I didn't really think she could have got unused to nursery practices in half a year, and she always did love it. Needless to say, we're both happy.
    A woman's home is, by damn, her castle, yes. Circumstances forced me to rent out part of my castle, damn it. […]
Kidd

Dear Kidd,

All I seem to do these days is compose difficult letters. I restrained myself on the phone yesterday, and shall attempt not to be too annoyed today, because the last thing I want to do right now is sever the somewhat strained bonds between you and me, you and Henry, Henry and Him, and the four of us in general. [...]

'Taint what you do, Kidd, it's the way how ... I think you might have adopted a less imperious and outraged tone, in view of the circumstances leading up to the somewhat one-sided discussion. [...]

I know the reaction at 787 must be largely in terms of That Zissman Woman. I should rather not have you think that I have made off with your friend Henry. I don't believe I could have "had" him, if I wanted to. [...]

I wish you'd think over some of the harsh words. I'm afraid, and again it's stilted, that I am placed in the position of proffering, and demanding, an apology.

with still some friendship,

Judy

DECLARATION OF INDEPENDENCE

On this date of September 19, 1945, we the members of the Futurian Society of New York, meeting in full and open democratic assembly, have declared that John Michel and Donald and Elsie Wollheim have shown themselves unfit for membership in a group whose primary basis is friendship. We are therefore in unanimous agreement that these three shall be declared no longer members of the FSNY; and that the FSNY is no longer necessarily in accord with any statements they may make.

The center of infection among the Futurians has always been Donald A. Wollheim-- Wollheim's paternalism, aided and abetted by the voderisms of egotary John Michel and the eager acquiescence of handmaiden Elsie Wollheim. The quarrels and strifes precipitated in fandom by the FSNY are well-known; the far greater dissidence within the FSNY has been kept a carefully-guarded secret. The events of the last few days have made it advisable that we now submit to fandom a candid accounting.

Because of the fanatical nature of their convictions, because of a morbid fear of any opposing political viewpoint, these people have:
a) abruptly and coldbloodedly terminated all personal relationships with four members of their group, among them three of their oldest and/or most intimate friends-- Lowndes, Blish, and Zissman,
b) automatically alienated every remaining Futurian, many of whom had no strong political adherences, and most of whom were equally close friends.

We are angry, but not surprised. It is the Wollheim-Michel method, and we have seen it only too often before.

Cyril Kornbluth, the FSNY's most brilliant writer, having come into conflict with the Wollheim standard of morals, was ordered by these three to conduct his life along strict lines laid down by them. Naturally, he chose to leave instead.

Harry Dockweiler was suspended by the Wollheim-controlled Executive Committee, because his vote might have brought the FSNY under Fred Pohl's leadership. Dick Wilson was not formally dropped from the roles, but was ostracized in exactly the same manner that the recent action was carried out against the four members, Blish, Lowndes, Baden, and Zissman, on the accusation that he was an 'untrustworthy character'-- that is, he was obviously more attached to Pohl than to Wollheim.

The "Statement of Independence," drafted by seven members of the Futurians, in which Johnny Michel and Donald and Elsie Wollheim were declared unfit for membership in the group.
Courtesy of the Merril estate

Before I became part of the Futurians, the early members had created a constitution that was quite elaborate. There were some interesting things about it. For example, it specified that any time three Futurians were together, the society was in session. Any time it was in session, members who had behaved improperly could be thrown out by the society in attendance. Basically Donald Wollheim and whoever was working with him at the time the constitution was written had created this section to maintain control of the group.

One day Larry Shaw came over to Parallax. He had been sent by his apartment-mate Johnny, but was not happy in that role. It turned out that Donald had convinced Johnny that he must stop seeing me because of my politics. Larry, who was a bit younger than the rest of us, had been sent over with this message and was upset about it.

Shortly thereafter, Damon Knight happened to stop by. We told him what had happened. As a result, Larry, Virginia, Damon, and I eventually came to the decision that the Futurian Society was in session, and we were going to eject Donald Wollheim and Johnny Michel because they were not good buddies.

Immediately we whipped out our mimeograph stencils and made a fanzine officially announcing that Johnny and Donald were hereby cast out of the Futurian Society: they were rats, and we would never associate with them again. We also included an amended version of the constitution, and quickly mailed it off to everyone we knew.

Donald brought a law suit against us for defamation of character and career damages. I think he had a relative who was a lawyer. The suit was for something like $5,000, an extraordinary sum at the time.

None of us had any relatives who were lawyers, so we had to think hard about what to do. In the end we paid a lawyer, who managed to get it thrown out of court, but it cost us a lot of money. In the meantime, Damon and Larry took upon themselves the punishment of Donald Wollheim. This they achieved by answering ads in the pulp magazines for weird, useless items that were on sale, like giant frogs, and having them delivered to Donald's home.

Donald was furious. He tried in vain to pin the deliveries on us. He even had postal inspectors coming around to inspect our typewriters, but they never managed to prove anything.

The Futurian Society, as an actual fan organization, was pretty much finished off by all this nonsense. But the Futurian Society, as a fan myth, has prevailed to this day, mainly because so many significant people came out of it.

In more recent times, Wollheim has had to use only the threat of ostracism; that sufficed to prevent the V.A.P.A. Board of Advisors from inviting Fran Laney to become a member of that organization. The same threat was applied, with a conspicuous lack of success, to Zissman, Blish, and those who were considered to be their 'followers.'

The threat has worn thin. We who have heard it so often are tired of it. We are tired of being 'handled' and of handling other people. We are an 'amorphous collection of individuals bound together by ties of varying magnitudes of social, literary, artistic, or science-fiction and fantasy implications.'*

We make no further claims to leadership, nor do we put our faith in leaders. No one person wrote or dictated this document. It was composed in democratic assembly, each person having full and equal voice. We have disposed of one Wollheim, and we will not tolerate another.

(LARRY SHAW   *Larry Shaw*

Executive Board: (JAMES BLISH   *James Blish*

(JUDY ZISSMAN   *Judy Zissman*

DAMON KNIGHT   *damon knight*

CHESTER COHEN   *Chester. Cohen.*

VIRGINIA K. EMDEN   *Virginia K Emden*

**ROBERT W. LOWNDES   *Robert W. Lowndes*

* From the Constitution of the FSNY, as approved by all of its then members, and published in October 1941 by the then Executive Committee, consisting of D. A. Wollheim, John B. Michel, Robert W. Lowndes, and Cyril Kornbluth.

** Reconsidering previously tendered resignation.

OF RECENT MONTHS, the digests and women's magazines have broken out in a rambling rash of rhetoric on that most unassailable of subjects, Mother Love. They are joyously enumerating the emotional and psychological pitfalls that lie in wait for the child cruelly deprived of the understanding and constant affection that "only a mother" can give.

The cause is clearer than the complaint. During the war, when women were needed in factories and offices, group care for children received a tremendous impetus. Young girls as yet unmarried answered the call for labour-power; mature women with grown children tossed off their aprons with no great reluctance; and young wives and mothers by the thousands, women with young children and husbands overseas, leaped at the chance to make some money, and to be doing something.

*Written in 1945, when Judith was twenty-two, for her ongoing Vanguard Amateur Press Association fanzine, TEMPER!, which changed names slightly depending on the content. This particular issue, four pages long, was called TEAPOTEMPER!.

Now the men have come home, and there aren't enough jobs to go around. For good wholesome frolicsome fantasy value, Henry Wallace's sixty million jobs is equalled only by the "two chickens in every pot" of twenty years ago. At the last reading, the number of unemployed had reached three and a half million. What jobs there are, says good old reliable Public Opinion, must go to the men.

"GIVE THE BOYS A BREAK!"

A good slogan, and with a veteran husband all my own, I'm in favour of it. Let's give the boys the jobs, the homes, the clothes and cars and little luxuries they're entitled to. And maybe if the bright lads who dream up the slogans put their slick-paper brains to work on getting the wheels of industry turning for peace, the boys would get all those things.

But it's really so much easier to create a smug illusion of peace, and prosperity, by getting the little woman back to her ruffled apron at the kitchen sink, and giving her job to her husband. The understanding fictionists and heart-throb psychologists assure us daily that whatever a woman may think she wants, she's really much happier in a submerged role, as wife and mother, and homemaker. Right after V-E Day, we started getting these little gems about the working wife whose problems are all solved when she discovers she's pregnant, can't work … and is really in love with her husband.

The only trouble with the ideas was that so many of the little ladies didn't believe. They liked their jobs and in fact didn't want to leave them. So the sloganeers sicced the paper-pulp industry on them. Now bland authority is issuing dire predictions about the terrible fate that lies in wait for the nursery-trained child.

The cover of the July 1945 issue (vol. 1, no. 2) of Judith's zine *TEMPER! The Family Magazine*, which featured poetry and writing by Judith and her friends. *Courtesy of the Merril estate*

GIVE THE KIDS A BREAK!

I have a daughter, and I admit I'm partial to her—more than somewhat concerned about her present and future happiness—even if I do work for a living. My girl is past three now. She's been in nursery schools, full or part-time, for two years already, and if I stopped working tomorrow, I'd still whittle the family budget six ways at once to keep her there. I've had too good a chance to make comparisons, watching the children in my apartment house, and the ones who go to nursery school, too.

If it's giving the kids a break to coop them up in an apartment designed for adults, where Mama's every other word, of necessity, is "No!" or "Don't touch!" —if it's giving them a break to let them play on the street, under the guidance and training of older children, better versed in street-lore—I'll let mine go underprivileged in a nursery, where shelves and sinks and furniture are designed to size, and built to withstand a child's powers of destruction, where a trained and interested person is with her all the time. If a child's psyche is really supposed to be better off under either the brooding care of Full-power Concentrated Motherhood, or the nervous yelling of a woman with more work on her hands than she can manage—I'll let mine risk the "deprivations" of nursery school life.

I've had some chance to compare mothers too, the carriage-wheelers and the ones who go to work. Next time you run across one of these "the worst home is better than the nursery" dictums, stop a minute, and think about the homes you know. How many of the women you know are able to give their children as much as one full hour of attention during the day? Are actually, physically, able to drop what they're doing at any moment to run and give Junior the admiration he wants, and needs, when he finishes building a particularly complicated block-house?

And just in case the women you know all have maids, and you think over-worked housewives and street-playing are "slum conditions," try this on for size; and see how it fits your preconceptions: in 1935–36, a "good" year, with prosperity just around the corner, approximately one-half of what the statisticians call economic units (which, on the average, is a family of four) had incomes under $25 a week. I could go into rents, the cost of food and household help, and the etceteras, but it's hardly necessary to get a fair estimate of how much time mother had for her two kids between laundry, cooking, cleaning, marketing, and making both ends meet. In the country, where kids at least have all the room they need to run wild, this might not be so bad. In urban communities, I fail to see how the child benefits from "home atmosphere."

And what about the other half of the "good" homes, full of plenty of free time for the lady of the house? How many women do you know who really care for their children? Who don't have a girl in the afternoons to take the baby off their hands for a while? Who wouldn't honestly rather go shopping, play bridge, work at the Red Cross than stay home with the kids?

What the self-styled authorities don't seem to know is that a real change has come over the world. The old cook-stove is no more, and farm-size families don't fit into city apartments. In the so-called good old days, when a woman had five to ten children to care for, and a big house to take care of, she didn't have to worry either about utilizing her excess energies or about the children's play. They had plenty of space, and a "natural" family group. We couldn't go back to that now if we wanted to, and nobody really wants to. The good old days were also the days when the infant mortality rate was almost three times what it is now; when hardly a family raised its brood without losing at least one child, and probably more than one; when there were no radios, refrigerators, or automobiles, let alone automatic clothes and dish washers, and imminent atomic power. Science keeps a-pushin' us, and the only loud complaints I've heard are from the people who can't afford yet to buy the new gadgets.

And while everybody worries about how to raise the standards of the lower half, the fortunate women on the top find they just don't know what to do with themselves. The same psychologists who are so busy warning us about our children don't mince words about idle women either. Theoretically, of course, all the modern innovations ought to set women free to take better care of their children. Actually, after Lo! these many years, believing every female was a natural child's nurse, we're finding out that when they get the time and freedom, most women don't give it to their children.

There are enough who do, though. Enough, that is, if they can take care of other people's children at the same time. Enough to provide nurseries with trained, intelligent people, who really want to spend time with children, who are doing it by choice, rather than accident of sex.

A mother in a low-income family is a better mother for being able to earn some extra money while her child is cared for in an atmosphere of affection and encouragement. A mother in a well-to-do family, who is only just discovering that child care is not her secret passion, will be doing more for her youngster by seeing him less, and having something to keep her own mind occupied. You have to see these "pitiable" children, leaving their mothers with a smile in the morning, and running back to them at night, to realize how very much both nursery and mother can hold a place in a small child's life.

SO WHY NOT GIVE THE GIRLS A BREAK?

The women of this generation were brought up to believe that they were individuals, free and equal persons with a job to do in the world. Let's quit kidding ourselves, then, that as soon as a woman marries she can run right back to the world where Grandma lived as a girl. Women don't even have a place in the home any more—the few who do want nothing more than to be deprived of it. They're free, among other things, of the place they held in an outdated society. Now they have to make a place for themselves in the modern world community. And they've got to do it at the same time that they see to it that their children are getting the best possible training for life in an increasingly complex and interdependent society. If the nursery schools can do a better job, why not give up and admit it?

EIGHT | A (REAL?) WRITER: HOMAGE TO TED STURGEON

It seems there was a travelling salesman. There really was. He was seedy and he was sad, and he travelled from door to door in Chelsea—that section of the lower West Side of New York lying between the more famous Village and the more infamous Hell's Kitchen. If he ever sold his wares I do not know, except as I may here bear witness he sold nothing to me; he did, however, carry news of me, a writer barely begun, to the ears of Miss Merril, a writer barely beginning.

There followed a letter and a meeting. Her letter contained some flattery of a nature quite overwhelming until tempered by the meeting, at which I was quickly made aware of the fact that nobody who had actually sold a story to a magazine—even a minor story to a minor magazine—could escape her awe. In other words, the status Writer was of greater importance to her than any writer. Even me.

At the time she had not yet sold a word, and her chant, her theme was, "I want to be a Writer!" and the anomaly in this was that she was one, and that anyone in the scrivening trade who ever talked to her knew immediately that she was; that she was a writer in every respect, from top to toe to inside to out, who could write and would write and must write if it was on wet cardboard in the pouring rain with a pointed stick; and she didn't know it!

— *from Theodore H. Sturgeon's introduction to* Out of Bounds, *a collection of short stories by Judith Merril, 1961.*

March 29, 1946

Dear Mr. Sturgeon:
Dear Theodore: (check one)
Dear Ted:

This is an impulse, long-delayed, but none the more carefully planned for all that. I hope you'll answer, and suspect you will, because you answered the ad … but better I should begin at the commencement, and work my way up to date.

Once upon a time I knew a character generally referred to as Horrible Henry. He knew and spoke much of a thin pale-faced lad, by name Peter Sturgeon. In the course of time, Horrible Henry being the type of character who attaches himself over a course of time, he discovered a copy of *Astounding Science Fiction* in my house, and told me with great pride and joy that Peter's brother wrote that junk.

Didn't mean a thing, then. Not till I got back to NY in the fall of '44, after a year or so bumping my baggage around the country, and read "Killdozer," and thought with great pride, "I know a man who knows the brother of the man who wrote that."

"Killdozer" was a powerful convincing novelette about a duel-to-the-death between a bulldozer operator and a sentient 'dozer in a construction site on a Caribbean island. (I know how that sounds; if anyone else had written it, it would have been schlock.) It marked Theodore Sturgeon's return to publication after a silence of several years (during which he had been running hotels and bulldozers in the Caribbean).

… Still didn't mean much, until shortly afterwards, when I was intro-duced to a Futurian, and through him to the whole world of fandom. Everybody else sat around all the time talking about authors they had known, and impressing me to no end, and all I had to hang on to was that I knew a guy who knew—etc.

Then there were more stories of yours, and one day I timidly suggested I'd like to meet this guy Sturgeon. "Him!" chorused the FSNY, "He's one of Campbell's group!"

"Campbell's group" were the established authors; regular contributors to the leading magazine in the field, *Astounding Science Fiction*, edited by John W. Campbell, Jr. Obviously we, rebels on the fringe, brilliant, unrecognized, could not consort with Establishment.

…When I first met them all, I'd suggested brightly, very brightly, that we put an ad in the *Villager* and see if we couldn't meet lots and lots of charming and intelligent fans in the Village. The idea got batted around, and somehow wound up with an ad in *The Saturday Review*, which I was informed you had answered.

But any mistakes I might have made about getting in touch with you were swiftly corrected. You were still one of Campbell's gang, and undoubtedly dull as dishwater … Things developed, as things do. Among other things, they developed into the end of the war, and my husband swapping a submarine for an unheated flat. They also developed into me being home, banging at the typewriter, with my files open, and my desk covered with the usual assortment of papers, books, carbons, coffee cups, toys, and paper bags, when the Fuller Brush man came a-knocking.

He saw me, desk, coffee cups, and plunged into a startling sales approach. It appears you once offered him coffee and absinthe, and it had a terrific kick. You used to live on 10th Ave., and now live on Eighth, and you write stories, and he guesses you do have quite an imagination, and no, I don't know what his name is, and anyhow, nobody but Hemingway drinks absinthe, so he probably has you mixed up with someone else. Although, come to think of it, Horrible Henry, who is in all respects a Hemingway character, also drinks the stuff, so there's no telling.

Me—I am a sort of a cross between a ghostwriter and research assistant, have published two middling bad detective pulps, written some poetry nobody likes but me, and put out a few amateur publications, about which nobody has gone into ecstasy. I am considered quite bright by those who like me well, and you'd probably like Dan, my husband, better than me, if you really know about things like bulldozers, or give a damn. He is about to become an electronics engineer. And it's all his fault, anyhow, because he spent a year after we got married propagandizing me until I finally picked up a copy of *Astounding*.

Now it's your turn …

Judy Zissman

449 W. 19 St.

New York City 11

We are always reinventing ourselves—our lives and our histories.

Going through these old letters, I was first startled, then bemused, to discover time and again how my memory corrects my life—not substantively, not in major ways, but almost exactly as one revises a carefully crafted piece of fiction—adding telling detail, pinpointing motivations, adjusting the view and the time flow to enhance emotional rhythms—making it all more believable.

Is it only fiction writers who do this, or does everyone instinctively revise reality when it falls short of dramatic credibility?

By the time Ted wrote his introduction to *Out of Bounds*, fifteen years after our first meeting, he remembered me as having "not yet sold a word," and (honestly) believed that "nobody who had actually sold a story to a magazine" could escape my awe. He did not know when we first met that my awe was for the first good writer I had known, simply because he did not, at the time, know that he himself was a very good writer. He began to understand that just about the time I began to understand that I did indeed want to Be A Writer more than anything else in the world. (But even later, he would never know it more than half the time: one of the most curious of writerly traits is the onion-like layering of outrageous arrogance and abject humility—on arrogance, on humility, on—etc.).

March 30, 1946

Dear Judy,
Thank you for your long-delayed, carefully planned impulse. What a wonderful blend of the studied and the spontaneous!

Your beginning at commencement calls up a wealth of anecdotal material. Wonder what ever happened to Horrible Henry Thomas? I mind me one evening going into Martin's 57th St. Cafeteria to be descended upon by nine of the habitués, all of whom were equipped with handshakes, backslaps, kudos and salaams. When the noise died down and the crockery had been swept up, I elicited the info that Henry Thomas had just been there and had announced, "You know, I'm not going to go see Ted Sturgeon any more. Somehow or other he makes me feel unwelcome." If you knew Horrible Henry at all, you would realize the earth-shaking nature of that statement …

The pale-faced Peter Sturgeon was elected in the Army and became a paratrooper. He married a swell kid from Brooklyn and then went overseas. After a worrisome time he returned last November.

Was much amused and interested—as was Stanton—at your remarks in re Futurians, and the SatRev ad. Wollheim answered us, you know. Hm. Seems we couldn't make the grade with these exalted people. Dull as dishwater. Those characters ought to see …

There followed half a page of outrageous name-dropping. In fact, when I met them later, the people he mentioned were almost as funny and interesting as he claimed—but you had to be there, eh?

He enclosed a cordial note of invitation from Jay Stanton, whose apartment he was then sharing.

… About Stanton. He is not a regular author of SF. He has lived most of that stuff—sideways thru time, the odd-numbered dimensions up to and including eight, and so forth. He was born on a satellite of Saturn twelve thousand years ago, and, being a little advanced for his generation (they live twenty-odd thousand years generally, and their culture is older than that of Mars, which has died out) was sent to earth to investigate our particular re-enactment of The Beginning of Things. He has donned human guise and does pretty well—you'd hardly guess that he wasn't a terrestrial. Of course, his playing of the banjo is superhuman, and his basic philosophies are too simple for most diffuse humans to grasp. He is very good about his electronics, pacing the knowledge he doles out to the top pace of humanity, since he feels that we already have too much on Earth which we can't handle. He damn near let that anti-grav thing slip the other day—that was close. Lunch with Campbell, y'know. You have to be careful. Dull as dishwater indeed.

Then, of course, there's Ree, the dark(eyed) angel, who writes exquisite (accent on the first syllable please) poetry. I could, by several hundred thousand words, say more about Ree. But you'll see for yourself, I'm sure…. I want very much to meet you and your spouse, and, extravertially speaking, I want you all to meet us.

Thank the powers I've found some reason to thank that Fuller Brush man. Of all the uninspiring, pity-generating, troglodytic accidents of human generations, he is exceeded in objective misery only by Henry Thomas.
Ted Sturgeon

What I had not told Ted in my letter was that I had actually bought his address from that Fuller Brush man. I had exactly sixty-nine cents in the world that day, and I told him so before he came in. After he told me Sturgeon lived only two blocks away I bought the cheapest thing he had—a toothbrush for thirty-seven cents—and he gave me the address.

We went over to the 8th Avenue apartment. I didn't like Ree. Ted didn't like Dan. Jay was fun. Ted and I didn't quite dislike each other, but I found him surfacey, over-mannered, almost affected. He made too many jokes, far too many puns. His blond good looks were too close to pretty. I had to keep reminding myself about the strength of his stories. I think he found me crude, too bold, certainly (rumours came back to me later) "unfeminine."

Ree left.

Dan left.

(Well, that's too flip. We'd been married seven years and we had a bright blue-eyed, beautiful three-year-old daughter; we had once been true and loyal comrades and now we were mutually embarrassed strangers—but that is another chapter.)

I fell—rebounded—into love with a man named Henry (not at all Horrible). Henry and Ted liked each other, so I saw more of Ted.

Henry left.

In January I moved from my now doubly desolate tenement apartment into an elegant East Side place loaned to me for three months by my Aunt Tim. Ted came to visit and we found ourselves really talking for the first time. He was going off to a friend's country house to do some intensive writing. He left me an address.

The next morning I began the first letter of the rest of our lives. The full correspondence file covers forty years. In its most intense period, between January and May of 1947, it deals specifically with the birth of a writer named Judith Merril.

Dear Ted:

I had no notion of writing you so soon, but I have a story to tell, brought back to mind, after almost a year's passage, by the discussion we had yesterday. I want to get it down on paper before I quite forget it, and I'd rather not use it anywhere in any way that might cause me to submit it for publication, or even to publish it in Vanguard. It must be in context if it's to be in print; and context in this case would be little short of a novel.

We were both members of the Vanguard Amateur Press Association, in which I published my occasional "fanzine" called *TEMPER!* The topic that had opened the floodgates was a newly announced government initiative against anti-Semitism. My anecdote concerned the inverse: Jewish community attitudes towards the "goyim." After three closely typed single-spaced pages, I wound up:

… There is a consistent effort being made by governmental authorities to stop prejudice. But before you can cure the Christian of his contempt, you have to cure the Jew of his fear; that is the harder job. In the meantime, the very imposition of authority on the weaker side, when it has till now always favored the stronger, is going to create such a wave of reaction that things are bound for a while to be worse instead of better.

This is admittedly self-conscious ... but how am I to bring up my child?

I enclose, as an afterthought, the clipping I mentioned. You'll be sure to return it, won't you? It has a good deal of meaning to me, largely because it's such an unrealizable dream. We can't start all over again, because there just isn't room in Palestine, and because our roots are else-where. We've got to achieve full citizenship here, somehow, or go without it. But don't miss the last two paragraphs, nor their connotation. A "new order" of some sort, is what we instinctively look for; it is much of the reason why even strong individualists, like myself, become Socialists (and the number who go through exactly the phases I did is great: Zionism; labor-Zionism; socialism), until we realize that that dream too, is not realizable.

Ten days later he replied.

And now the answer. Sorry I couldn't do what I wanted to do—namely, throw up everything and write right away. I've got to do an awful lot to fully justify this period of hermitage.

How odd   Of God
   To choose   The Jews

said a wit whose name I can't recall. How odd, too (speaking with the detachment of a visiting Martian) that a group of sensitive, intelligent peo-ple should strike such a dismal medium in clannishness! ... This frightening reaction would not occur if most people regarded their fellows as individu-als. Further, such an attitude is the strongest possible defense against such tragic social pressures.

Merril will be persecuted because she is a Jew. You can no more stop every occasion of it than you can prevent her from catching cold. Sooner or later it will happen and only if she is fore-armed with a deep-seated, habitual regard of individuals as individuals will she be able to defend her-self. Defend herself not against the little boy who says she can't come to the party because she's a Jew, but against the flux of poison within herself which will be set up. She must be able to say, with conviction, that Hans is excluding her because there is something the matter with Hans. She must be able to do this without beating Hans over the head with it: Hans is out of it, and it must be her own conviction...

Conclusion: that the member of a persecuted minority must not only be an acceptable individual in his own right as an individual. He must cast himself as an ambassador of his kind, as long as "kind" is important to the rest of society. I told that to Phil Klass recently, and he got very angry indeed at me. I could not persuade him that by ambassadorship I did not mean knuckling under, turning the cheek, and so forth.

Phil Klass is better known as William Tenn, arguably the funniest serious writer science fiction has ever had. (Arguably: Stanislav Lem, after all?) When we met, Phil had recently published his first story, and the second, "Child's Play," was about to appear.

Phil and Ted and I were like the Three Musketeers for much of that magic year of 1947. We laughed and argued and roamed the New York streets and picked each other's work apart, brain-trusted, cooked fine food, got drunk, and argued about everything and sang and loved (each other and others) and argued some more.

One thing that now baffles me: at one of our frequent joint financial bottomings, we invented a cheque-kiting system that enabled us to pass a single sum of ten dollars successively through all three bank accounts for days and weeks on end. (In 1947, remember: ten bucks was money!) Of course, banks were not yet computerized, but all our accounts were in the same branch, and I can no longer figure out just how we did it.

Feb. 13, 1947

Dear Ted:

… Your stuff about ambassadors makes me mad too. Not because it isn't true, but because it is, and I'd bet a pickled penny that's really why Phil got mad. What we resent, or I at least, is the knowledge that because I'm a Jew, I mustn't talk too loud or wear too bright colors, or show any ignorance of the social graces. I don't want to be an ambassador; I want to be me.

I can get by; I am, on the whole, a "white" Jew. But I don't like being among people who talk about the "yids" and I don't like being told, "You're different. They're not all like you," as I have been, too often.

The damnable part of it is that we are ambassadors, whether we choose to be or not … and you see, you contradict yourself when you say "Be a person." Within my own circle, I am free to be the best person I can be. Out in the very real world, where people insist on classifying and categorizing, whether you or I like it or not, I am not free to be the best person I think I can be; I must first be certain that I am not, by my behavior, shocking anyone in a way that would be regarded as particularly Jewish …

Incidentally, this does not weigh on me as heavily as these letters might make it appear. I live with certain restrictions as a Jew, certain restrictions as a woman, certain restrictions as a civilized person. I disregard these restrictions when it seems not too dangerous … so I need not think about being a Jew most of the time any more than I have to think about wearing clothes in the street…

Right now, I am all wrapped up in another argument entirely. Henry's CO friend Vitold was in town, and we spent a long winey evening talking about it. *TEMPER!* is full of it, an article by me, done months ago, before I knew H., or had had much chance to discuss it with anyone, and one by HES … I keep saying "it." The reference, of course, is to the entire subject of pacifist resistance to war, conscientious objection, and for that matter, any sort of resistance to war. I shan't get into it now, because it would probably run into pages and pages, and anyhow, *TEMPER!* will be run off tonight, and I'll send you a copy. Opinions?

"H" and "HES" are (Wonderful) Henry, who was a "CO"—conscientious objector—in World War II.

Feb 22, 1947

Jeer Dewdy,
… Your friend to whom you never said, defensively or otherwise "I am a Jew" was a jerk. If you must run with wide-eyed innocents who drift around blandly unconscious of the facts and facets of life, you will have to pay the consequences. (I wish I was a consequence. Those things seem to get pretty well paid.)

I truly like the way your mind worked on that matter of ambassadors. You please me, at times, you do…. By "be a person," then, I meant that it is desirable … to live in the greatest concentration of "good taste" as is compatible with sincerity. Civilized functionalism is an overall cover of the human animal, it's true. But it isn't a hard glossy veneer. (That's affectation.) It's "oil plating" like it says in the ads—a fine even layer of clean lubricant, through which the basic steel shows well …

For God's sake get a new typewriter ribbon.
See you soon …
Ted

Feb. 24, 1947

Dear Theodore:
Sometimes I like you, too; and sometimes you irritate from here to way out there. Anyhow, I get more backhanded compliments than anybody. Women, in particular, apparently with the best of intentions, are always telling me I should do this, that, or some other damn thing, because I really "could be beautiful." Now this is to start with a contradiction in terms. Beautiful is something that is or is not and never could be if it isn't; the joker in this case is that experiment has made it clear to this particular might-have-been that the best I can do is look like "if I only bothered," I'd make top rating, on account of when I do bother, I may look chic, but I also look plain-and-painted, and who wouldn't rather look almost-beautiful? All of which is doubtless of no interest to you whatsoever, except I'm so glad you like my mind sometimes …

Also about Jews; frankly I'm sick of them. I haven't talked or thought so much on this subject for years …

Naturally, it's up to the individual, of whatever background, to adjust himself to the accepted tastes of the environment he seeks out. Only we can't, if we happen to be an intellectual minority, live in the favored environment all the time. The good taste, for instance, that allows you to wear whatever clothing you like among friends of similar standards is hardly acceptable to the police force of the City of New York …

Ted was, by policy and frequent practice, a nudist. He used to point out gleefully that answering the apartment door bare was a great disincentive to solicitors (whether for votes, payments, or sales). In high school, he had trained to be a circus acrobat, and he had a gorgeous body. We didn't live close enough for home visits when the sagging years came, so I don't know for sure whether his nudism outlasted his beauty.

… The intellectual tastes and emotional attitudes that led me to become a member of a left-wing group at one time are equally unacceptable to the police, as I have had occasion to learn.

Now I'm coming to my point: I have spoken at I don't know how many street-meetings, after which the cop on duty informed me in one way or another, and in varied language that he would, if not for my presence, probably run the whole bunch of Jew-bastards in. But I was much too nice a girl to be dragged in with them, and would I please go home and let the officers do their duty?

Of course I never did go home; the thing that made me join in the first place was a similar incident. I'd been holding out for months because the whole thing seemed so futile and so ingrown, and then I agreed to go to one meeting; after the meeting, we were singing old Joe Hill songs, and a batch of Christian Front lads, out for an evening of fun, started tossing rocks through the window. At that point, the well-known pit of the stomach got the better of the top of the brain, and I decided anyone good enough for those boys to throw rocks at was good enough for me to join.

This was an individual action, as were all my actions in the Party. I spent about 14 months as a member fighting the Party Line, and finally got out, still unconverted to the idea of a party line.

… What are Cajuns?

And have you had the mailing yet? Vanguard I mean? I'm curious about your reactions.

When are you coming back? I want to have one great big party in this beautiful place while I have it, and it might as well be when you're here as when you're not.

This was neither the first, nor by any means the last, friendship in my life that began with all-out debate; it is only the best-documented. There have been perhaps a dozen such friends I have cherished as People I Can Really Argue With: cogent thinkers with views that are thoughtfully different from mine; tough talkers who can't be easily bamboozled; friends who might conceivably convince me or be convinced, but will in any case still be friends at the end.

Of course it was not all debate. I told Ted how moved I was by his new story, "Maturity." And I sent him some of my poetry.

March 4, 1947

Dear Judy,

Sometimes you irritate me too. Like now. I'm supposed to be working. (Wait'll I fix that margin. Talking to you I got to get a little farther over to the left. Shaddup! I can temper your TEMPER with one of my own.) So instead of working I spend the time I'm not looking for your last letter in thinking about where the hell I put it. I found it stuck between one of my pastel nudes and an atlas. Now what am I doing? How the hell can I get any work done while you sit there goggling at me out of those mad eyes and wait for me to talk to you? Shaddup! Least you can do is sit quiet and listen.

This "beautiful is a is or is a is not" deal is for the birds. You know better than that. All things are beautiful, at times, to a degree. Have you ever thought about beauty, just beauty, as a thing apart from other things, rather than as a quality, or appurtenance to other things? I wonder if you have … do you ever sit quietly long enough to do that? So much beauty is quiet stuff…. Mostly you go around like a man with a paper scrotum in a forest fire …

I'm not going to talk to you about being beautiful any more. This infant, this newborn, puking, pink-and-mustard friendship of ours has already reached the stage where I can sense the old "there he goes again" reaction when I say anything about it, so the hell with it. Know what that reaction is? Prejudice. Yes it is. Put a stroboscopic beam on the split second reactions of any bigot and you'll see. Here comes the set of factors; I recognize them; I don't like them already.

Beautiful is a state of mind. It is a state of mind where it starts and it is a state of mind where it goes to. It is an abstract compounded of harmony and/or contrast with the environment of the beautiful thing. The environment does not have to be concrete, but it has a hell of a lot to do with the reflexes of the beholder. So be beautiful, and I shall react to beauty to the degree of yours. Be uninteresting, and I shall not react. Be downright ugly, and I'll probably think that you're beautiful, so don't ever worry about that again.

In all this business of bad taste and good taste and so on, I'm beating my brains out against the very things you are—the desire for the right to rebel against that which does not suit my standards. It's a tough battle, particularly when you evolve to the point where you are a hypocrite if you don't face the fact that all too often you are substituting "convenience" for "standards." I can only know my own definition of graciousness, and it is one that precludes hating a man for his black skin, pissing on other people's rugs, going naked when it will distress others, sleeping with other men's wives, violating privacy, and any number of other delightful or uncomfortable or fun-making things. A gracious man avoids many difficulties, true. So does the professional rebel.

" … but with a whimper" is damn good. I'm going to give you a present.

The discerning reader may be surprised to hear that neither of us knew we were conducting a courtship—not until the night he came back to New York, in the first week of March.

He phoned me from a bus station in the morning, said he had a gift for me, and that he did not want to go directly to Jay's: could he come to my place first? Of course! I had, from somewhere, a bottle of sparkling wine; I had an old high-school prom evening gown, and the makeup my aunt had given me (and shown me how to use) before she left. I went out and bought some balloons. It was a fine party, for two.

```
VISION

                Somewhere
                there is a lucid plane of beauty
                where we two might live
                without obstruction;

                somewhere

                we'd taste more wholly
                savor without fear
                fullness,
                a richness of the life we've touched
                and glimpsed
                and dreamed and talked of
                longingly to one another.

                Here
                now
                we're part of the disease
                that preys on us
                surrounds us
                saps our strength;

                the air here
                is not clear;

                too much
                we cannot see or know
                too much
                around us
                too much of us
                is sick as well as sickened.

                Somehow
                the trap of horror
                can be broken;
                our eyes can pierce the murk;
                our limbs grow strong to
                bursting;  minds gain courage.

                We number two
                among the fortunate of men;
                we have the vision
                and we know the world
                of uncontaminated atmosphere
                exists
                        somewhere
                                somewhen.
```

A poem Judith wrote for the July 1945 issue of TEMPER!. Courtesy of the Merril estate

The gift was a copy of Clement Wood's *The Complete Rhyming Dictionary and Poet's Craft Book* inscribed, "I give this so that Judy can/Become a god-damn artisan."

He advised me to practise formal verse, if only for the sake of my prose. Although we were now seeing each other almost every day, we continued to write letters—often hand-delivered. In fact, he had carried his last letter with him. I answered it the next day, after he woke me with a phone call.

Dear Ted,

Thank you for calling. I feel well-slept, well-pleased, and, well—very well …

About the beautiful deal, as I've since explained, most of what I wrote was sheer ugly defense mechanism. After all, there's bound to be some reaction to a character who goes around telling everybody how unfeminine I am …

Beautiful, however, is what our numerous [Alfred] Korzybski-mad friends would call multiordinal. I was talking about beauty-parlor-beauty, not sunset-and-soul beauty, and wouldn't have said what I did about the second variety even in a defensive mood. I agree with you completely, and now what are you going to do?

Listen, there's something serious I want to talk about. I mean practical-serious. I told you the mercenary calculating reasons why I cultivated you, and they still hold. I like the way you've taken me up on my poetry-scribbling, but I'm much more concerned with prose cause it pays. The more of what I write you're willing to read and comment on, the happier I'll be about it …

The current admonition is just to warn you that any time you do comment, you'll have to make sure it's rounded. It's easy as hell for me to decide it's all wrong if nothing's said at the same time about its good points. This is not in reference to anything you've said or done in the past … just a request for the most useful variety of criticism in the future. And for as much criticism as you can take time to give me, too.

Hey the hell with this stuff. Happy New Year. Spring is here. I just took [my daughter] Merry to school and came back, and there's an ad in the paper for a five-room apartment, and I've been reading my new book on the bus, and I got some fine pictures of Merry in the mail today, one of her looking into the living room mirror with a little-girl's grin at the delights of a mirror.

Spring is here!

It feels so funny to feel happy all the way through … clean nice fresh fun young happy. Thank you, Theodore, and thank the nice man who mixed today's clear sky.

The five-room apartment was in the basement of a big old low-rise on E. 4th Street near Second Avenue. (Ten and twenty years later this would be beatnik and then hippie territory; I was premature.) It was too expensive, but the rooms were big, the ceilings high, the windows large, and the third bedroom meant I could rent out a room. I took it.

And I wrote a sonnet—or thought I did:

The world's a whirling ball of fire;
The world's a slowing mass of ice;
My world's a wistfully precise
Geometry of my desire.
My world's a passionate love-lyre
Played on a bed of lava and gneiss;
And I'm an articulate, concise
Spier and crier and versifier.
I'm an integral part of the ruse
We play on us in the same old game,
Shaping the stars to the eyes of the Muse.
At the door of my cell I bid for fame
And codify my cosmic clues
In the human hall of freezing flame.

Ted pointed out, with some restraint, that sonnets are not ordinarily in tetrameter. I revised it. Achieving greater technical perfection did not improve the poetry. Ted wrote me a five-page letter:

… It says stuff. There is little evidence of the worst fault of the sonneteer: the forced shaping and pruning of words and thoughts to fit the rigidity of the sonnet form. It is a rigidity. You are at liberty to write any form, or any kind of vers libre, that you choose. Nobody says you must write sonnets. But if you do, write a sonnet and not something approaching one …

I shall go overleaf and consider your final version line by line. Is it necessary for me to write here things about "don't take this the wrong way" and "I really think you have talent, and am only trying to help you in a field in which you would exceed me except for the accident that I got into it many years before you did"?

I trust not. Suffice it to say that this is a hell of a lot [of] trouble…. If you had no talent in these matters, I know I could say as much, and do it freely. I'd even gain from it. You'd respect me personally for it. So draw your own conclusions.

There followed a detailed, painstaking analytic dissection of each line—sometimes a sentence, sometimes a paragraph. Then:

Now, you wrote a sonnet. You did it as a challenge, and as the taking up of a challenge. Your next sonnet will be better if you follow these suggestions:

Keep pure and faithful your respect for the form. Violate it nowhere, ever, not in the slightest shift of syllabic value. Our language, with all its faults, is one of the most completely expressive in history.

I find little fault with your punctuation, but it might help you to assume my view of it; namely, that punctuation is inflection in print. To me, "She loves me—" is heard differently from "She loves me …" and from "She loves me." There is a speaking difference between a colon and a semicolon and a comma. With this quite clear in your mind, punctuate the sonnet as if it were prose; for, as far as idea-content is concerned, it is prose, just as fine prose is poetry …

Now, about the "rules." They can be violated, and are, by the great. You can cite me hundreds of examples. There are tetrametric lines in Shakespeare. If you would do this, go ahead. But be Shakespeare first.
T.H.S.

I was incredulously grateful for both the faint praise and the detailed criticism. I had by this time sold three or four more stories—detectives and westerns—to Doc Lowndes, and Ted was pushing me to try science fiction. The writing, and rewriting, of the sonnet, and Ted's reactions, had quite confirmed my confidence that I could learn any literary technique, but good science fiction was not just a matter of learned skills. I believed I did not have the capacity for imagination-cum-detailed-visualization it required.

It never occurred to me that the same quality might be a prerequisite for poetry: I took refuge in Clement Wood. (I never did write another sonnet, but I did do one each of some other tricky forms.)

While I practised precise meter and scansion and rhyme, I was cleaning and caring for my aunt's elegant apartment as I had (and still have) never done in any place of my own. I was still doing some of the research and ghostwriting jobs, and writing the odd filler piece for Doc Lowndes. I was taking Merry to nursery school every morning, picking her up in the afternoons, putting Band-aids on her knees, playing with her, reading to her, making dinner and giving her a bath every evening, and I was getting ready to move on April first. (Henry had told me once that the way to deal with painters and plumbers was to smoke unfiltered Camels and offer them during discussions. As usual, he was right. For my new place the painters mixed me the exact shade of grey-blue turquoise I had fallen in love with on the walls of Aunt Tim's apartment.)

I found tenants for my new spare bedroom: Friedel and Asher, immigrants from Latvia.

Meanwhile, Ted and I were all the pleasures proving, orbiting at e2, the limiting speed of emotion; and I was deciding, Yes! I was going to be a professional writer. Between times, I coped with my mother, who was delighted, but worried, about the last item, and worried-and-upset about all the rest of the above.

I was twenty-four years old. Now, forty-five more years down the line and a practised teller of tales, I know that if I were inventing this story, I would never try to convince a reader that so much could have been packed into so short a time. I did not believe it myself; my revisionist memory had stretched six weeks into six months—but it's all there in the letters.

How can time be so compressed? Where did the energy come from? When did this young woman sleep?

Just nine days after I opened the door for Ted in my old prom dress I wrote:

March 17, 1947
Monday morn, before 3

Ted dear,
I left the phone, and stumbled over to the typer, full of unfinished scraps of conversation, thinking how, since I'd been awakened early, I could spare time to write you and explain something important.

Imagination … I didn't realize, I think, until tonight, quite fully that it was something that could be developed and wasn't just an "is an is or is an is not" deal. (I love that!) I don't know what factors you had in mind when you said my imagination had been stifled, but I think I can follow it pretty easily. Start with the kind of reaction I had to music when I was a kid—someone would laugh at me, so I'd go away from whatever was beautiful, and forget about it. Toss in an intensely socially conscious environment during my adolescence, where the searching out of the Facts became the ultimate desideratum. Add a husband who called poetry "poultry," which would have been all right if he had ever called it anything else, even when he wrote it. Run through this a thread of enforced independence, personal, and then financial, which kept the sheltering roof anywhere but overhead, and let the sunlight in a little too bright a little too often, so that many things were seen in sharp relief that might have benefited by shades and tone. Combine it with a sharply analytical mind, which I have. My dreams went underground.

So now Sturgeon comes along and tells me sure I've got an imagination, all I have to do is relax and I'll find out.

I started in this game wanting to be an editor, because I was pretty damn sure I'd never make the grade as a writer. I began to understand applied technique from Johnny Michel, who lives by it. Johnny's a guy who's been disappointed by life so damned often he's taken the delicate quivering little center-piece and carefully callous-camouflaged it, till hardly anybody, including Johnny, knows it's there. He could, and did, teach me what I had known when I was ten, but since forgotten, that writing was something you did by figuring people out, and working hard at the images in your mind, and expressing them in certain symbols, with meaningful allusions and touches as often as direct statements. The only thing he couldn't teach me was where the images came from and how to let the pictures come out without having to figure them out.

Anyhow, after a while along came beautiful lovely deep-purple Henry. (I told you I only learn from other people; books help, but I can't get it without people.) Of course he had this business all confused with romance, which made it hard for me to get at sometimes, because the romantic smoke-screen is something I bypassed a long time ago, and haven't much use for. Romance, fun-and-gayety, yes; romance, slick-style love, no. I told Henry things I'd almost forgotten about, like the long involved games I used to play in the attic "observatory" with my one close friend. I was generally a modified version, or an exaggerated one, of Richard the Lion-Hearted, mixed up with Robin Hood, Kim, and a few early Greek gods, and she the lovely, but independent and troublesome princess, and we spun it out, near as I can recall, week by week, and sometimes day by day, for four years or so, and when I moved back to NY it was probably the thing I missed most. I should have been writing it, not playing it, but my mother plagued me so to write, and kept talking about what my father had done … and there was always the excellent chance I'd do less well than he.

Anyhow, there wasn't much outlet after that. I did write a little, though unwillingly, when I was fourteen and fifteen. By then I had friends, two budding chemists and one ditto economist, and I thought I was a young economist myself, so I started college and quit after a year in a passion of disgust with the school and myself and the world. It was the summer of 1940, the draft act, and war coming, depression still, and I was the Forgotten Generation, almost all by myself.

The five years between us make a difference here. I was 17 that summer; war was something direct and personal and too hurtful to do anything about but be logical. If you let yourself feel it, at 17, it damn near killed you. I met Danny and got married, fast, and discovered sex, and found out how many things sex can make unnecessary. Sex and a Cause, together, can take care of all the tag ends of emotion and imagination.

You know most of the rest of the story. I was a Party worker for a year and a half, a housewife for two years, and then I was suddenly alone, with a baby, allotment checks, time to experiment, and eventually John Michel, and all the people and trains of thought he brought with him. I couldn't let myself go all the way, and make full use of his (and their) limited value, because there was Dan, in the background, Dan whom I loved like crazy, and who would be back, probably still laughing at all that sort of thing, Dan who was pleased as punch at my first published story, and loved having a writer-wife to brag about, but wasn't likely to go for anything much purpler than *Crack Detective*. I very consciously did not want to unfit myself for living with him. It happened anyway, but I tried goddam hard not to let it happen.

Alright, here I am. I'm full of lovely little words that bust up near the top and run away again, because they're not used to coming out. I still feel a little embarrassed when I talk about the effect good writing has on me, because whenever I said anything to Dan about it, it didn't seem quite to make sense. His view was 'taint how it's said that counts, it's what. I never accepted that, but I couldn't fight it, because the attack was on something too intimately part of me to be allowed to set itself up in opposition to my love, so I shut it up and turned away from it. It wasn't his fault, because he didn't know; I just subsided into the understanding-without-words of the sensitive inarticulates. He felt things, you see, but found it shameful to say them.

Now I tell you I want, more than anything else in the world, to be a good writer. I do. I want the power of it, the kind of power you described in a bulldozer, the kind that comes from looking at what you wrote in a second-hand store, and knowing it has become a part of at least one person who read it, and that if it was good—if you had something to say and got it across—well, whatever it was, it's part of somebody else now, and you better goddam well hope it was good. I want to be sitting up there pushing words around the way the guy on the dozer pushed the levers, and getting results the same way. You can't insult me or hurt my feelings about it, not if you start from the basic premise that I can learn it, that I've got all the levers and the necessary weight and strength and the machine waiting to be used, and all I have to do is learn its workings. Hell, Ted, just accepting that premise is as big a compliment as anyone can pay me right now.

Now tonight, on the telephone, you tell me I've got imagination after all, and for the first time I realize what happened to it, where it went, and how to get it back, and you ask if I'm insulted!

I'm goddam mad at the people who stifled it; I'm goddam happy and pleased and grateful and full of love for the guy who's willing to let me practice its somewhat dulled workings on him himself, personally, even though it means asking questions and getting inadequate answers a lot of the time. Thanks, Ted.

with love and gratitude,

Judy

Ted got a wire from the British magazine *Argosy*: his story, "Bianca's Hands," had won its annual contest. A thousand dollars, but more than that: a mainstream literary award. I watched him, that afternoon, just beginning to allow himself to be aware that he was, by anyone's standards, a good writer, and I began to understand as well the true nature—beyond money or even glory—of the satisfactions a good writer (a Real Writer) might experience. I went home and tried to write what I'd seen and felt.

This was the taste of victory. He slid it in and out of his mouth, examining it for a moment apart from himself, tasting it then as a thing of himself. This was the flavor of triumph, this music, this message, these words, words of himself that had brought forth words of another, life and pain of himself that had come clean and beautiful onto paper, the essence of his own person translated by the message in his hand, by the private meaning of the music he had chosen to hear, into praise and dollars. This was the thing that had happened to him, the memory with which he lived. And a telegram and a thousand dollars changed it, purged it, made it only a memory, no more a part of himself, now only a thing that had come from himself, that would belong to a hundred, a thousand, and tens of thousands of other human beings.

This was the taste of triumph, this once-intimate, once-personal savor that had gone out of him onto the paper, out of the paper into the check, that set him free from pain without losing the knowledge of pain, free from love without losing the glory of love, free from being human without losing the humanity.

Two days later we were in an ice-cream parlour with Merry, and Ted announced he had the perfect pen name for me. I had already decided I did not want to do serious writing under either my husband's or my father's name. I had, in fact, two pen names already, men's names required for Doc's pulps: Ernest Hamilton combined Henry's and Ted's middle names; Eric Thorstein was in homage to Thorstein Veblen. But this new name had to be just me.

Ted printed out on a napkin in elaborate characters: JUDITH MERRIL. I loved it and Merril thought it was great, but I said I couldn't use it: it sounded Anglo-Saxon; I wasn't going to try to pass.

Ted got pissed off. For two days I didn't see him. Then he arrived on my threshold and handed me an envelope, with a letter and another envelope inside.

March 18, 1947
5 a.m.

Judy darlin':
Enclosed is a thing.

Now I'll tell you all about it. But first—please! If you can curb your curiosity, just this once, please don't read the enclosure until you are by yourself and will not be interrupted. I'd like to think of your reading it under those circumstances.

I got the idea for it when I doped out the pen-name for you in that ice-cream parlor the other day. The thing you did that I said was bad was to thumbs-down the Merril spelling, trying to work out a Merol or Meloroll or Merylstein or Cmerilskowski or something. I saw it as Judith Merril; it looks well, it says well, and I can't see it as anything else.

Your reasons for wanting it like that annoy me. You are a far less self-conscious Jew than Phil Klass, yet he means to make his reputation and get his skill as William Tenn and Kenneth Putnam before he uses that patronym. Phil won't eat butter with his meat for anyone at any time, and here you won't publish under an Aryan handle. Is everyone crazy?

The thing that happened that made it all right for me to go ahead was remembering something you said about your Hebrew name. I went to my trusty old encyclopedia and looked it up. It was right in there. It means Jewess. It doesn't mean anything else but Jewess.

Or would you like better I should circumcise you?

As for the pome (this is the Poet's Craft-book Dep't.) it is a Petrarchan sonnet, which means that its form is extremely rigid and complex. The rhyme-scheme is 1 2 2 1, 1 2 2 1, 3 4 5, 3 4 5. Notice that there is no rhymed couplet at the end, as is found in Shakespearean and Wordsworthian sonnets.

The idea is presented in the octet (the first eight lines) and resolved in the sestet. I'd rather build something like this than eat, which is demonstrable ...

The rest of what I have to tell you I have told you before and will tell you again and again and again and again and ...

T.H. Sturgeon

And in the second envelope:

> The Birth of Judith Merril
> As if your life were in itself a god
> And pondered on its past, and on the pain
> And pleasure that composed it; all the grain
> And polish of its growing; how it trod
> The ways of trouble and the flowered sod
> Of laughter ... So created, it again
> Created, Jove-like, from its careful brain—
> A child was born mature, armed, clothed and shod.
> This miracle-Minerva is as wise
> As all the wisdom you have shown. Her strength
> Is yours, and all your gentleness and heart.
> Creative, like her forebears, she shall rise—
> She will be heard! and all mankind, at length,
> Shall know her for her worth, her truth, her art.

Yes, he was (briefly) besotted. And yes, I knew it. What was my worth, my truth, my art? Two pulp detective stories, three pulp westerns, and a handful of half-good poems.

But I was—and am—overwhelmed by the knowledge that behind the infatuation was a kind of love—love of writing as much as of me—that could make him give his time, his energy, his knowledge and inventiveness, not to make me his disciple—I was already that—but to help me become my own self, a writer-woman who just might, with enough work and inventiveness of my own, become a colleague. And this extraordinary effort never faltered, even after he fell in love with another woman.

Of course I was blissfully besotted myself, but on a slightly different potion. When he came back the next day, I swooningly acknowledged my new name, never once challenging his specious arguments. But when he began talking about marriage, I stopped swooning.

Maybe there was some worth and truth, even wisdom, after all (if as yet no evidence of art). Where did I get the sense or the strength to back off (just a bit)? Consider not just the honour, the glamour, and the flattery, but the fun and excitement. I knew I wasn't ready yet (if ever) for another marriage, and I suspected Ted was a better lover than husband, but what saved me—saved us— I think, was that I was still partly in love with Henry.

Only partly: not so much that I ever lost sight of what I was getting. On March 20 I wrote:

lissen, lug—-
you just called and woke me out of a sound sleep and some fantastic dreams. my imagination's improving. you know i never used to dream? mostly i just want to thank you for last night. for the stars and the crisp air and the way the air whirled and the stars jumped up and down and hugged themselves. also i thank you for the sea surf and the palm trees and the crescent moon lying on its back. these things do not endure for me in the way that the concentrated essence of people does. i'm a people-lover … new york is so full of so many people's loves and hates and daily livings. there is a short whitman poem, which i do not seem able to locate at the moment, that says he loves manhattan not for its shops or streets or any-thing, except the way his eyes meet the eyes of lovers and friends as he walks through the city. that's it …

i left you quite disturbed, not unhappy, and not disturbed for me, but full of beautiful tears because i wanted very badly to be able to give as much as i was getting … oh well, why hash it? thank you for last night and just for being in my life.

How can time be so compressed? Reading through these letters, I was astonished to find that the affair I always remembered as lasting about six months was only six weeks long. Welllll—seven? Eight? There was this ambiguous lap-over period between me and my successor—but part of the reason for the ambiguity was that in that same dreamtime I was, in fact, at last, Becoming a Real Writer.

For years I have been telling the story of how I wrote my first science fiction story—the first Judith Merril story—and telling it wrong.

Once there was a little green man who was not running up the wall. The wall was on the landing outside the Stanton apartment. Ted—who had never stopped badgering me about writing an sf story—was standing there with me.

"Look!" he said. "Look! See the little green man running up the wall?"

I looked. "No," I said. "I don't see any little green man."

"Look," he said again. "See? He's taking quick little steps and he has a long pointy hat and it's sticking straight out—"

"Ted," I said. "I don't see any little green man, and if I did, he'd be taking long slow draggy steps, and his hat would be drooping down."

Ted used the smile that sometimes made him look like a sardonically sweet demon. "Right!" he said happily, "I write fantasy. You write science fiction."

Now this happened as told, I think. (I forget names, faces, places, times; I do usually remember dialogue, precisely and with intonation.) But for years I have believed, and reported, that I went home after that and started work early the next morning on "That Only a Mother," the story that made my new name famous in the little pond of science fiction almost overnight.

Not true.

I made reference to the Little Green Man later in that letter to Ted on March 20. The story was written a month later, while my daughter was having the measles and Ted was dallying with Mary Mair.

April 15, 1947

Dear Ted:

This is no doubt feminine, irrational, and unfair; but I've got to get it off my chest, and if I do it this way you won't get it till tomorrow, by which time it will be a little fairer, if still true.

You started writing a story Saturday. You were hot; you were going to stay right with it till it was done, and not let anything or anybody interfere. Even me. OK? I was right with you, and still would be, if same held true. But you let George Smith interfere; you let Phil Klass interfere; you let a vaccination interfere, and the *Argosy* girl. They're all either "unavoidable" or "justifiable," I know. But today is Tuesday, and I'm beginning to feel I might be either unavoidable or justifiable myself.

I'm sorry; I know I'm being unreasonable. I am feeling mildly sorry for myself, and that is a dreadful thing to do. But knowing, as you do, what it's like to be cooped up with a sick-but-not-deathly-sick kid (and going slowly crazy at the same time because there's work I've got to get done, and can't)—"Judeee," it yells from the other room right now, "you were going to fix my racing car—"

The spring was busted. And I don't like the tone of voice I used to her. I would give my left ear to be free to stay at this machine steadily for a while, maybe eight whole hours without an interruption. So I take it out on you because you don't come to see me.

No, there isn't a god damn thing you could do if you did come over. I'm sorry, Ted; this is one bitch of a letter. I just hope you've finished the story by the time you get it, because I don't think I could forgive myself if it did make you interrupt your work.

Ted wrote to me the same day, telling me about Mary.

Intuition? ESP? Call it what you like; we're talking about the times you know stuff you don't know you know. It happens to some of us more than others; it happens to everyone who doesn't simply shut it out.

A few days earlier, when I could still leave Merril with a sitter because I thought all she had was a cold, I had gone over to the 8th Avenue apartment, and met Mary for the first time. There were several visitors that day, among them an extraordinarily beautiful woman, very quiet, very pleasant. I did not sense anything between her and Ted; at that point there was nothing—she had just arrived.

Next day or the one after, Ted stopped by, and something important happened. Merril still had a "cold": she was being kept indoors, but not in bed. Ted—unlike me—was fastidious, possibly to a fault. After an hour or so he said, agonized, "Will you wipe that child's nose?" I looked, surprised, and saw a worm of mucous running down to her mouth; recalled vaguely that it might have been there for quite some time; wiped. Of course it was back ten minutes later. After Ted left, I stopped seeing it again.

The same day there was a tiny article in the *New York Herald Tribune*—page 52 or thereabouts. The U.S. Army of Occupation in Japan was denying rumours that many infanticides were occurring in the areas around Hiroshima and Nagasaki. Migod! I thought, remembering the pictures I'd seen in *Science Illustrated*: brain tumours and missing limbs on baby rats whose parents had been exposed to atomic radiations.

Those were the seeds from which the story—The Story—grew. While they gestated Merril's cold became, officially, measles. I couldn't go out: she had to be kept quiet and resting in a darkened room.

Whenever she was sleeping, or temporarily undemanding, I worked on a western story for Lowndes. Ted was supposedly holed up with a story of his own. On the 15th, he wrote to tell me Mary was still there, and he had made love to her. He was big on monogamy in those days, and could hardly believe he now wanted both of us. He was, actually, in torment.

So was I, but I didn't know it yet. My Story was getting ready to be written. It was about a mother who didn't—wouldn't? couldn't?—see her baby's missing limbs. All my passion, all my sensoria, were bound up in the feelings, the awareness, of that other mother; with what was left over, I wrote Ted a reply that was affectionate, analytical, and quite astonishingly objective.

The best we had to hope for was that, if it went on long enough, and was convincingly good, it might become, "for the rest of our lives." It wasn't made of forever-stuff. I could have played with you and pretended and kept you with me till I didn't need you. It says here. I could do that with some people, I think. I can't, and couldn't, do it with you. No more than you could do it with me, now, when you could have avoided stepping on my ego-toes at a bad moment by playing with me …

I don't think you will be hurt, or misunderstand, when I say that it wasn't losing you that made me cry. I don't think I've lost you; I never had all of you, and I think I still have most of what I did.

… I barely know Mary, but I've often found I do better analytically when I don't know people too well. She's good for your ego. She'll probably be good for a lot of other things. But you won't be content to have her bring the coffee. You'll want her to talk, too. You'll want her to talk and bring the coffee. She'll either learn to mimic the talk, or else she'll really learn to be part of it, and then she'll stop bringing coffee. You'll give her everything she needs from a man, and she won't be able to give you everything you need. You'll come to me for some things, or someone like me. And because she's not stupid, not "just-woman" enough to sit back and say, "That's my man; he can do no wrong," she'll resent not being able to give you everything.

You've got marriage and love and comfort and companionship all mixed up your mind. But if you want a woman devoted to you, with all the most powerful and endearing connotations of that word, then stick to the beautiful-but-dumb classification, Mary's not dumb enough. She's got too much brains and sensitivity to be happy as a doormat, and, I'm afraid, not quite enough to be the other kind of thing.

Watch your step, darling …

If you're not in love with Mary, don't tell her you are. It will hurt less, at least, if she knows what to expect. If you are in love with her, the sort of way that makes a man stop noticing other women's shapes, then do tell me. I don't want to knock myself out against a stone wall of refusals, but just now, if you're still available, I'd rather have you than anyone else who is.

Four days later I sat down to write the story, and it came in a rush, the fastest story I have ever written: eight hours straight, with time out for calls from the other bedroom. When I finished, I decided I could leave Merry with my tenant Friedel for an hour. I knew it was a good story: I thought it was right—but how could I tell until Ted saw it? (I don't think it even crossed my mind that I might run into Mary.)

Ted read the story, glowed, made some small suggestions to tighten up the ending, and said to send it to his agent. It should not, he said, go to the science fiction magazines until it had been tried on the big slicks. I floated home over the rooftops.

That was Monday. Wednesday he wrote me the definitive Dear Judy letter. Of course I had known it was coming; that didn't make it hurt any less. Friday evening he came over and we had the Inevitable Horrid Rehash. I cried a lot. We made love one last time (we thought). After he left, I wrote a piece of very tricky verse:

Another last sweet childhood treasure died
This night; and love became a dream that once
Had lived. I don this mirthless night the dunce
Cap of sophisticated fun to hide
The child who cries inside while I deride
The logic of her tears. I let her live.
This cap's protection I shall gladly give
To keep the child's fierce passionate wide-eyed
Protest alive within the calm outside
Adult who came to growth this tired night,
When scalpel words dissected, in the light
Of a new love, the moon for which I cried.

And the next day I wrote a letter apologizing for tears, explaining my miseries away—and exulting!

(Sat afternoon)
… Monday I sat down and wrote that baby, saw you Monday afternoon, came home, went to sleep early, got up at three, and rewrote. I knew I'd done something. I had to see how other people took it. I put it in the box for [agent Scott] Meredith, and came home to wait.

This is my first story, really. I've watched people read, and they start slow with a chuckle here and there. They read quickly thru the midsection. Then they get to the last scene, and they read slower and slower, turning the pages as fast as they can. If you make a noise they say "hmmmm?" but they don't look up. And I haven't heard from Meredith.

I can do it, Ted, by God, by God, I can do it! Have you the remotest idea what it is to find that out after the years I've been convinced I couldn't? I can sit up there on the dozer and MAKE IT GO.

If I can't sell it now, if I have to do something else for a living, it's gonna break my li'l heart. I'm in a state of excitement like nothing I've

Judith's short story "Dead Center" appeared in *The Best American Short Stories 1955*, edited by Martha Foley.

known I think since I met Dan when I was 17. And no one to let it out on at all! When the depression hit, valid or not, it hit hard.

I can see how it looked from your end and I'm terribly sorry it had to come when it did. Try and see how it was from here…

Please call on me if there's anything at all I can do.
Love,
J.

I wonder what sort of "anything" it was I thought I might do?

"Everything" might have expressed my state of mind better, but my conceit of being in command of the dozer was considerably premature. I know now "That Only a Mother" was not a skilfully written story: I knew it as short a time as a year later. It was—still is, perhaps—a powerful story: a combination of raw emotion, overweening conviction, and nine years—from age fifteen—of suppressing the nascent Real Writer.

In the following weeks I wrote some more stuff for Lowndes and some love stories aimed at the women's slicks. Of all the stuff I've written, one time and another, straight love stories (including my single try at a confession-magazine story) are the only things I have been completely unable to sell.

I learned that Mary had a voice even more angelic than her face. I arranged for her to sing at Merril's nursery school; it was a great success. Ted was a singer too; in those days he played a great 12-string guitar. (I am a tri-tone: not mono-, mind you; I have three notes, with no sense of pitch and no memory for melody.) Obviously, they were made for each other (for a while at least; I think it lasted two years). I found another lover, and wrote some forty pages of unsent letters, learning the ways to think of Ted and Mary as a couple, without having to lose Ted's friendship and criticism.

I WAS LIVING ON WEST 19TH STREET when I met Fred Pohl.

Shortly after Fred returned from overseas, Doc Lowndes brought him over to my apartment. They came with a bottle of vodka and immediately began to have a drinking contest. I drank a little bit, but they were doing most of it. When the first bottle was finished, one of them went over to beg another full bottle from my neighbour.

Lowndes made it out of the apartment on his feet.

Fred collapsed on the couch and was really sick over the side. He woke up in the morning in the kind of state one does after being thoroughly drunk and terribly sick. That was the beginning of my romance with Fred.

(I later found out that Fred rarely drank. However, when he did, he had to get drunk. The only time it got that bad again was when another writer, Cyril Kornbluth, was visiting. Cyril and Fred, as soon as they saw each other, had to get drunk.)

☙

I had been in love about three times when Fred and I began to get involved. I really didn't want to be in love, but I liked Fred. I enjoyed Fred enormously.

Fred is probably the wittiest man I have ever known. Not the most brilliant, although he has a lot of brilliance. Not the most erudite, although he has a lot of knowledge. But he has a certain dry wit, to such an extent that during my life, I have never met anyone else who rivals him.

I remember one time when we were in bed, making love. Suddenly I had this tremendous need to know how he felt right then. He said, "Bumpety, bumpety, bump." It was gloriously funny, but it didn't tell me anything about what he really felt. In fact, a lot of his dry wit was used precisely to keep anybody from ever knowing what he really did feel. Except with small children, he would not permit himself to open up or even show that he had too much feeling.

For quite some time, the most attractive (not to fall in love with, but to be seen with) male personality for me was the extreme Anglo-Saxon one. Fred was intriguing. He was dry, cool, tall, and slim; not quite dapper, but certainly fascinating. Intellectually, the man's life has been incredible.

Fred was surprisingly marvellous with babies and small children. He was a terrific father to our daughter, Annie. He was also fabulous with my older daughter, Merril, who regarded him as a father. (Merril effectively lost her father twice: when Dan and I broke up; and then again when Fred and I did.)

On the down side, I truly believe the things that both appalled and fascinated Fred about me were usually delivered as complaints: "There's no other woman in the world who can get her hair fixed perfectly, get in the car and between the car and the door get it in a total mess." He also frequently commented on how "Russian" I was —a reference to me supposedly always getting hysterical about things.

For each of us, in opposite ways, the cold dry and the hot temperamental personalities were equally attractive and repellent.

I was always horrified that he was called "60–40 Pohl" because as a young editor of science fiction pulps he published his friends' stories and then split the already meagre payments to keep 60 per cent for himself as a kind of finder's and editor's fee. His defence of the situation left me not just unconvinced, but completely contemptuous. Nevertheless, there was something about the spirit of competitiveness and exaggerated chicanery of it all that was attractive.

Fred was indeed clever. He was knowledgeable. He was powerful. He showed me I could be a great success as a writer and editor. And he knew how to make people do what he wanted. That didn't work to a great extent with me, but it made him the central man in any crowd. While we were together, from 1946 to 1951, Fred and I were a total centre in the SF community.

A group of us who lived in New York started something called the Hydra Club. It was a social organization composed of people in and around science fiction. Everybody who was anybody anywhere around science fiction became part of the Hydra Club. There were seven of us who met to write a constitution.

The constitution wound up simply being, "The name of this organization shall be the Hydra Club. The purpose of this organization shall be …"

Once a year, we would hold a business meeting and anybody who wasn't there was likely to be elected secretary, which was the only elected function the group had. The secretary had to make sure that notices for meetings got out. Neither Fred nor I was ever secretary, but for quite some period of time the meetings/parties were held twice a month at our place.

The Hydra Club became the big meeting place for S F writers. Isaac Asimov would attend. German-born scientist and science writer Willy Ley was there. The meetings became the big marketplace for writers and publishers, and editors from the various publishing houses would be there. It co-existed with the development of science fiction as a commercial genre.

Fred and I were able to bring all of this together.

By 1947 I was getting started as a writer. Scott Meredith (who later became infamous as Richard Nixon's agent) was a brash young man with a brand-new agency that supported itself with "reading fee" customers. Unpublished authors were not ordinarily accepted as regular clients. But Arnold Hano, who was then chief reader in the agency, apparently sent "That Only a Mother" in to Scott with a note saying, "If you don't get $1,000 for this, you ought to quit."

I was a client, and Scott Meredith began circulating my story to the first-rank magazines, all of which bounced it vigorously. The first and best rejection letter was from Collier's.

Scott put me on his sports-story roster. He had a deal with a giant pulp publisher to supply the full contents of their (ten? twenty? thirty?) sports magazines. If you were in Scott's "stable," you brought your story in every Friday morning and got a cheque for one cent a word (less 10 per cent commission) and an assignment for next week: "Football, 5000," "Baseball, 6000," etc. In the afternoon a messenger came and picked up the two-foot stack of manuscripts. (Did anyone ever read them before they went to the printer?)

I knew nothing about team sports, and cared less. I wrote with the rule book on one side, a stack of pulps opened to stories of the assigned sport on the other, for the slang, and the *Encyclopedia Americana* propped up behind the type-writer for the history of the game. Characters and plot in these stories needed only the sketchiest consideration; formula requirements were rigid, permitting exactly four permutations of one basic situation (win/lose, fair-square/crooked). It was great draftsmanship practice in simple story-telling. And I was earning money every week, by writing stories!

(Toronto entered my life for the first time when I brought in a story called "Golfer's Girl." Scott frowned at the title, skimmed a page or two, frowned again, and told me I knew the girlfriend could not be a major character. No cheque that week, but the story was sold to the *Toronto Star Weekly* for $300: six times what the pulps would have paid.)

I brought out *DISTEMPER!*, an all-poetry issue of my fanzine *TEMPER!* —the final issue as it turned out, the last of my amateur publications.

In August (still 1947), I went to Philadelphia for my first science fiction convention. At a drunken hotel room party, Sturgeon introduced me to the great editor John Campbell. It was friendship-forever at first sight.

"John," I said, slurring only slightly, "John, I wan' tell you, I wrote a story so good I can' sell it to you, 'cause you couldn' pay enough for it." (His magazine *Astounding Science Fiction* paid top rates for a pulp, two to three cents a word.)

"You' right," he said, with his own bit of a slur. "If you' story is that good, I can' pay enough for it." We beamed at each other.

Next morning I woke up more horrified than hung over, but six months later, when the story had finished its rounds of the slicks (Scott, obviously, did not quit), John did buy it. The story was published in the June 1948 issue of *Astounding*.

At the time, Campbell was king. He used to write a monthly editorial in which he presented some idea about the future. He would take authors out to lunch and discuss that month's idea with them. A lot of the stories he published in *Astounding* came out of these lunch discussions. One issue of the magazine stemmed from discussions about an editorial he was writing that concerned love as a weapon. I don't think any naive reader of that issue would have had a notion that all those stories shared a conceptual genesis—because everybody went in completely different directions with their stories. My short story "Whoever You Are" did not appear in that issue, but it definitely had its origins in one of those Campbell discussions.

Anyhow, by that time I was an editor. In the fall of 1947 I answered a newspaper ad for an experienced mystery editor at Bantam Books. I applied for the job even though I had never done any editing work. Before I went in for the interview, I did careful homework. (My mother had been a big mystery reader, so I knew a lot of the authors' names, but I myself had never read the genre that much.) I was able to respond to their questions, and make conversation about how Mignon Eberhart did this, and some other writer did that.

I thought I had really done a good snow job when they hired me. It turned out afterwards that my attempts had been absolutely useless. The managing editor at Bantam by that time was Arnold Hano—the same Arnold Hano who just before that had been working for Scott Meredith and said, when my first SF story arrived, "If you don't get $1,000 for this, you ought to quit." Arnold knew right away that I didn't know anything about editing mysteries in particular, but he recognized my name and persuaded the bosses, including then-president Ian Ballantine, that they would get a bargain out of hiring me. He insisted that whatever they hired me for, I was going to do well. And so they did hire me—instead of at $60 a month, at $65. That's about $500 a week these days, or $30,000 a year. Mass-market paperbacks then sold for twenty-five cents—there's the comparison—whereas they are now eight or nine bucks, or more.

Bantam was new. It was struggling to make it in the paperback field. One of the really great things about working there was that it was still a relatively small operation, and (aside from Ian Ballantine, who led a totally separate existence from everyone else) there was a lot of humour and face-to-face argument and intensity in the office.

The four of us in the editorial department were in a sort of unstated competition to write the most interesting possible reports. Our publishing was entirely reprint —we didn't do any original books—so the reports we wrote on the books we read were almost incidental. Witty, intelligent, educated, devastating reports were being written on books daily.

Ballantine was different. He was an interesting man with an unconquerable naiveté. He had a special status at Bantam Books. He was the first president of the company, and stayed there until he started Ballantine Books. The truth is, Ian didn't know books. He knew selling books, but he didn't know literature. His opinions were almost always totally different from those of everyone in the editorial department. He seldom tried to overrule the editorial department, but Ian had one golden rule: what people wanted was new information.

Time and again, Ian proved to us that any book that contained what was new information for him would sell out in the market. For example, we had one book, *The Chinese Room* by Vivian Connell (1942), that was our all-time bestseller during that period. The reason *The Chinese Room* was a big bestseller was because the woman in the novel rouged her nipples. This was a novelty for the readers.

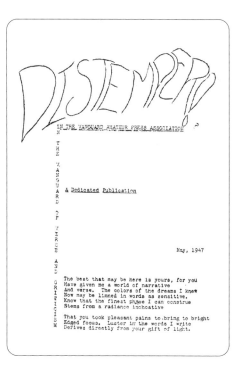

The cover of Judith's May 1947 all-poetry issue of *TEMPER!*, temporarily renamed *DISTEMPER!*. The subtitle says, "In the vanguard of verse and criticism."
Courtesy of the Merril estate

After my first year at Bantam (and many halts, much hesitation, and repeated Gallup-testing) the rest of the editorial department finally agreed to my proposals for a science fiction anthology. (This was the single career move I can remember actually fighting for.)

Meanwhile I was (really!) writing, and I started a short-short story that grew. When it reached ten thousand words, I began to understand that it wanted to be a novel.

I went into agonizing reappraisal: I had a full-time job, a child in first grade, an anthology to learn how to edit, and a new husband. Fred had a full-time job and was also building up a literary agency on the side; he had no time to pick up the pieces for me.

Ian Ballantine's secretary, Corinne Rosenthal, was a highly literary one hundred-words-a-minute typist; Corinne had read some bits of the story as it grew and, astonishingly, volunteered to stay after work each day and take dictation, then type out a draft for me. I arranged for the Scots warbride who was coming in to look after Merril after school each day to stay a bit later and get dinner started.

I hit twenty thousand words before Christmas. Then, during the school holiday, Merril's teacher came to see me. With tears rolling down her cheeks, she told me how my daughter's fiendishly clever disruptions were destroying her class and her self-esteem. Okay. Too much warbride, not enough Mom. My dream-plan didn't call for a novel till 1957 anyhow. I stuffed the messy draft-and-revisions out of sight in the bottom desk drawer.

Then I went to a party and met Walter Bradbury, Doubleday's first-ever science fiction editor. Brad had heard I was writing a novel; could he see what I'd done? No use, I told him, I couldn't even take time to retype the scribbled-over pages for reading. Brad was insistent; if I had a publisher's advance, he pointed out, I could take a leave of absence from work and finish the book. He took the stuff as it was, read it and produced a contract.

When I left Bantam, it was not my intention to do so. When, after many ups and downs, and typical young author psychoses, Doubleday finally bought the book—that is, they signed a contract for it, it was then maybe twenty thousand words—I had to finish the book and didn't think I would be able to do it within the time limit if I continued to work full-time at Bantam. I wanted to take a year's leave of absence.

I told all this to Ian Ballantine (who in his strange and marvellous know-nothingness was so often right), and he responded, "No, you can't have a leave of absence. You're going to quit." I was heartbroken, but then he explained, "You're not supposed to be an editor, you're supposed to be a writer."

Ian was right again …

I did quit that job, and never again in my life have I gone back to work in a full-time job where I was doing something, day after day, for somebody else.

Judith's first novel,
Shadow on the Hearth, 1950.

My novel *Shadow on the Hearth* (Doubleday's dismaying title), which was about life in America under the threat of nuclear war from the point of view of a young housewife and mother, and my anthology *Shot in the Dark* (a good description of how Bantam felt about it) were both published in 1951. The novel was a "critical success," but made only a few dollars on the side from a small book club. The anthology sold out in two months and went back to press.

The title of my book had been chosen by the publishers in preference to about a dozen other titles I had provided, all of which pointed towards the idea of atomic war. On the cover was an attractive young mother, obviously in great distress: it could have been a gothic novel, or basically anything.

At the time they warned me that the book would get me a little money but no critical reaction. The publication of the book was an absolute non-event. There was no launch. There was no card from the publisher. Nothing.

It just happened that on the morning of the first day it was out, the washing machine in the building where I lived went on the fritz. I had been washing my baby's diapers, and had to cart them back to my apartment. I was cleaning them in the kitchen sink when a friend of mine called to say, "Congratulations."

"On what?"

"The *Times* review," she said.

"What?" I was in disbelief: I mean, a review in the *New York Times*!

Although the baby was sound asleep in the crib, I violated all my principles and went dashing out to the corner to buy the *Times*. I read this marvellous review, which said that they didn't think I was as good as H.G. Wells or Orwell, but allowing for that, *Shadow* was a pretty interesting book.

I called up Doubleday and got a hold of my editor. "Hey, what did you think?" I asked him.

He said, "About what?" They hadn't even bothered to look at the *New York Times*. They didn't know the review was in there.

Doubleday had also, without consulting me (only my agent, who had sense enough not to consult me, if it was going to be done), changed the ending of the book. In my version the husband was trying to make his way home through the atomic catastrophe, getting to the alley behind his house and being shot by civil defence patrollers. Doubleday changed the ending so that he made it into the house and survived.

Sometime afterwards, *Motorola TV Theatre* bought the novel and made it into a television drama under the title "Atomic Attack." Motorola pulled out all the stops, trying to pick up on some of the things that had happened to Orson Welles in his famous radio broadcast of *War of the Worlds* in 1938. The program hired John Daley, a popular news broadcaster at the time, and had the news broadcasts in the novel done by him. They put little squibs in the trade papers and whatnot that people should not get worried when they heard John Daley making broadcasts about an atomic attack—it was part of a work of fiction.

Here it went the other way. *Motorola* expected it to be a big thing and it was sort of a fizzle. But one of the things I really want to write about here is my reaction to watching the show. *Shadow on the Hearth* was a very political novel. It was written for political reasons, and one of the central characters was a physicist who understood about atomic warfare and what it meant. Of course, this content was all modified in the TV presentation. For the first time I became aware of the major differences in the media: not in terms of misusing television (*Motorola* did attempt to maintain the essence of the novel), but in terms of how writing for television is entirely different from writing for presentation in a book.

Watching the adaptation was sort of like having a different lens on each of my eyes. One part of me was saying, "They've killed my book. They've killed my book." The other part was saying, "But they did the best they could to translate it into television."

TEN | KORNBLUTH AND LEIBER AND ALL ...

I MET CYRIL KORNBLUTH right after my second daughter Annie was born in 1950. Fred and I had been married and were living in an apartment on East 4th Street in New York City.

While all of the friendships within the Futurians were very close, Fred and Cyril were particularly close, so I had heard a great deal about him from my husband. Most of what I heard was recognition of his tremendous talent—there were a lot of good writers in the group, but Cyril was up there, above all the rest.

Physically, Cyril was a very small man, just a little taller than five-foot-three. He was short and stocky, not in a cartoon style, but in a typically New York, Jewish-looking style. He was dark-haired, and had not quite olive skin. He wore thick glasses.

Cyril was away overseas during the war, and when he eventually came to visit Fred and me, he stayed for a week.

About that time I had started to write a story based on an idea of Fred's, something that he had never been able to put down on paper. He was, in fact, not writing any fiction at the time, so he just handed me the idea and I began to develop it. I finished about twenty thousand words of what was turning into

Judith poses for an author photo in front of the big house in Redbank, New Jersey, with co-author Cyril Kornbluth (*Gunner Cade* and *Outpost Mars*), circa 1951. *Courtesy of the Merril estate*

a novel, but as soon as I got pregnant with Annie, I couldn't cope with work at all. I became totally submerged in biology and couldn't do anything. The manuscript ended up sitting on my desk for months and months.

When Cyril came, he read what I had written, loved it, and asked, "Do you mind if I have a go at it?"

"Go ahead, I can't do anything with it," I told him.

Cyril proceeded to hole himself up in the office of our apartment for three days, and produced something that was thirty or forty thousand words. It was considerably changed, but not in such a way that I felt violated.

Then he went back to Chicago, where he was living and working for a wire service.

❧

When I was ready to work again, I wrote Cyril and suggested that we pursue the project as a collaboration. He liked the idea, and we started to work on it by mail. I rewrote his section, as he had done with mine, and then sent it to him in Chicago. He would rewrite mine, and all the previous sections as he went, then continue the story with another new section, and so on and so forth. By the third or fourth pass, we had about half a novel. Fred showed it to Horace Gold at *Galaxy Science Fiction* magazine, and Horace decided to buy it. Shortly thereafter, we had two serial installments ready for publication.

We had one more installment left to write, the last third of the novel, but the manuscript was starting to just go back and forth between us—the story wouldn't end. Finally Cyril and I decided we had to do something differently or our novel wouldn't be ready in time for *Galaxy* to publish the first installment.

We decided I would have to go out to Chicago for a week so that the two of us could work directly on it. I would stay at the studio apartment he shared with his wife Mary.

Mary was thin, stern, and sculpted. She was a sculptor. There were at least six or seven guys who had all wanted Mary, but Cyril got her. By the time I knew her, she had been through all kinds of shit and seemed to me pretty sour, so I never really understood Mary's attraction for all of them. Perhaps she was the first really bright, creative woman they had known—maybe there weren't many who showed their spots in those days.

For the week I was in Chicago, Cyril and I had a tight schedule. He would go to work every day at the wire service. While he was working, I would write. Then Cyril would come home and write more or less all night, grabbing only two or three hours of sleep somewhere along the way.

This meant that while Cyril was writing, I had my evenings free. Cyril and Mary's apartment in Chicago was close to where Fritz Leiber lived. I started going over to see him at night. Fritz and I had met at a couple of conventions and had started to become good friends. There was a great deal of attraction between us.

☙

I first met Fritz at a science fiction convention in 1949. It would have been a memorable night anyhow; I met a lot of people either already legendary in that tight little world, or—like myself—novice myth-makers who would be friends and colleagues later. Poul Anderson, Randall Garrett, Joe Winter: we all wound up at a uniquely bemuraled restaurant called The Purple Cow (such as could only happen in Paris or the American Midwest).

But that was later. At the beginning it was just a crowded hotel room, and I was the almost-unknown author of two published stories, and I could not seem to find a single face I remembered meeting earlier in the day.

I was quite certain I had not met the man sitting on the window ledge, darkly handsome, remote … brooding? a bit amused? Our eyes met, and he began to stand up. (It took a while. Fritz was six-foot-four.) We both smiled tentatively.

"I'm Fritz Leiber," he said.

I said nothing. (This was a man I had been in love with through his writing for six years.) When I got my breath back, I said, "I'm Judy Merril."

And he said, "Judith Merril? You mean YOU wrote …?"

The next thing I remember clearly is that I was in deep conversation with Leiber (Fritz Leiber! Who remembered my story!) and that the room was even more crowded. (Eventually we found talking air in a bathroom, and had a memorable discussion of, among other things, men's clothing.)

His interest in fiction had started at college, where most of the time left over from his education in utopian socialism, pacifism, fencing, and chess (the only subject in which he would gain an official "expert" rating) was devoted to literary correspondences. The most significant of these were with H.P. Lovecraft (and other members of the "Lovecraft Circle") and his friend Harry Fischer of Louisville.

His writing, therefore, began under the sepulchral Lovecraft spell. His first efforts were all directed at the "weird" market—stories of neuromancy, midnight, murder, and madness. In the early years he published the novels *Conjure Wife* and *Gather, Darkness!* (1943) almost simultaneously, and his first collection of short stories, *Night's Black Agents*, with Arkham House, came out in 1947. He continued to write throughout the fifties (*The Green Millennium*), sixties (*The Wanderer*), and seventies ("Catch That Zeppelin!" and "Fahrd and Me").

Erratically, inconsistently, and sometimes clumsily (often, one felt, almost absent-mindedly), Leiber continued, astonishingly, to introduce and combine concepts, images, and techniques that kept him not only abreast of the best in the field, but also—in his own best work—recurrently making quantum jumps that landed him (sometimes unsaleably) far ahead of the rest again. Altogether, he won some six Hugo Awards, four Nebulas, and twenty others.

That was Fritz Leiber.

Two significant things happened during that collaborative time in Chicago.

One was a real problem, and also the reason Cyril and I had to get together in the first place. Our manuscript was turning into a four-installment novel, instead of the three installments Horace Gold wanted to publish. Somehow we had to bring the whole thing to a conclusion a hell of a lot faster than it wanted to go.

In the process of doing this, we made a fascinating discovery. We had introduced a character early in the second installment who had begun to take over the novel. He was interesting as a character, and just kept intruding in all the scenes, but he was totally irrelevant to the plot or the thesis of the novel.

We discovered this when we tried to lift him out entirely. We realized he wasn't really involved in the book at all. We found we could remove him from most scenes, and the character who spoke after him was really answering the character who had spoken before.

It went well after that. Cyril and I ended up spending most of our time taking this guy out of the novel, and doing some other muscular work on the manuscript. By the end of the week, we had finished the book in three installments in time for Horace.

The other significant thing that happened during the trip was that my relationship with Fritz Leiber was taking shape.

There was one extremely humorous (in retrospect) day, somewhere in there, when Fritz and I had gone to a hotel together. After we came back, we were sitting in an old café across the street and down the block slightly from Cyril and Mary's apartment.

I remember that two songs kept playing on the jukebox. One, which was very popular at the time, was called "If," which I associated with *The Thing*, a science fiction movie made from John Campbell's story "Who Goes There?" about the Antarctic (the movie location was changed to the Artic). The other song was "She Had a Dark and Roving Eye." Fritz and I were just sitting at a table, gazing into each other's eyes and having lots and lots of laughs.

All of a sudden Fritz looked over and said, "Isn't that Cyril at the door?"

There was Cyril, with his nose pressed against the glass door of the café, staring in at us. I don't know how long he had been there. When he realized we'd seen him, he turned and left. He didn't come inside.

Fritz and I stayed there for another hour or two and then I finally went back to Cyril's place, where I was staying. Their apartment was a storefront converted into an enormous studio space for Mary. It was filled with long sawhorse tables and such. I walked in to find Cyril sitting by himself at one of these tables. In front of him was a large jug of his favourite drink, Vin Chartreuse. Cyril was leaning over the table with a glass in his hand. He looked up as I entered and slurred what became a recurring line of his: "There she is. The little mother of science fiction."

We did no work that night. We never even discussed the matter of Fritz. He knew what had happened. I knew that Cyril was not pleased with my spending that much time with Fritz—because Fred was his buddy—but we were not to talk about it. So far as I know, he never said anything to Fred, but it was a live thing sitting there between Cyril and me all the time.

Now there are authors one admires, authors one agrees with, and authors one loves. Fritz Leiber was my good friend, but the fact is I had fallen in love with him years before we met. This is not at all to say that my passion was a purely literary one: simply that the man and his work are not separable.

Anyone in the author-meeting business (critic, editor, anthologist) quickly comes to know that the writer of the grisliest murders will turn out to be a wiry, milky little man; the author of the "Noble Doctor" story probably suffers from chronic acne complicated by gout; and the authoress of those innocent ladies' romances will undoubtedly not just be a tart, but a tweedy one.

Not so with Leiber.

The rhythms of his prose were those of his speech. His letters and conversations seemed to pick up where the last story stopped, and run into the start of the next, if not in topic then in theme and style. Writing about him, I find it difficult to remember whether this phrase or that image was from our public or private communications.

This kind of personal response—although less accountable and much less self-conscious—is shared by thousands of other readers, and has been made clear on several occasions. For instance, the November 1959 issue of *Fantastic Science Fiction* had the big black headline on its cover: "LEIBER IS BACK!" He had just come out of one of his recurrent dry spells, and editor Cele Lalli bought up all his new material until there was enough to fill an issue.

There was also the memorable occasion when I saw—and heard—an ovation from hundreds of fans and fellow-writers when Leiber took an award at a convention hotel fancy dress ball. His costume? A cardboard military collar slipped over turned-up jacket lapels, plus cardboard shoulder insignia, an armband, and a large spider black-pencilled on his forehead. It was designed to turn him into an officer of the 'Spiders' in the Change-war of The Big Time, and "No Great Magic."

Judith's short story "Survival Ship" was printed in this anthology edited by Robert A. Heinlein, called *Tomorrow the Stars*, 1952.

Horace Gold published that first collaboration between Cyril and myself in three installments under the title "Mars Child," later reprinted in book form as *Outpost Mars*. Shortly afterwards, Fred and I bought an enormous house in Red Bank, New Jersey. Cyril quit the wire service, on the strength of having made the one sale of ours and his having written a couple of other things. He decided he was going to work full-time as a writer. He and Mary came to live in the house Fred and I had bought.

The house was not actually in tiny Red Bank; it was across the river in a "suburb" of Red Bank. It was located on an acre of land right at an intersection, with roads bordering two sides of the property. The only architectural detail I still remember about the outside of the house is that it had a great verandah that wrapped all the way around two sides.

Inside there was a spectacular living room, which ran the full depth of the first floor. When we moved in, right in the middle of the room, there was a huge mantelpiece over top of the frame of a fake fireplace. We replaced the fireplace with a full-length mirror, which dominated the space. This became the only distinctive feature of the room.

Cyril and Mary arrived while I was suffering from hemorrhaging after an abortion. Fred and I had been having an increasingly difficult time keeping our marriage together. Annie was then about a year old, and it had seemed inadvisable to have another baby considering the state of affairs between Fred and me. So I had this abortion and then hemorrhaged, and was laid up in bed for quite some time.

My situation coincided oddly with the arrival of Cyril and Mary, who had been trying to have a baby for years. Mary had been a serious alcoholic, and although I wasn't aware of it at the time, I think she was already on heroin. Anyhow, she had sustained a lot of body damage, and the doctors thought she wouldn't be able to have children.

Somehow, finally, she did become pregnant. But she had been told that if she was going to have the baby, she would have to stay flat on her back for the rest of her pregnancy. So that was when Mary and Cyril decided to come live at the house with us.

It was a really big house. There were about thirteen large rooms. There was even another Futurian buddy named Jack Kilovski, and his girlfriend Lois, who were living with us. Jack had a full-time job in a factory or some such thing.

Lois, Cyril, and I were doing all the housekeeping because, in each case, the other partner was unavailable.

May 11, 1951
A room on Christopher Street
To Fritz Leiber

Well, I did finally get a couple of thousand satisfactory words past the title—a tithe, literally, of what is still to be done, but the rest now begins to seem possible—and the whole world proceeded to revolve once on what must have been its four-dimensional axis. I have a room of my own to work in—for four weeks, anyhow.

Firstly, as you know, I was having all sorts of troubles, not yet entirely conquered, rooted in lack of confidence and all types of neurotic difficulties; I was mad at everybody, on account of they ought to have been encouraging me and helping me, and were they? No!!! Poor me. About the time I wrote you the last couple of miserable letters, I went over and had a heart-to-heart with ol' Horace, whose only contribution outside of the most needed item, two ears, was to try and talk me into taking analysis. Now this far I don't go, but he did succeed in pointing out to me that I couldn't very well expect other people whose problems were at least as great as my own, to solve mine for me—not free anyhow. Those characters get ten and twenty bux an hour. [...]

Still one page is my self-imposed limit until I am farther along. For other news, I'll say only that we have our vegetable garden planted out at the house, that we're increasingly preoccupied with house and moving problems, that we've acquired some wonderful picture of Ann by grace of her charm and L. Jerome Stanton's camera. When we get prints, I'll send you-all one of her and Merril together which is a beaut. That is, if you've written me by them. I take it, from your silence, that you're working like mad, but I'd be more constant knowing it's that, and not further troubles at the office, illness, unhappiness, ghosts or demons.

Back to work!
Affectionately, Judy
P.S.—I think it's next week's *Life* your name will be in, if not the week after—this info by way of THS [Theodore H. Sturgeon].

May 14, 1951
An Office on Ontario

Dear Judy,
Have a lot to get into this letter and not too much time to get it in. Ah for those glorious days of carefree youth when one could dawdle away a whole day or two evenings just writing a nice long letter, sinking into its atmosphere as if it were the beginning of a fantasy!

I've been waiting to finish *Sex and Temperament* before writing. Incidentally, I've also been reading Horney's *Neurosis and Human Growth*, so will probably start the novel with my head all stuffed with women's ideas—to say nothing of the ones I get out of "Mars Child." (Still watching the stands for #2.)

The main thesis of *Sex and Temperament* (cut off the AMEN-T and you have a fine paperback title?) has influenced so many other books and become a part of my thinking in such a number of ways, that I find myself thinking most of incidentals. Especially the transitoriness and catastrophe-proness of these small sub-cultures. [...]

The general effect of all this is rather melancholy, yet not unpleasant. [...]

Writing's always been hard for me and I've gone through enough unproductive periods. I've been especially hampered by a tendency not to let myself go, not to take advantage of inspiration and feel, but to hold back and quit too soon in the good stretches. Freud said something about Oedipus Complex and, I imagine, the idea of a person being able to attach affection to another only by a slow process of transference, of grafting onto the new person feelings that one had toward a parent or another love. I think writing has worked the same way with me. Started with supernaturals and only painfully learned to write s-f by grafting supernatural atmosphere, etc., onto s-f (*Gather, Darkness!*) and then slowly winning free of the supernatural influence. Now, maybe, by writing about the near instead of the far future, I am starting another graft—with realistic, or rather, present-setting fiction. Of course along with the graft there's always growth, it's no simple, literal-meaning transference. [...]

Much agog at the news about the *Life* SF piece.
Affectionately, Fritz

Thursday, May 24, 1951

Dear Judy,
Spent yesterday evening being jealous of the second installment of "Mars Child." You know, it's the things closest to us, most intimately linked to our own thoughts, and that stir our own feelings most, that we're most jealous of. But it's with such things that jealousy is most inappropriate, least to anyone's advantage—and always best (I mean jealousy) when one rides out the feeling until it fades into a warm sense of appreciation. (Ye jealous people everywhere take not of this profound principle!)

I think you and Cyril have produced a landmark of American SF in "Mars Child." A combination of realism, competent writing, political and social sophistication, and imagination. It's odd that last year's best SF novel was, in my opinion, Heinlein's *Farmer in the Sky*, while "Mars Child" will likely be the best for 1951. Very different stories in treatment and attitudes, but alike in being stories of colonization, with the prospect of a doomed earth in the background. But I like your cooperators better than Heinlein's noble space-patrolmen. Of course, Heinlein has a weakness for thinking the best of people (except tiny coteries of villains) while Cyril Judd is rather bitter about folks (an understatement?). You press Heinlein closely when it comes to technology (the description of spaceship landing was succinct and effective, while the treatment of Martian agronomy shows a lot of scope), and I think you outclass him in social-political insight. [...]

The gunther is a nice surprise, the liquor dealer a good character, and I like the way the non-individualistic feel of the Sun Lake colony is maintained—also those constant behind-the-scenes peeks at family life that having Tony a doctor makes possible. It isn't easy to make a colony a hero and you do it well. Needless to say, the raw realism of abortions, brothels, suckling problems, etc., is one of the best things in the world for present SF and one of the items that makes "Mars Child" a landmark. [...]
'Fectionately, Fritz

Tuesday, June 19, 1951

Dear ol' Fritz:
The sun is shining, the sweet-peas are blooming, the tiger lilies are riotous, and the corn is three feet high. We are eating lettuce out of our very own garden, and are promised beets any day. Lois is sulking because Jack is taking a job she doesn't like; my mother is fussing interminably around the

kitchen; Merril is trying to talk somebody into going boating with her. And I, after two endless weeks of housewifely chores, chauffeuring duties, shopping, moving, unpacking, arranging, rearranging, straightening out, organizing, and squabbling all around, I have retired to my top-floor seclusion and am actually, literally, and truthfully at work again.

I have set up "office" hours for myself, and anyone who so much as speaks to me between the hours of 9 a.m. and 2 p.m. is likely to have his, her, or its head bitten off, which vastly improves my temper the remaining nineteen hours of the day. We also have an intercom system (salvaged from Transradio when they moved their offices last year) half set up. It is to be all connected tomorrow, and after that no one will be allowed even to come tapping at my door (which they do little of; two flights up), then I just flip a switch to growl warningly at them.

Now I can try to match your speed, which I still find impressive. Yes, I do know what you mean about that kind of jealousy; I am more than prone to it myself, but I think you ought to bear in mind the old noblesse obliga business. When you're so far and away ahead of the field you've no right to envy us any of our small achievements. (Overstated, but meant; I do think you're about the best in the business today, in science fiction, and am far from alone in my opinion. [...]

Have just reread *Poor Superman* by the way, in page proofs. And by the way, though the new title is a stinker, I don't think changing it was too bad an idea. It gives the last line a little extra something. [...]
Judy

Fred was then running a literary agency called the Dirk Wylie Agency full-time. He sort of inherited the agency, where he had been working on and off, from Dirk, another Futurian, who had been injured during World War II. I never met Dirk—he came back from the war to the hospital, where Fred used to visit him. Then Dirk died, and for some time after his death Fred kept up the agency as a non-participating partner with Dirk's widow.

So although we were living in Red Bank, Fred was spending by far the largest part of his time in New York, working at the agency. I had a year-old baby and a nine-year-old girl. Mary was flat on her back, determined to have her child. Lois wasn't all that much help either. As soon as Mary went flat on her back, Lois became ill and had to spend all her time in bed as well. So, basically, Cyril and I were running everything in this enormous house.

From the time Cyril arrived, it was also part of our agenda that he and I would be doing another novel together. This second novel turned out to be *Gunner Cade*, and it started from a complete synopsis that Cyril had for a book. We began with his existing synopsis, broke that down, elaborated on some stuff and added more. Then we broke the whole project into sections that we estimated should be roughly five thousand words each.

Our intention was to write the book in three weeks. Then we would sell it to John Campbell at *Astounding Science Fiction*. We were all desperately broke. It did, in fact, take us six weeks to write it. And we did, in fact, sell it to John Campbell. (Or maybe Fred sold it to John Campbell—somebody sold it to John Campbell, at any rate.)

On this second novel, the way Cyril and I worked was that each of us had a major responsibility for the household, the baby, and all such things. But every night, one of us would work on the manuscript. So that from the time I was able to get up again after the hemorrhaging, we were both working alternate nights. As far as our basic writing went, Cyril would write what was supposed to be a five-thousand-word section in about three thousand words. I would then go back and rewrite his section to make it five thousand words. Then I would write the next five-thousand-word section in eight thousand words. He would rewrite my section to shorten it, and so on, and so forth.

A portion of the novel *Gunner Cade*, written with C.M. Kornbluth as "Cyril Judd," serialized in *Astounding Science Fiction*, 1951.

In the end, when we looked back at our first novel, it was really difficult for us to ever untangle who had written what. That was because it had been rewritten over and over again. With *Gunner Cade*, although each piece got written and rewritten by both of us, later we were able to say that Cyril wrote the barracks and war sections—I had hardly changed anything in those. I wrote the love sections, and he hardly touched those. But aside from those particular sections, neither of us was able to say definitively who wrote, thought, ventured, or generated what.

While Cyril and I were planning *Gunner Cade*, the whole time we were consciously trying to write something that John Campbell would like. We did a really interesting analytical breakdown of what Campbell would and wouldn't buy. The scientific stuff had to be there, but the sort of spiritual fantasy element had to be there as well. Also, the novel had to contain the sort of humor that made sense to Campbell, and so on. We analyzed, in particular, Robert Heinlein and Fritz Leiber as prototypes. In the end, the way we plotted this novel, departing from Cyril's original outline, leaned on Leiber's *Gather, Darkness!* as a model. We really came to the conclusion that *Gather, Darkness!* was the ultimate typical Campbell story.

So when Campbell did indeed read it overnight and bought it the next day, we went out and did two things—bought $70 worth of groceries, and sent a telegram to Fritz saying, "Congratulations. *Gather, Darkness!* has sold again."

As far as I know, with all the authors Cyril and I talked to, we never met any other writer of quality who ever recognized that they had done something like that. No one has had our level of awareness about the extent to which writers

The cover for the second printing of *Gunner Cade*, by "Cyril Judd" (C.M. Kornbluth and Judith), 1952.

plagiarize, model themselves after, or derive inspiration from other writers' work.

At the time I knew Cyril, he really did not have any integrity about being an author, or sense of self. He might have developed some later, I'm not sure. He knew how good he was as a writer, but he lacked the integrity.

I could only morally justify doing something like this because it was a collaboration. Somehow that made it totally different for me—I could never have done what we did if I had been writing under my own name. By that I mean it was just a cheap evasion for me. I assumed that by putting another name on it, I could do something I wouldn't normally do.

I did a similar thing years later in an entirely different context. That time there was no issue about having less integrity, though. As a result, the second piece of writing might even have had more integrity. The second time I did it was when I wrote under a pen name, and was able to work with male protagonists in a way I had never before been able to do under my own name. I was able to get completely into the men.

What I mean is, my image as a writer demanded certain things of me, so long as it was under that image that I was writing. As soon as my work shifted out from underneath that image, I could be what I thought of as less honest.

But it is truly extraordinary that Cyril wrote a lot of the stuff he did, with all the power it has, when these things really didn't matter to him. All his earliest writing didn't have his own name on it. All his Futurian writing was under pen names. His image of himself as a writer had nothing sacrosanct in it. He felt that kind of integrity or holiness for Mary as a sculptor, but not for himself as a writer.

Meantime, we were all living together in this close situation. I never got to know Mary well. I mean, I knew her the way you know someone you're living in the same house with, but Mary was a strange, faraway person. She was also experiencing this weird pregnancy, whereas I was living an extremely active life with a baby and a toddler.

Cyril and I got to know each other like only two people who are collaborating can, but our relationship was entirely confined to the office I used on the third floor of the house. In that room, we got to know each other absolutely and intimately. There was nothing in the world we could not talk about or did not sometimes argue about. We were exploring our feelings and exploring the world through the book we were writing.

We were both thinkers who could be quite detached, analytical, and frequently cynical. But we were also intensely involved with our characters, and passionate about our views. I also learned that Cyril and Mary had a trunk full of Victorian equipment, like black lace corsets, that was part of their married life. If we were up in that office, there was never a problem discussing these things.

But when we were in the living room downstairs, Cyril and Mary suddenly became the old-fashioned couple. If Cyril thought of a dirty joke that he wanted to tell, he would take Mary out of the room, tell it to her, and ask her to tell me. He couldn't do that kind of thing with both sexes present.

Fred and I, on the other hand, were barely talking. Fred was usually not at home. When he was, he and I were a sort of super-sophisticated Manhattan couple.

☙

Sometime during this whole period my friend Katherine MacLean, yet another budding SF writer, came to stay at the house for a month or so. One significant day Kate, Cyril, and I had an argument about morality, ethics, and the whole smear of personal human behaviour.

It went on all day long, throughout the entire house. It started, I think, in the kitchen, but I have visual flashes of it continuing in every part of the house. It ended on the third floor. Not in my work room, but in the room across the hall, which had a little kitchenette in it.

One of the things that kept coming up in the argument was Cyril's time in the service, and his real belief in the virtue of World War II. He utterly rejected a lot of the cynicism I had about it. In fact, he got quite angry that Kate and I did not sufficiently honour his experiences.

He seemed to feel that the war had been a holy war against Hitler, and wholly a war against Hitler. The notion that there were other elements to the situation, and that perhaps it was not entirely a virtuous war, was an anathema to him. He was also, for a long time, of the school of thought that would not buy or have anything to do with anything German.

I also remember that down in the kitchen, there was a funny point in the argument when Kate said to Cyril, "You know, when I was in college, I had very little opportunity to experiment with anything like this for myself, but I really believed in free love. Now that I'm a little older, and have had a lot of opportunity to experiment, I still believe in free love."

Cyril got this look like a fish gasping in air.

Finally, hours later, when we were upstairs, the argument came to a close with Kate saying to Cyril, "Now I suppose you believe you were born fully clothed!"

Cyril drew himself up to his full five-foot-three and said, "I certainly was." Then he turned and walked, in a dignified manner, right out of the room.

❧

I realized years later that I knew virtually nothing about Cyril Kornbluth. I've learned more about him now from reading Damon Knight's book *The Futurians*, with its background material on people in the group. But in all that time we spent together, I don't recall him ever telling me about himself as a child, for example. He talked a lot about some things, such as his time in the service, meeting the Futurians, and his development as a writer. But never, to my recollection, did he talk about himself growing up, or his family.

It's important to remember that Cyril was the youngest of the Futurians. He was about fourteen or fifteen when he began writing, and associating with all these other guys who were anywhere from two or three to eight or ten years older than him. Despite this, he became the Significant Writer, to a great extent.

I cannot recall Cyril ever being happy. I can recall Cyril being very much amused. I can recall him chuckling with glee about accomplishing something. The day we made the Campbell sale, and went rioting through the supermarket, was the closest to happiness that I ever saw him. But no, Cyril was not a relaxed, happy person.

❧

Eventually, during the time that Cyril and Mary were still living in the house, Fred and I decided to break up. Contrary to public appearances, things between Fred and me had been getting more and more unhappy.

It was one of those situations where you sit in the middle of it all, saying, "What is my problem? I have everything. I have this house. I have had a novel published on my own. Had two novels published with Cyril Kornbluth. Fred and I ghosted an anthology under the name of Robert Heinlein. Fred has all these publishing connections and I have many others, because I worked at Bantam and he has worked at other places."

But after a fairly prolonged period of problems, I had got to the point where I felt I could not continue living with Fred. My biggest hesitation, the biggest barrier to breaking up the marriage, was what it would do to the science fiction world in general. We were glued together by everybody else's awareness of us. We agreed that I'd say I had decided I could no longer hack it, which wasn't exactly the way it happened. We started making plans for separation.

Cyril became tremendously upset about this, and delivered to me, for several days, a protracted lecture about the copybook marital virtues. Chief among which, for Cyril, was loyalty. I was being disloyal to Fred. This was so important to him that it totally terminated any possibility of our doing work together again. As soon as possible, when they knew I was going to stay in the house and not Fred, Cyril and Mary moved out. Cyril started immediately working on a novel with Fred. I believe they wrote five or six books together. Fred hadn't been writing at all up until that point, so this was a big event.

The dissolving of our marriage created a certain distress on the part of our mutual friends, because there was an immediate feeling that they had to line up behind one of us. When we found ourselves on the same platform at a convention, or in the same room at a party, we had to be completely civil. Not just barely civil, we had to be able to argue about differences in literary opinion together, if necessary. We were excessively careful not to do any public quarrelling about our intimate problems, and not to ask for people to pick sides. Nevertheless, people quickly decided to which team they would remain loyal.

꙳

Fred wrote a novel while we were together. This was a serious novel. He only let me read one chapter of it before he burned it. He didn't think it was good enough to be read. The opening sentence of this novel was something like: "He ran around inside his own hard shell for twenty years, until he met the woman he could take inside the shell with him."

This opening sentence was so sad. It expressed, better than I ever could, the emotional constraints on Fred. Feelings were not allowed to come out of that shell. If you wanted to get close to him, you had to climb inside. I think several people got inside his shell to a certain extent, but I don't think anybody ever got Fred out of it. Cyril Kornbluth probably got inside more than any of the rest of us, and little children were able to run in and out at will.

After he burned the manuscript, Fred stopped writing altogether for a while. Only when he and Cyril started writing together, after we split up, did he begin again.

꙳

A few years after this whole period, Cyril and Mary were living in Long Island. They had, finally, two children, both of whom had serious development problems of various kinds.

There was a snow storm. Cyril went out to shovel the snow, and fell down with a fatal heart attack. He was only thirty-six or thirty-seven.

ELEVEN | KATHERINE MACLEAN AND THE ESP LETTERS

AFTER FRED LEFT the house in Red Bank, Katherine MacLean came and lived with me for a while. At the time, she and I were doing a lot of ESP and associated investigations. One of the things that really interested us was whether we could change our appearance by deciding to do so. I had brown hair and had always wanted black; straight hair and wanted curly. Kate wanted to change the shape of her upper lip.

Kate and I spent hours in front of the huge living room mirror, looking at ourselves and working at changing our appearance, such a tragically funny female thing to do. Part of our strategy was to imagine the change. But in order to do this, we also had to find out things like what makes a hair curl. I discovered that the way a hair's root grows determines whether it will be curly or straight. So I just kept thinking about changing the shape of the root. Same thing with the colouring.

My hair did not turn black, but everybody began to see it as black. It did become a darker brown. And it did get curly.

Kate didn't manage to change her lip.

No one ever believes this story, but I have before and after photos. My hair stayed curly for a long time—it still has some curl in it. When I was younger, my hair had absolutely no curl in it at all.

Kate was impressive (and so lucky!) because she was a second-generation science fiction person. I don't mean that she was a second-generation science fiction writer, but that her father had read science fiction, so she sort of grew up with it. (This is in contrast with my own situation and my mother's extreme disapproval of the genre.) Kate's father was a food scientist. Her mother was absolutely charming, but completely off the wall.

Kate grew up in a part of New Jersey called the Nave Sink. The Nave Sink is in the same basic area as the house in Red Bank, although I knew her long before Fred Pohl and I moved out there because she was already writing science fiction. She got to know Ted Sturgeon and Phil Klass, who were close friends of mine. It must have been through them that I met her.

Science fiction author, scientist, and friend, Katherine MacLean, circa 1955.
Courtesy of the Merril estate

When I met her, she was relatively new as a writer. She must have published only two or three stories by that time, whereas I had published quite a few. My first consciousness of Katie is at a party that Phil Klass was having. Phil was, at that point, close friends with Cyril Sells. He also had a brother named Mort, who subsequently became an anthropologist. The party was being held at Mort's studio apartment in the Village. We had all converged there, and had been doing quite a bit of drinking. At some point in the evening, we decided to go to Carnegie Hall, where a friend of Sells named Reuben was living and performing as some kind of artist.

We all poured out of Mort's place, and went to get a taxi, in a state of enormous hilarity. We had trouble flagging down a cab, so we spread ourselves across the street and stood there waving.

To this day, that scene is one of my recollections that has the most complete joy in it. The essence of poetry, the essence of happiness; the bunch of us spread across the road trying to get a taxi at the risk of our lives. In fact, I have a distinct memory of one us suggesting we were too drunk to be on the road, and that we might get hurt.

Eventually, we did make it alive to Reuben's place in Carnegie Hall. Reuben was playing Beethoven's "Seventh" on the hi-fi as we arrived. There was a little passageway where the hi-fi was, and then there a big back room.

At one point I wandered out of the music area and down the hallway. At that instant, Kate was coming back from the big room. We met in the middle of the hallway, threw our arms around each other, and swore eternal friendship.

The first woman with whom I could really feel level was Virginia Kidd. Katie MacLean was the second. A total human being, not somebody designed to be another person's sidekick. Kate was also a good writer, much more scientific than me. She had and does have a natural understanding of science and logic (which I, to my chagrin, have never had). She did her B.A. at Barnard University, New York, and later did postgraduate work in psychology. She's also a little crazy, and I say this in the fondest way imaginable, but part of her is a little batty like her mother. However, most of her is smart and logical.

She had four brothers, and a wonderful father. These were the people she grew up admiring. She had always felt protective towards her giddy, silly mother, but she had a very low opinion of women in general.

During that long period when she stayed at the house in Red Bank with me, we were all experimenting with extrasensory perception and early Gestalt therapy, the school of psychology concerned with the tendency of the human mind to organize perceptions into "wholes." At around that time, Kate and I realized we had a strong sexual attraction for each other. It has always been impossible for us to act upon it, but it has always been there.

Over the years we lived together in a number of different situations. She was always much less practical than I was, in terms of the outside world. Our relationship had a kind of symmetry. She has always been muscle-bound and agility proud. She was the one who would do things like carry bundles, and repair the roof. I was the one who could get us invited to parties and cook.

Kate lives in Maine now. Every time we've seen each other over the last fifteen or so years, which is maybe six times, we've had not necessarily a quarrel, but some sort of sharp digression or estrangement.

Every time, after a few months, we're eager to see each other again. So when we swore eternal love, I guess we really meant it.

THE ESP LETTERS (1952–53)

When I wrote this first letter to Kate, I was already separated from Fred and still living in the big house near Red Bank. She and I were starting a series of long-distance ESP tests, and experiments in Gestalt therapy.

Feb. 1, 1952

Dear Kay:
I am running around in circles these days, trying to catch my own very elusive tail.

Anyhow, I now have my own private Delphic oracle and crying shoulder tied up neatly into one sturdy stocky bundle of masculine charm and eager curiosity. Some results are surprising; others are bewildering. My temper is unpredictable, my work runs slow but much smoother, and I am sitting around wondering why I have to be so damn responsible?

Take one gob of panic generated by pressure and apply to same.

Do I really have to do this? What is the worst possible thing that will happen if I don't? (The answer in every case so far is, I don't have to, and nothing more than trivial will happen if I don't … except in the one single case of taking care of my kids, where if I don't, someone else will … horrible thought!)

Since I don't have to, let's examine … am I able to? (Answer has in every case so far been, yes, I am able to. There seems to be nothing I can't do while busily introspecting.)

The catch … do I want to do this? If so, why and if not, why not? and if the answer comes first, yes I do—but I'm not doing it—find out what the reasons are for not wanting to, and decide what I really want. Also vice versa.

This worked fine for the silicon story, on which I had come to a dead stop …

Did I tell you about the hard-cover anthology I was waiting for the word on? It's sold; contract in a few weeks, semi-secret till then.

Back to the silicons…   and love, Judy

Thursday, April 10, 1952

ESP Test—starting 11:30
(written by Kate)
The first that happened is that in putting on my coat, which I'm using for a wrap, I knocked over a paper cup full of watery coffee into my letter box—(cardboard box full of paper & misc.). Now business of checking key-in idea. Reading it I think of winter.

I planned to visualize to you the anagram looking diagram in the symbolic logic article in the *Astounding* with William Tenn's short story "Firewater," but didn't get to it, what with one thing and another—it puzzles me because I haven't read the second half of the article yet.

Interested to see what you wrote.
Great Love, Katherine

(Was going to type this but typewriter broke. Hope you can read most of it. will send typed copy later.)

April 17, 1952

Katie darlin'
After days and days of no mail or just bills, comes today from you and Sol and also (surprise!) from Les Cole (surprise because it's a nice rational letter like his early ones). And yours gets answered first, yet, already. Why? I'll tell you.

When I left you at the bus station I had a sudden swirly conviction of grief-loss-tears I'll-never-see-her-again. Couldn't rationalize it any which way. Couldn't account for it. Decided to decide my pre-cog was out of order, but didn't really believe it. Didn't expect to hear from you, ever.

[…] Hano took the novel without further revision.

FIVE HUNDRED DOLLARS ACTUALLY COMING IN! GLORY BE!

more soon, love Judy

April 19, 1952
12:10 Saturday afternoon

Kay—
Just got your ESP transcript.

You caught some stuff. What I was doing Wed am was finishing Joe's book—not sure exact time. He does wear similar doctor-glasses …

Did you curl your top front hair or just looks that way? Something red, too—red corduroy dress maybe? No, not cord dress, red in hair or near head, no sleeve, somehow bow? collar?

Here's a picture of a room—

Any relation to yr. or a memory room?

Judy

Tuesday, April 22, 1952
noon

Dear Kay:
A transcript of period of ESP just ended:

Lay down on couch in my office, face down, one arm leaning on your big red Hubbard survival book, on which I had yellow paper ready to be written on. Your letter, not recently re-read, was on the couch within touch, as were my notes of Saturday's attempt at contact. Did not read any of this material today.

Lay still and tried to visualize you. Got pretty clean visual image, then another, several in different dress and position; some trouble filling in face, though hair was there. Finally saw the face after I felt it. (below) Couldn't get your voice-tones at all. Felt distinct tension in diaphragm as visualizations became clearer. Then shoulders-upper arm to lower arm sensation which felt the way your shoulder-arm carriage looks. Pulled in muscles over upper lip to resemble yours before you changed it; clenched lower jaw similar to yours—all this semi-deliberate, partly compulsive. Could have stopped it; wanted to do it; hard to tell whether action or wish came first. [...]

Began to get "gone" feeling, scalp was actually prickling—chill prickles, like in horror stories with ghosts around—consciously tried to empty conscious thought from mind; words in mind: "I'm here. I made it." (triumphant ... greeting ... happy) "How's the painting going?"
Judy

April 23, 1952

Judy,
ESPers Unite. We have nothing to lose but our chains.

So here it is, 11:30 and I haven't anything specific in mind except pictures of people's mothers. That's what I get instead of pictures of me—most unflattering—it takes constant reassurance of looking in the mirror to feel I don't look like that. Must be my maternal expression. Can't resist occasional There-There broadcasting and sometimes get immediate hasty retreats and escapes by students. Afraid I'm spoiling this class' production too. Everyone has a sniffly cold anyhow so I can't test by that anymore.

Love—concern—I love you too Judy. Please not so much—you'll make me cry. Send something like a message—something specific.
Kay

Sunday, April 27, 1952

Raining. Has been
raining for three days.
Judy,
Jeeze, how are you getting along without a baby-sitter? Your Mother standing the grind? Hope you can get someone. [...]

By the by Judy, you've never seen me really operating. I'm speaking strictly from pride, ordinarily thru' my life I work like a fiend, sixteen hours a day of doing anything and happy doing it because nothing to do makes me restless and or sleepy. And I like using my hands and brain to the top of the dial (lousy wording). [...]

At all the up levels work is play and done for fun, at the middle levels it's no fun, and there's no energy surplus for play, at the bottom level, which I found myself on once when I thought my brother Don had crashed in a plane he was supposed to be passengering in that crashed, life all of a sudden is real and life is earnest and no game and you get efficient and do everything that ought to be done without wasting any motions or asking yourself whether it's fun or not. [...]

About ESP. There was some definite contact on two points, but Jeeze Judy your technique! Telepathy contact, if we both wrote down our mind contact and reactions at time of contact, should be a generally fused or parallel thinking around the points of contact, like the identical key thought of ESP being perhaps possible now because therapy-knowledge makes it shockless and safe. But holy smokes if you empty your mind you're emptying my thoughts out with yours. How can you tell one from the other off hand? And what am I supposed to be picking up from you? I had a tremendously strong feeling of emotional contact, a feeling of your personality that was more intense than anything I'd felt in your presence, and great friendship colored both as from you and returning from me. It was practically overwhelming, but hell no wonder I didn't get anything but emotion if you were lying there trying not to think. You were not thinking my thoughts as well as your own. Also, kid, I don't think in words. I think fast in concepts.

Kay

Thursday, May 1, 1952
10 Baltimore Avenue, Reholseth Beach, Delaware
11 p.m.

Dear Judy,
Anything happen to anyone Saturday night? I felt a jolt of loss-sorrow around 10:15 PM and an impression of fright through to 10:30.
    How's with you?
Katherine

May 14–15, 1952
Wednesday–Thursday 11:30–3:20

Wot I'd like to know Judy is how much your fluctuations of yen for Joe correlates with my fluctuations of yen for Phil. I suspect we're sharing a common yen battery, keying each other off ...
Kate

In September 1952, during the time Katie was staying with me in Red Bank, the writer Walter Miller (author of *A Canticle for Leibowitz*, among others) came to visit, and my relationship with him immediately began progressing apace.

Wed, Dec. 17, 1952

Dear Kay:
I hoped this wouldn't be necessary. The fact that I owe you a large sum of money makes it very hard to do; is only the reason I've waited so long; and is partly, I guess, the reason behind it.

Look, kid, you shouldn't be here. I don't want you here. I wish to hell there was some way I could give you what I owe you and know you could leave with some comfort and security. I'll give you all I can as quick as I can. Starting with a miserable ten bux out of Fred's check. [...]

I need to be alone, Kay. Either alone, or with someone a hell of a lot more sympathetic to my current emotional state than you are. I'm not alone when you're in the house, even up in your room. [...]

I'm moody, these days. Regardless of whether you can empathize with it, or understand it, I am going through a tough time for me. I'm up and down all the time. The only kind of people I can afford to have around are indifferent or calm ones, or people who will subordinate their moods to mine.

You won't and shouldn't. You're also going through a different kind of crisis and you ought to be the hell away from me—and my kid. I WILL NOT LISTEN TO ANY MORE CRACKS, COMMENTS, OR BITS OF ADVICE FROM YOU ABOUT ANNIE! Maybe irrational, too, but I want to shriek at you and hit you when you tell me something I'm putting on her is too small, or some food I'm preparing is something she doesn't like, or how she never whines with you, or anything else about her. I'm taking care of her. I don't, by God, even want to have anyone around to leave her with for an afternoon or an hour on short notice. I need the full-time responsibility right now. I'm jealous of it. I need something to make me sleep and eat at fairly regular hours, and do the marketing and sweep up a little.

I write better when you're out of the house, and Annie behaves better. I suspect I may be provoking trouble with Annie, just to express the rages I don't let out on you.

All right, so you're growing up. You're turning female. You want to be a mother. YOU'RE NOT MY MOTHER. [...]

I'm not living entirely in present time and place, Kay. I'm just trying to get along as best I can while staying as close to Walt, past, present, and future, as I can.

That means all kinds of reactions that are perhaps unfair and unreasonable. Maybe even my conviction that you feel so much hostility toward him is unfair. Nevertheless, I feel it. Let's just say I owe you a grudge to the extent that you were an extremely irritant factor while he was here. Which doesn't mean it was your fault. Maybe it was his. [...]

Regardless of where what started, I don't want you living in the house with me now. [...]

AND BEAR IN MIND that I wouldn't be writing this agonized thing at all if I didn't, very much, want to stay friends with you. I wouldn't get mad at all if I didn't love you. But if the present state of affairs keeps up much longer, I think I'll be full of too much suppressed rage against you to be able to be your friend for a long time to come.

In short, and in last: GET OUT QUICK, PLEASE, BEFORE I ATTACH ANY-MORE OF MY TROUBLES TO YOU, AND START HATING YOU!

Love, yet!   Judy

Feb. 19, 1953
440 Riverside Drive, NYC 27
Gloomy Thursday 7&8 p.m.

HELLO JUDY
Feeling basically happier and dancing slightly as I walk, and it's turning into spring so my window opening on many trees and some river will really mean something besides a cold draft soon. Feeling sulky and neglected, nobody loves meee. But I love myself better than yesterday when I felt cold and isolated and efficient and love never even got within thinking distance, and everything was bleak. [...]

So far my studies have consisted in buying Durant's *The Story of Philosophy* in Cardinal Pocket Edition and reading most of it. Startlingly levelheaded and clear. I'm for Spinoza. There's a good process-structured view of life! [...]

Honest Judy, living with you these last two months was like being keel-hauled twice daily, especially after that startling stuff in the first letter that I should stop being antagonistic or get out, and in the second letter when damned if I was anything but overflowing with love and unsuspectedness, saying the equivalent that you loved talking with me in the kitchen and couldn't stand having me in the house when I was upstairs. After that time, when I was with you I just hid in a shell and tried to be absorbed in some-thing else and not there as much as possible. [...]

This "antagonism" between me and Walt I always thought was a lot of fantasy, since I never noticed any.

Love K

May 2, 1953
Congers

Lo Judy-honey

Wasn't writing before because no good news.

It's a really beautiful spring, with only a few dreary drizzly dark days stopping yesterday. Yesterday afternoon was wonderful and so was today. Arthur C. Clarke was over for dinner and stayed the night and was a very sweet slightly distant man, very shy. Marion made a wonderful paella which is a sort of sea food jambalaya, startling Clarke, who apparently is traditionally English in avoiding anything but mutton chops, beef and mashed potatoes and had never tasted lobster or clams and was suspi-cious of shrimp. [...]

I think [Walt's] "I Dreamer" was superb and it twisted my guts so much at the end that everybody in the damned subway where I was reading it started coughing and sneezing at once while I sat trying not to bawl. A story as complex in surface and background and as simple in depth and undercurrent as that gives me the kind of theme music I write to when I write my best. From stories like that, as well as from life, I have learned feelings to use in my own stories. Do it again Walt. Do it some more. Jesus Judy, has your kid anthology been filled? Could you grab that story?

Any attractive men out there? Send them to New York?

Don't fall over backward to be tactful to not write me about Walt for Christ sakes. I'm not mad at Walt, that was a mad based on a misguided suspicion and he pled not guilty. [...]

A week later,

I'm now in the typing homestretch of the first half of the novel we're collaborating on. It's tedious steady work but should be done by tomorrow, unless I can get Phil on the phone and persuade him to offer some diversion and sabotage [...]

A piece of my typewriter just fell off, trying to cooperate ...

Love Katherine

May 9, 1953

Dear Katie—

Just a note to express pleasure at your letter.

In case you've been seeing people, like it sounds like you have, why don't you maybe write me a news-gossip type letter? I don't want to know anybody's bed-secrets. Just what's going around, and who's talking about what? I find myself very timid about re-entering the water, what with the shoals and undercurrents and all that. [...]

I feel real deepdown satisfied about things, Kay. [...]

Back to work. Write me quick before I leave, huh?

Love, Judy

Oct. 23, 1953

Dear Katie:

Do me something. Write to Walt, will you? He's still at the same address. Offered to show him carbon of the letter I wrote you, but he was drunk-mad at the time, and refused, being certain I'd so written it as to try to get your one-sided "sympathy." If you write him (I hope) in the same vein you did me, I believe he will understand I didn't do that, and also, more importantly, will realize HE HAS GOT ONE FRIEND. [...]

You mind if I babble on some? I just this morning finished the termite story! (at 30,000 words, the last 10,000 of which was written out of about 8 pages of notes and draft, since I left Orange City—and the last half of that in the past two days, since I left the last place in which Walt could come.) Now I feel like I've earned an afternoon off and some letter-writing time, and Annie is being self-reliant for a change this afternoon (she always is in the mornings; in the PM, somehow, she feels she needs me for every small step), and your letter cut through me like they say a hot knife through butter, though I never tried that. But as long as I had the story to finish, on account of Walt having got into such a thing every time I tried to work on it at home, I was sort of buoyed up with a "this is necessary" feeling. Now it's done, all that remains is to think up stories to write so's to earn back money and prestige and public respect, so's to keep Annie. And where'm I gonna be then? A famous writer, maybe, with an only child too possessed and too possessing. [...]

Not married, I don't think. Love in this same sense I don't really believe will happen again, and marriage without it I've tried too. I got one outside chance, but it'll be too late for Annie, I'm afraid. So far, my old friend Mark Clifton has been startling accurate, though cold-blooded (which I recall from my own cold-blooded days is a good way to be accurate, but no way to live), in his predictions and criticisms. Among them a letter I got in Chi last Feb. which I simply ignored and never answered I thought it so petty and mean-minded, full of phrases about guys who "hide behind an altar" and clearly implying in his world-weary opinion I had a snowball's chance in hell of ever getting married to Miller, so why didn't I wise up and decide I wouldn't marry him?

I've found this out a lot of times before: that the more you empathize, the more you try to understand motivations, the less likely you are to be able to predict futures. You have to do that on patterns, strictly, I guess—observed behavior extrapolated toward an objective. It doesn't matter that I know all the reasons (and have not tried to explain more than a little) why Walt couldn't marry me right now, and understand them, and love him and miss him, and know he loves me and misses me ... all this is irrelevant from the point of view of anyone watching the events. There are other circumstances under which Walt could and would have rushed to put a ring on my finger ... but maybe part of the predicting business is knowing which circumstances the folks are likely to get into. So Mark was right about that, as about not kidding myself that I'd be able to write and be wife to Miller both, as about several other things. My hopeful note here, which started this dissertation, was that he hinted once I could get married okay when I'm a lot older. But that'll be too late for Annie, like I said. [...]

Well, I can sign their goddamn slave contract. I guess I was breaking my neck coming as close to it as was possible for me (woman, artist, "brain," 20th century America) in what I was trying to do together with Walt. For him the union was a visit to Bohemia; for me a voyage to conformity. Neither worked. But I've gotten along with society before in two different kinds of ways, pretty effectively. One, which I tried for only a short spell, and is suspect because it led me to where I am maybe, is just plain openness and affection infinitely extended in all directions. I was getting along happily that way, but have a hunch it was a fool's paradise, even without the Big Love development.

The other, tried and true, way was a lot like Clifton's. Sit on the outside, do as you please pretty much, but calculate your chances ahead of time. Never make an impulsive move unless you plan it to be impulsive. Etc.

Oct. 26, 1953

Dear Judy,
Since you said nothing about keeping the news quiet I went around keening the news abroad like an ambulance siren. […]

I took the lack of request for secrecy in the letter as permission to run around and retract statement that you were married and necessarily explain why not, and since it had me pretty hard hit I probably sounded like I was announcing world's end. Consciously I just felt furious at you for getting into troubles I have to empathize with (my friends should be happy) but for a whole day and a half I felt sick when offered food, though not aware of being sad. After sad came up to awareness I started eating again. I worried like hell about you maybe not being able to write now, and now I'm glad as hell to hear you've finished Termites at last. You've still got that old-back-against-the-wall ability to stop feeling the hurts and begin to work with total efficiency, when things get too tough,

Mad at Judy but instinct for self preservation = instinct for Judy preservation.
Very strong aff., Katherine.

TWELVE | WALTER MILLER AND THE CUSTODY BATTLES

A man lives all his life inside the wall of his own skull, making words into sentences, moving muscles to form gestures, so that he can make his existence and purposes known to others; and in the same way, absorbing his perceptions of the people and things around him, trying to interpret as best he can, so as to understand some part of their meaning for himself. But he never gets outside the bony barriers of his own head, or past the hardening defenses of others. For every human being, the word or gesture has some slightly different meaning.

No two people ever meet completely without some slight or great distortion of intent or understanding, occurring in the jangled complexity of living cells that make up the expressive and interpretive mechanisms of the man.

Todd Harmacher made this discovery, as most men do, when he was very small. Each contact of the thirty-odd years since had served to confirm it. Each contact until, for a few brief minutes this evening, he had let himself believe that he was truly, entirely in communication with another human being, rather than with some strangely shaped and ill-portented section of his imagination.

Now he paced the city streets, oblivious to rain and cold, defying noise and light, aware of the potentialities of total loneliness as he never quite envisioned it before.

He crossed another street and turned a corner, for no reason except the inner urgency that said, Turn! Here!

Stop!

He stopped.

Perception invaded him. He was standing in front of an old stone building, a relic of the city's first pride in size and strength, grey and massive and dirty. A lamppost down the street threw a flood of light along the rainsoaked sidewalk, but the doorway directly in front of him was dark. And her smiling face was in his head again, framed by the soft scarf, the drifting mist of her hair touching gently against the bitterness and anger in his mind.

I'm sorry dear, she told him, but I got scared! I used to think I made you up, then for a while I thought you were real. Then I told myself that was nonsense, and I learned to live with a dream …

I know. I know!

And then when I saw you, I got frightened. And when I started doing things I didn't mean to do …

Poor darling! I shouldn't have …

No! Don't you see? That's when I knew it was real!

But then … ?

But then I knew you still didn't believe it yourself, and I thought, if I did as you asked each time, you'd never never know which one of us it was, or whether I was really here. So … so when you weren't looking, I ran out, and came here and called you and waited …

— Judith Merril, "Connection Completed," 1954

WALTER MILLER AND I first collided, the way two stars collide, in September 1952, at the big house near Red Bank, New Jersey. I had just separated from Fred, and Katie was temporarily living with me. Walt was working for a short time in New York City on a script for the TV program *Captain Video*. At Katie's invitation, he came out to our place for a visit and ended up staying for three days. Then he went back to New York to finish his script.

When the script was completed, his wife Anne came up from Kyle, Texas, where they were living. They had a long-standing arrangement that as soon as the script paid off, she would make a trip to the Big Town. Then the two of them went back to Kyle. While he was staying with Katie and me, he told us he had an assignment for another script, which he thought would give him enough money to make a break from Anne. They had been discussing separation for some time.

Later on, when he was on a trial separation from Anne, Walt lived with me in Red Bank for a couple of months. We decided on our course of action: he would go back to Anne to reach some kind of custody settlement, and to arrange for a divorce. He figured that the lump of money he would receive from his contract to write a sequence of *Captain Video* scripts would give us some freedom to get together and figure things out. We thought at first that it would all wind up with their children being separated: two would stay with Walt and two with Anne. It didn't though, because Walt and I ended up caring for some or all of his four children at various times.

Meanwhile I changed the separation arrangement I had arranged a year prior with Fred. As part of the settlement he had given me his interest in the big house in Red Bank. I made arrangements to sell him back the house and go down to Mexico to get a divorce.

I waited for my next move until I heard from Walt that things in Texas were settled. We met in a motel in Austin, Texas, during my trip out to Mexico. During our few days together in that motel, we were happy. There was one night in particular when he said to me, "You know, the two of us are like absolute hams. We have each found the perfect audience for our work. And now the question is, having found the perfect audience, will we ever think of performing for anyone else again?"

On my way back from Mexico, I met him again in Austin, and then he was ready to go.

We spent a few months driving around Colorado in a big wooden station wagon with his two small daughters and my Annie. Then we drove back to Texas to pick up his little boy, Mike, because Walt had to fly to New York about a two-day script he was working on, and he was taking his children on the trip. He also took Annie back with him when he went, so she could spend some time with Fred.

In the meantime I took the train back from Colorado to New Jersey in order to meet Merril, who was coming to live with me for the summer. I needed to find a place to stay. When Walt was finished with his work in New York, he was going to join up with us. We would have all five of the children together for the first time—my two daughters and three of his kids.

It was while I was travelling on the train to New Jersey that I wrote the short story "Connection Completed," more or less to and about Walt. It's about what was going on between us, how two people can find each other and no longer feel at all alone.

In New Jersey we first set up house in a little apartment over a garage in a small town. The garage was owned by the parents of my friends Catherine and Dwayne. By that point Fred was living in the big house in Red Bank again, which was only about five or six miles from where we lived.

One day Fred came over and told us he wanted Annie to spend two weeks with him. Fred was about to marry Carol, his fourth wife, and her mother was coming to visit. Carol had a daughter from a previous marriage who was living with them. Fred wanted to bring Annie back so that he could present this whole happy family to Carol's mother.

"No," I said. "We're just getting these kids to accept each other as one family, it's not a good time to break them up." I was holding Annie in my lap at the time; she was just a baby.

Fred stood up and went as though to take her from me. I refused to let him.

Suddenly Walt was standing in the room with his deer rifle pointing at Fred, yelling, "Get out!"

Well, this is what you call old-fashioned cultural violence. Both Fred and I were New York City raised, basically. I had lived in some other cities, but they had all had pretty much the same socio-cultural rules. Walt was from Florida and Texas. He kept a rifle with him all the time. It was never loaded because there were kids around, but it was a definite statement to Fred: "You're in my house. Get out."

Fred must have felt his life was in danger, because he leapt at Walt to grab the gun. Next thing I knew, we had a movie-style wild western battle going on, except that neither of the men had ever been in a fight before. Fred had the reach on Walt, and Walt had the fighting instinct. The gun fell forgotten on the floor.

Finally, it reached a point where Fred was holding Walt off, and Walt was swinging with both arms and legs. All the kids had been in the house with us when this started. I chased them out, but I still held little Annie to my chest, soothing her and telling her not to look.

Finally Fred put Walt down.

Merril, who was standing at the screen door watching all of this, came back in. She picked up the pieces of Fred's glasses and put them in his hand. Fred went off to find a cop. In desperation I phoned Milt Amgott, an old and trusted lawyer friend in New York, and told him what had happened. I ended by yelling, "Fred's gone to get the cops!"

His response was, "Well, this might not be so bad. In New Jersey, like Transylvania, a man's home is his castle. If he tells someone they've got to leave, they've got to leave."

So Fred came back with a cop, and told him the entire story. The more the cop heard, the more disgusted he became with Fred. Eventually Fred and the cop left, and we finally managed to get the kids into bed for the night.

As Walt and I were settling down onto our own mattress in the living room, he turned to me and said, "If anybody thinks they're going to push you around …"

He didn't finish the sentence because we both broke up. We realized there were two completely different, and equally ridiculous, endings to that sentence:

"If anyone's going to push you around, they're going to have to deal with me" and "if anyone's going to push you around, it's going to be me."

☙

The first custody suit occurred during the summer of 1953. Early that summer Walt and I and our combined family moved to Florida, to Arm City, a town near Orlando. (Since then Arm City has been subsumed into Disney World.) Merril came to join us after having spent a year living with her father. It was her first experience of living with Dan for that length of time. She had previously always stayed with me. Dan and I had made an

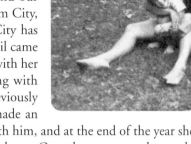

Judith with her two daughters, Ann and Merril, circa 1954.
Courtesy of the Merril estate

agreement that she would spend a year with him, and at the end of the year she would come back and spend a summer with me. Over that summer, she would decide what she wanted to do.

We had very little money and our scant subsistence level was very different for Merril after the way she had been living with Dan. Towards the end of the summer, Dan came down to see Merril and took her into Orlando for a weekend, where he bought her a lot of clothes and touristed her around. When they returned from the trip, he announced that he wanted her to return to his house. It was a terrible thing to put her through. Merril had already clearly said that she wanted to stay with me and Walt. She was placed in a difficult situation. Dan and I were both in the house, and she was being asked to say what she wanted to do. She had to decide between us. She reiterated that she wanted to stay with me in Florida.

Dan left in a fury.

Shortly after that, a man I didn't know came knocking at our door. He asked if I was Mrs. Something-Or-Other Miller.

I responded, "No, I'm Mrs. Walter Miller."

It turned out he was a private detective who had been hired to establish the incriminating evidence that I was living with Walt as man and wife. We were, in fact, at that time. Walt's divorce from his first wife was about to become final in a couple of weeks, and we were planning to get married.

After the private detective came, everything changed. Two days later, Dan and a sheriff picked up Merril from school unannounced and drove off with her. As it was happening, Walt and I saw the car pull off with Merril in it. We had absolutely no idea whose car it was. Terrified, we chased them down the road, trying to figure out what was going on. Merril was frantically trying to talk to me through the window, and being pulled back into the seat. Eventually we recognized Dan in the front seat.

Walt and I went back home to wait. Finally, about an hour later, Dan made a stop to pick up Merril's toothbrush and clothes, and some other personal things. I don't remember whether the sheriff was still with them. That was when Dan informed me that the custody hearing would be held in the Florida district court, and Merril would be staying with him until a custody decision was reached.

He knew that Walt and I were flat broke. I mean flat, flat broke. We certainly couldn't afford to pay a lawyer's fees—we were just barely making ends meet. Once again I phoned Milt, my lawyer friend in New York. I explained the entire situation to him and asked, "What do I do now? Can you find a lawyer for us?"

He said, "There's no sense hiring a lawyer because you have no money. If you have to borrow money in order to pay a cheap one, it isn't worth it. It's better to throw yourselves to the mercy of the courts and conduct your own defence. I'll give you all the guidance I can." Which he did.

Then Walt and I approached his family, who were truly a strange mixture of people, and asked for help. His father, Walt Senior, was of German extraction, and a really hard-headed atheist. His mother, Ruth, was a southern Baptist lady. Her mother, Walt's grandmother, lived with them as well, and she was even more of a southern Baptist lady than Ruth.

His family turned out to be very supportive. Ruth totally astonished us by volunteering to come to court as a witness on our behalf.

Looking back with the distance of time, I can say that some really funny things happened during that hearing in Florida. Dan had hired an aggressive lawyer who tried to bulldoze his way through when he realized we didn't have anyone representing us.

The judge, though, was a local boy, so the fact that Walt's mother, who was a local lady, was testifying for us held a lot of weight. In his eyes, Dan was a damn Yankee from New York.

Most of Dan's testimony had nothing to do with our immorality, although that was the grounds on which the hearing was being held: it had to do with our poverty. Dan emphasized that he could properly provide for this child, and we could not. At one point he described a meal he had eaten at our house. Walt used to go over to an empty lot next door to our place that had a lot of cabbage-palms growing in it and pick the cabbage out of the palm, put it in a pot with an enormous joint with shreds of meat that he got from the butcher's, and we would eat that with rice and biscuits. We considered the cabbage-palms to be our green vegetable for the meal.

Anyhow, cabbage-palms are weeds in Florida. But Dan was unknowingly describing a meal which was, by Southern standards, not only fairly conventional, but also downright delicious. And he was describing it to this Southern judge in terms of utter contempt—including the fact that the biscuits were made from scratch. This did little to influence the judge in his direction.

Then Walt's mother came in and said she could not imagine a home in which she would rather see her own grandchildren raised. Her testimony went a long way.

In the end the judge's decision was based entirely on the matter of adulterous cohabitation. He said, "Well, the laws of Florida do not permit me to make any other decision except that this child must be in the custody of her father."

Judith's third husband, Dan Sugrue, in Milford, Pennsylvania, circa 1962. *Courtesy of the Merril estate*

Cohabitation meant sleeping in the same bed. We could, perhaps, have occupied the same house if there was no indication of cohabitation—if it were possible to establish that we slept in separate bedrooms. The laws of Florida required the judge's decision to reflect the fact that we were known to be having an adulterous sexual relationship. We were living together; I think the wording was "as man and wife." Although my divorce was final, Walt's was still at least two or three weeks away from being official.

The judge said that under the circumstances, he wanted to provide for liberal visitation rights. He specified that Merril was to spend summers and all school holidays with us—at her father's expense.

After the hearing, Merril returned to our house to get the rest of her clothing. She had half an hour to talk to me away from Dan for the first time since the sheriff had grabbed her. She told me that she had overheard phone conversations between Dan and Fred, and that all along the plan had been for Fred to now come down for Ann.

So I called up Milt again and asked, "What do I do now?"

He said, "Well, the first thing you do is get out of that court's jurisdiction. The next thing you do is make sure that if you maintain any contact with Walt, nobody finds out about it. You do all your communicating with people through me, and nobody is to have your address."

Indeed, there was more than a bit to be concerned about there, because our terribly broke status partly had to do with the fact that Walt and I were running off together and to all appearances, there was poor, virtuous Fred being left behind—and Fred was a notable figure in the science fiction world at the time.

When the custody calamity hit, I felt a huge rush of parental guilt. We had destroyed this child's life for lust. We should have waited. We should have heeded Milt's advice so that I wouldn't now lose Annie.

The biggest problem was that neither of us was getting a lot of writing done—which is why we were so damn broke. We were both trying hard, but as long as we were in the same house, we weren't writing.

We kept wondering how prophetic Walt's statement in that Austin motel had been, because as soon as I found another place to stay near Orlando, which was a different jurisdictional area, we both started writing like mad. This productive phase continued for a long time—what we were still, at that point, thinking of as the remaining weeks of waiting—during which we were both getting an enormous amount of work done.

Florida also happened to be having one of its epic flood spells, so the business of communication between Walt and me became really weird. He knew every backroad and byroad in that part of the state, so he simply assumed he could come see me by being careful he wasn't followed. But when the floods hit, there were only certain roads that could be used, and it became harder for him to drive around. It turned into a major marathon for him to come at all.

Meantime, Walt wrote his almost-ex-wife Anne that we were going to get married. As soon as he did this, he got a phone call from his almost-ex-mother-in-law telling him Anne was having a nervous breakdown, with asthma attacks, and had taken to her bed. She was crying all day. She only wanted him to come back.

Both Walt and I were writing like mad again, because we were apart. Under those circumstances, it seemed as if the only sensible thing was to let somebody get what they wanted. So he told Anne he would come back.

I had meanwhile found a room for Annie and me in an ancient mansion in Orlando (this is pre-Disney Orlando, mind you) just off skid row. This huge estate was broken up into small rooms, and the slave quarters were slightly refurbished to turn it into cheap housing.

The first time I arrived at this place, I pulled up in front of the Big House in the old wood-panelled Ford station wagon in which Walt and I had travelled all around the country with our kids. Sitting there in rocking chairs on the verandah, like a cover illustration for an Erskine Caldwell novel, were four or five old Southerners. There was one woman and several men, and they were all either very skinny or very fat.

One of them yelled out, "Where's your man?"

I yelled back, "Ain't got one!"

Then they saw me getting out with a kid, so the woman turned to the men and said, "Guess you're gonna have to help!"

So the men got up and helped me unload all my boxes, which were mostly books and records.

I had loaded up the station wagon with all the stuff I could manage, and left everything I didn't think I needed right away to be picked up later. I had to make several trips back and forth to get more stuff from Walt's. For a while I was doing a lot of driving back and forth on circuitous routes in the midst of this terrible flooding.

So here I was living in this great old Southern ex-mansion as a woman alone without a man. People were quite startled, but not at all troublesome when I explained that no, I was not a working girl. They couldn't imagine a woman being alone, at least in that area, but they were fine with it.

There is an interesting story about one of the men who lived there. His name was Old Buddy, and he shared a room with his friend Herbie. Old Buddy was a sweet man who had been in the "death march" on Bataan, in the Philippines. He was taken prisoner by the Japanese and incarcerated for two or three years. Most of the thirty-six thousand troops captured died of starvation and ill-treatment when they were forced to walk barefoot through seventy miles of jungle to prison camps.

When U.S. forces recaptured Bataan, the Japanese released all the prisoners, including Old Buddy. He came back to the United States and gradually regained some weight. He still had trouble with his feet, but they were largely healed.

Then he developed a severe drinking problem. He and Herbie were both drunk most of the time, but Old Buddy was a really interesting guy, and very sweet. The friendship of Old Buddy was one of the things that softened somewhat my experiences of that period. At one point, he even said to me, "We should get married."

"Why?" I asked.

He answered, "Well, if we're both going to be miserable, wouldn't we be better off being miserable together?"

Interestingly enough, about six months after I left Florida, Old Buddy moved back up to Cape Cod, where his family lived. He stopped drinking, met a woman, and fell in love. They got married. About a month after the wedding, he stepped out into the road, got run over, and was killed. That was Old Buddy.

During that Florida Mansion period of my life, the only things other than Old Buddy's friendship that made life bearable were the visits from Walt's parents. Once he was back with Anne, Walt was not seeing me. But Walt Senior used to drive over from Daytona and take me to the supermarket. He would bring gifts for me and little Annie, and visit with us for the afternoon. It was utterly astonishing that these people had remained my friends—I didn't even know they were my friends until all the trouble came.

Throughout all the trouble, and even afterwards, they continued to come visit. I was no longer taking care of their grandchildren, and Anne was back with Walt, but they kept coming. It made an enormous difference in my life. I also borrowed two hundred dollars from them that I never returned. Not for lack of wishing to, but because they had the bad taste to die before I had the two hundred dollars to pay them back.

The only other really good thing I can remember from that period was a package I got via Milt from Ted Sturgeon and family. It was a care box filled with a little of everything for me and Annie: there was Ted's new book, a rag doll, some silly sweets, even some black lacy underwear.

☙

Eventually I left the gloomy Southern mansion and I ended up living with my mother for a while in a minimalist Florida hotel.

She had decided all of a sudden that she should come down and help me out. The whole thing was a trial for both of us.

My most vivid memory of that time is my mother sitting in a sort of courtyard outside our room. There was a small cat that used to run around the motel, and my mother would sit there calling to it, "Here pussy, pussy, pussy."

(She was, of course, totally ignorant of the Southern meaning of the word pussy.)

Her attitude towards my career at the time was mixed. She wanted me to be a writer, but she certainly didn't mean a science fiction writer. She was impressed with my publications and my reviews, but not with the writing itself. Her attitude was, "Why are you writing junk when you could be writing something good?"

To be honest, I cannot remember what she wanted me to write instead. I can only remember I didn't want to do any of it. Apparently I had a complete block against her and anything she said. Eventually my mother decided she couldn't do much for me, and she returned to New York.

A couple of months later, in the spring, I was thinking about my visitation rights with Merril. I realized that given the current situation I certainly wasn't going to be able to take her for the summer—I couldn't even write directly to her—all my letters had to go through Milt. If I wrote directly Dan would know where I was and he would tell Fred.

I didn't know what to do anymore. I counted up all the money I had left. I had enough to take the train back to New York, with about fifty bucks left over.

So I called Milt and asked him, "What do you think? If I came back, what do you think would happen as far as Ann's custody is concerned?"

He told me, "Come back. We'll make it work."

So with Annie, who was then about three and a half, I took the train up to New York. We had a whole bunch of parcels and boxes, but once again I had to leave a lot of my stuff behind. I paid for one week in a hotel room out in the West 50s—the cheap-living hotel area—which cost me twenty dollars. It had a little hot plate, so I went out and spent everything else except ten dollars on enough groceries to last us the week.

In the meantime I made a few phone calls. I was supposed to see Milt the next day, and I also called a couple of old friends.

One of the friends I called was Margaret Bertram, who came bopping over to the hotel that same evening and handed me twenty bucks, saying, "I bet you thought you were never going to get this back!" I knew for sure I had never lent her the money, but she had a job. She also lent me travelling around money, which I desperately needed.

Within a week, I had a contract to do a book for a man I had worked with before.

Amazingly, Milt phoned Fred and managed to convince him, without ever directly saying it, that I had returned to New York because I had come into some dough. It was a stroke of genius on Milt's part. He told Fred I was prepared to battle him up and down the courts for Annie if necessary, so, considering the circumstances, wouldn't he rather come to some kind of agreement?

Fred decided to make a shared custody agreement with me. Ann would spend half her time with each of us.

☙

The second custody suit, the big one, happened in Pike County, Pennsylvania, which is where Milford is located. I was living there at the time. It happened because Merril came for her summer visit, and decided she was not going to return to her father's. Merril's custody had been won by Dan in that first suit in Florida, and she had been living with him for the last two years.

This occurred at a curious time for me, because during the spring that preceded her visit, I came to the conclusion that my kids were going be better off if their fathers had custody and I had visitation rights. That way, at least, I wouldn't have to live constantly looking over my shoulder. I would be in a position to be totally honest with them instead of having to compromise continually between what was expected of me by the courts and neighbours, and how I wanted my relationship with them to be. I also realized that Fred had much more freedom with Annie than I did.

I almost talked myself into surrendering custody of both my daughters. Then Ann came home from a visit with Fred. She had been spending half the time with him and half with me, but she was getting ready to start school and would have to live with one or the other of us. And Merril came back to me and said she wasn't going back to her father's. Then Ann, who was six years old, announced she wanted to live with us instead of with Fred. She liked living with Fred, but she wanted to stay with Merril and me and go to school in Milford.

I didn't have an option. You can't tell your kids, "No, I'm going to send you away because it would be better for you in the long run." You can't do that even if you fear it might be best. You particularly can't do it if you really don't want your kids to go.

I went to see Sid Krawitz, the best local lawyer and a member of the only other Jewish family in Milford besides us. I laid it all out to him and asked, "What are my chances?"

In Merril's case there was a previous custody court decision, and she had been awarded to her father. But Sid told me, "Because she is thirteen, her wishes would be paramount. She is the one who is going to have to decide."

I said, "That's what has already happened."

He said, "Yes, but now she has to tell her father. If she is prepared to tell him she wants to live with you, I think we can win this in court."

So I went back and explained this to Merril, who said, "Yeah, I'll tell him." I assumed that what she meant was, "Yeah, I'll tell him, as long as I don't have to go face to face."

She wrote him a letter, and from that point on, all hell broke loose.

I only saw Walt on two occasions after that time in Florida.

One of those times was in 1956, during the time I was still living in Milford, Pennsylvania. The big custody suit had already commenced, but was not yet completed. I was enjoined not to take the children out of the state until things were decided, but the World Science Fiction Convention was being held in New York.

I had told Walt earlier that I wasn't going, but it was very tempting. I wrote him to ask whether he would be there and he answered that he couldn't possibly go. So I thought it was safe for me to consider it. Based on the fact that he wasn't going to be there, I made quite complicated arrangements for the kids, which I felt were safe.

The first thing that happened when I arrived, when I was still in line to get my credentials, was that people were coming up to me and asking, "Have you seen Walt yet?"

I couldn't believe it. We spent the weekend walking around the hotel together, side by side, and once in a while we would touch slightly. It was like lightning struck and we would bounce apart. Fred was there, mind you, so we had to be careful.

The second or third night Walt made a big pitch—he wasn't staying at the big hotel, he was at a small hotel in the Village—attempting to get me to come down to his hotel room. The only thing that prevented me from going was that I was having my period, and it was an extremely heavy one. I was practically hemorrhaging. This kept my urge intact.

However, having grown up in New York, something I had always wanted to do was take a hansom cab ride through Central Park. So we took a hansom cab ride, and necked like mad. Unfortunately, the entire time I was conscious of the fact that I was not only wearing a pad, but had a whole wad of cotton stuffed inside my pants. And that despite all this, the blood was still coming through. In those days, we used to worry a lot more about this kind of thing than people do with the current menstrual technology. That alone is what kept me from going back to his hotel.

SF: The Best of the Best, 1967. Included stories by Walter Miller, Jr, Isaac Asimov, J.G. Ballard, Damon Knight, Theodore Sturgeon, and others.

At six or seven the next morning, there was a knock on my door. I was sharing a room with another woman, and we stumbled to the door in surprise to find Walt! He wanted me to come to mass with him. I had not previously deduced the Catholic element in him, but it turns out Walt had been not quite excommunicated—there's a step before that—for allowing his wife's tubes to be tied after the fourth child was born on the advice of a doctor.

So I think that time in New York was the first chance he had to attend mass in a long, long time. We went to St. Patrick's Church, a church where nobody knew he shouldn't come. I had never been to a Catholic mass, and this was a high mass with two cardinals. One was a visiting cardinal from somewhere in Europe. It was an incredible experience.

At the absolute emotional peak of this whole procedure, right before the raising of the chalice, a funny thing happened. All of a sudden, everything stopped. In walked a little priest from a tiny little spot near the arched roof, and he started this long monotonous speech, "Ladies and gentlemen, I want to welcome you. I particularly want to welcome the visitors from the shrine in Ohio, who are here today …"

This really dull speech went on and on. I looked around and saw quite a few people moving in the aisles. I realized that this was when mothers took their children to the toilet and stuff like that. Suddenly this made me remember my own situation. I started to feel really wet, and I was wearing a powder blue suit. I nudged Walt and told him I was going to the ladies' room.

I got up and left the church. I edged my way back to the hotel, which was about two blocks away. I didn't want to show my backside to the street, because I had no idea what it looked like. I edged my way around the lobby of the hotel, into an elevator, and went straight to my room.

It was all sweat.

I thought, "Well that has done it. That has really finished it off."

About three-quarters of an hour later, there was a knock on my door. When I opened it, Walt was standing there saying, "This had better be good."

☙

During that whole period, and for several years, we maintained contact through written correspondence. Walt stayed with Anne for the rest of his life. They raised their four children, none of whom I ever saw again.

Walt died about a year and a half before I sat down to tell this story. It always startled me that there was no longer any chance of seeing him again. However, it may have been even more of a blow to find out that his wife had died six months before he did and he made no attempt to see me.

THE PHRASE "MEANINGFUL RELATIONSHIP" was not yet current when Mark Clifton and I plunged into our long-distance mutual exploration. Done-to-death as it is now, still it is the phrase that fits.

I was twenty-nine years old and a fledgling writer. He was "established." A vividly meaningful relationship of personal, literary, and ideological valences exploded to fill some seven hundred pages of typed, single-spaced letters—nearly five hundred of them in the first three years.

June, 10, 1952
Red Bank, New Jersey

Dear Mark Clifton:
If anybody had asked, and I don't see why they should, I'd have said up till today that I'm far too professional, blasé, and sophisticated to write a fan letter to anybody.

But nobody hereabouts seems to know anything about you, so I can't just let if off in talk. And I couldn't raise a response when I tried to ESP you

*Originally published, with minor changes, as "A Memoir and Appreciation," in The Science Fiction of Mark Clifton, ed. Malzberg and Greenberg, 1980.

yesterday, after I read "Star Bright." So here I am, reduced to the simple direct system of writing to tell you how much I liked your story.

And to ask, of course, who are you anyway? It's not often that a new name hits science fiction with two stories like this one and "What Have I Done?" Even less often that a writer, new or old, happens to hit so close to my own current preoccupations with two stories in a row.

I don't know ... maybe you're a true Bright, and worked this stuff out for yourself, all alone. Seems more reasonable (or at least more comfortable) to believe you are part of what impresses me increasingly as a really widespread trend of thought, coming up from all rooms at once, and beginning to achieve some sort of direction that points to the possibility of a new synthesis of social sciences.

Obviously, from the two stories, you have some familiarity with what the book *Gestalt Therapy* calls "experiments in self-awareness." Does yours come from the same source, or some other derivation? And the psychosomatic approach to psychology is not often as thoroughly integrated into thinking as it appears to be in yours ... not to mention the application of the self-awareness "techniques" to ESP ...

I send this, I might mention, with some hesitancy. Maybe you just got a couple of ideas for a couple of damn good stories, and the philosophic-scientific background that hit me so hard was pure invention; but it doesn't seem that way in the reading. Seems much more like a significantly successful effort at exposition of some very difficult subject matter. Anyhow, I risk being Intense, which as we all know, is the Great American Crime. He who laughs first gets laughed at least. In any case, maybe I'll get to find out who you are, and whether you meant what you were writing?
Sincerely, and most curiously,
Judy Merril

June 15, 1952

Dear Mark Clifton, hello again ...
After I wrote that one, I decided to hold on to it, was going into NY that evening, and figure Horace Gold might have your address. I could have sent it through Ackerman of course.

HLG not only knew your address, but so much more about you too that I'd had most of my questions answered. However, he added that you are a fluent and fascinating correspondent, and that you brag incessantly about how fast you can type, so that you will write to anyone at the drop of a postage stamp. This I want to see.

Dead serious: Horace satisfied my first curiosities and piqued some new ones. He seems to think well of you; so do a goodly number of folks who've read the two stories. I was particularly startled to learn that you're a new writer, not just a new writer to SF. Still find it hard to believe. You have a smooth and expert touch in the difficult job of interweaving the emotional and informational ... was propaganda writing part of personnel work?

Hope to hear from you ...   soon?

(A scribbled postscript to this letter expressed dismay and puzzlement about the problem of writing with a ballpoint pen on "corrasible" paper in warm weather.)

A rare photo of science fiction writer and friend, Mark Clifton, circa 1955. The hand-written caption says: "Dear Judith: A camera is sometimes more accurate than E S P ."
Gladser LD

June 19, 1952
Redondo Beach, Calif.

Dear Judy Merril:
At the drop of a postage stamp—

So Horace has disillusioned you. My friend! Still, perhaps it is just as well. I'm accused of enough oddities without allowing any illusions to stand. You see, hesitant pause, I too am intense. I bridle a bit at his accusation that I brag incessantly about my typing skill. I did a little personal favor for him once, and to remove any sense of obligation he might have, I tactfully pointed out that since I was a rapid typist it really was no chore. If this be bragging—but then it is the sad lot of man to be perpetually misunderstood. Heavens, how would we ever hang on to the shreds of our superiority without it? Understand a man and you have dealt him mortal insult. So Horace, as usual, does the most gracious thing of all.

I was delighted with your letter. Never, never get too blasé. Think how much pleasure you would have denied me had you not written and sent it!

Your fourth paragraph on the widespread evolvement of some new form of awareness. Again our thought parallels. I quote from a letter I wrote recently to a chap who was being pretty bitter about it all:

"I have the feeling that things are not as black as they seem. I have the
feeling that we are, right now, stumbling around the door of our next
evolutionary level, that if disaster can only be staved off a little while

longer, man can take such a step. I have the premonition that only the thinnest door separates us from the landing above ours, from homo superior. I think there is an astonishing number of people ready to take such a step—perhaps a critical mass which can explode into homo superior, if we can find a way of passing through that door."

Not to him, but to you who have progressed farther: I am convinced that the door is composed of editorial fear. Something is happening to our editors and publishers. The fear of getting a few objecting letters, of losing an advertising account, of being hauled up before a congressional committee, has pulled all the teeth, and the literature served up is no more than premasticated pap. I suspect this is the reason why people flock in great droves from one damn fool-ism to another. It is as if our flood came from worn-out soil. It looks good on the surface. The volume is certainly there. But the trace minerals and vitamins are gone. It does not sustain us.

There is enough food to be found by searching in literature for a youth to get his growth. But beyond that point, when he gets into current literature, he finds carefully predigested volume, carefully packaged and wrapped in cotton wool so that no one might feel the impact—and no substance. However much he may absorb of the volume, if there is no value in it, he will start looking to other sources. I do not need to cite examples of such crazes, or why a good American man will be caught up in the fallacies of Communism. He hungers for food substances which we fear to provide him. A man, hungry enough, will do desperate and foolish things. And if he still hungers, he dies.

I wonder what our nation would have been had that small but critical mass of patriots responsible for our nation been fearful of the criticism of a few stupids, or the raised eyebrows of England's social set.

I hadn't realized this until lately, for I am new to the writing game. You complimented my work, but I know I have a long way to go before I can make my written word match my skill in the spoken word. I do not react in pique when an editor tells me that a story is thin, fuzzy, or unconvincing. But when a whole series of editors write, in essence, "Gad Clifton, this is wonderful stuff. I wish I dared print it but I don't," I am filled with foreboding and concern for the future.

I am accustomed to hearing editors and publishers talk about the low mass level of intelligence, and how the writing must be slanted to that level; saying nothing because it will either be misunderstood or not understood at all. I am accustomed to hearing this, but I do not believe it. For more than twenty years I have been intensively interviewing people. Very early I learned the skill of shearing away all the froth and getting down to the real body of the brew within a few sentences.

I mention, not as horn blowing but as fundamental, that it was the custom for a number of years for psych professors, students, and others to come into my office in pretense of applying for work, so that they might study my interviewing techniques. An amusing sidelight was that within a few sentences they not only confessed their identity, but also confessed they had not intended to reveal it—but that since this had turned into a man to man discussion and was entirely off the record they now felt free to do so. It never occurred to them that that was the technique—that all my interviews were man to man and off the record, and therefore each person felt he could talk freely—without fear.

I have had over 2,000,000 such interviews, almost all of them off the record and man to man. During all this time I looked for this stupid mass level. I never found it. With only a small percentage as exception, I found each man was open for thought, hungry for thought. True, the educational, social and emotional levels varied greatly. I have interviewed everyone from Mexican peons to bank and college presidents, but I was seldom able to find anyone who was not receptive to thought or a new idea—if it was given in his language.

The practical application? During all those years, either as a labor relations director or as a consultant, I never had a strike. Most of my companies were strong union, most of them had been hot spots, the challenge; but I never had even ominous labor trouble because I had never been able to find that stupid mass level, and therefore could not treat the people as such.

Invariably, when I was called into a hot labor dispute, I found it existed because management persisted in giving the workmen what it thought was good for them, instead of finding out what the workmen really wanted. And in the majority of cases it would have cost management far less in dollars. For the problem was, perhaps surprisingly, not one of wages—that was merely a symbol, a "get even" mechanism for subtle frustrations which would sound foolish if expressed to unsympathetic ears.

This God complex of feeding the people what the publishers think is good for them in literature is a parallel.

People are far more willing to think than we give them credit; and the younger generation—we'd better start giving them something solid, something they can get into, instead of the frayed old hokum, or we're really going to have a mess on our hands.

With me it is not idle speculation, or science fiction extrapolation, or amusing sophistry—I know the evolvement is there, that it is springing up on all sides, the force of new life behind it. What is this terrible fear we have that our egg will crack and a chicken emerge? Why are we clamping steel growth? Either the steel bands themselves will shatter and destroy us with flying shrapnel, or we will succeed again, as has happened so many times in past civilizations, in killing the chicken still in the egg.

Intense? Perhaps. But when a civilization arrives at a point where the only acceptable reaction is to titter scornfully, that civilization dies. England arrived at that point. "Look here, old boy, there's some things one doesn't say, don't y'know"—and England died. In Japan it was bushido—the one correct reaction to every given circumstance—and Japan died. And in our culture? It may be quite the thing for the flower of our culture to raise a delicate eyebrow, shrug a white shoulder, and die gracefully on the vine; but I believe the plant is still powerful and strong, and if we concern ourselves too much with the flowers and not enough with the roots, there soon won't be any flowers.

To me, it is basic tragedy that our literature of today does no more than titter scornfully. There are tremendously powerful things to be said, and there are the writers to say them, and they may not be pleasant to the delicate shell-formed ear of the flowers of our culture; but as long as this door of "I wish I dared print it, but I don't" is closed—

Well, Judy, I touched on one point of your letter—and somehow it just lengthens out and out. But you can't say Horace didn't warn you. At the drop of a postage stamp—

Drop another, will you?

Cordially,

Mark Clifton

Mark and I met, in person, on only one occasion: the Thirteenth World Science Fiction Convention, in Cleveland, in the summer of 1955 (where he and Frank Riley took the Hugo award for the novel *They'd Rather Be Right*). The meeting was cordial—at times delightful—but some curious inverse chemistry sent each of us away with a sorely wounded sense of rejection by the other. The feeling was strong enough that neither of us found a way to articulate it until several years later. Our correspondence lapsed entirely for a while, and when it resumed (for another five years) it was both less obsessive and more intimate—rather like the letters of old, fond, but spent, lovers.

We were, of course, never lovers in the usual explicit sense. Indeed, the symbol of rejection on each side in Cleveland was our failure even to embrace upon meeting. And it may well have been that this wounding abstention was necessary: that the sort of sounding-board function we served for each other, through most of a decade of critical experience for both of us, could only work between people whose actual physical lives were in no way interconnected: that we were instinctively, however painfully, protecting the very meaning-fullness of the relationship.

In any case, most of my thinking and awareness, during that dramatic fourth decade of my life, was filtered, or refracted, through Mark's extraordinary perceptions, and modified by his philosophies.

Of course, I was not alone in this. Everyone who read his prolific output (in the days when other writers irritably referred to *Astounding* as the "Clifton House Organ") shared the experience to some extent. Because the important thing to understand about Clifton is just—

He meant every word of it.

When he was not writing simply out of his personal history, he was writing with excruciating honesty out of his personal beliefs and ideals. Among these were his years of "extrasensory" or "paranormal" phenomena—and his years of practice of one particular ability—a sort of hyper-empathy that he called "somming" (from somatic), because it required the physical presence of the other person, and which consisted of experiencing the other's somatic awareness.

Aug. 4, 1952
Mark Clifton to Judith Merril

… My difficulty lay not in the reluctance to accept ESP (or, as we called it, "esper") phenomena, but in the realizations that all didn't have them developed to a high degree. Much of the pain of my childhood and youth lay in my belief that everybody knew these things and were simply hypocritical in not conducting themselves accordingly. I was quite grown up before I began to realize that what I thought was hypocrisy was simply blindness. It still requires conscious effort on my part to make allowances …

And yet, everyone is. That was what bothered me in childhood. I sommed that each person could esper—it was the fact they didn't, and would not, act accordingly to their esperance which gave me my difficulties. It was like the hysterical blindness so often found in case histories of psychological trauma. Nothing wrong with the eyes, the nerves, or the brain mechanism—the patient simply refuses to see light and therefore is blind. Now if that trauma was a widespread thing, a majority-of-the-people thing, we'd have a good analogy of the esper factor. Perhaps it has roots in the eons of savagery, when the witch-doctor saw to it that he had no competition— and the racial fear became fixed. A real fear then—the possessor of the quality would find himself eliminated. It wouldn't be the first folk trauma to persist down through "civilization."

Mark was a private person, almost a recluse: but this was primarily for reasons of (ill) health. He began writing after suffering a general physical breakdown that led him to retire from a long and successful career in personal and industrial relations. This also coincided, roughly, with the breakup of his marriage. He seldom referred to his physical problems in any detail (a reference once to some problem with his heart, once to a disturbance in his white cell count). His own diagnosis was that he suffered from essentially psychogenic ailments—that he had, in effect, OD'd on people. He shared a small house with a close friend who functioned to some extent in the capacity of nurse and made sure he kept himself to himself sufficiently to avoid serious setbacks.

He was reticent, then, about personal affairs but even more concerned about the privacy of his statements concerning his interests and beliefs.

With rare exceptions, he exposed his experiences and convictions only through science fiction. There were reasons for this.

The first was simply deeply ingrained wariness. Mark was the classical Amurican Success Story: from poor orphan boy in the Arkansas hills to manicured executive in forty pain-packed years. Some of his stories of Christian Charity in Arkansas are blood-chilling. This one was rather mind-chilling—for him. His letter of Aug. 4 continued:

… When I was thirteen years old I got a job teaching school in the swamp country of Arkansas, a little one room country school, sixteen miles south of Little Rock. (I might mention that I, myself, had never been to school; but I could read and write, which was something of an accomplishment in that community.) I was fired for teaching that the world is round—you see this was 30 years ago. There was a sort of school board made up of farmers, the justice of the peace, the preacher-moonshiner. The J.P. (know how the southern country folk love sonorous oratory?) handed down the decision in these words:

"Solomon plainly says that the earth is flat, has four corners, and is the center of the universe; that the sun and stars revolve around the earth for the glory and benefit of man." Then with an avenging look of stern reproof, "Who are you to set yourself up as being wiser than Solomon?"

Individually those men might possibly have admitted privately that there might be something to this round world business, but collectively—

I have traveled over most of the world. I have been lucky in knowing some of its great people. I have mingled with scientists, philosophers, the rich, the poor, the educated, the ignorant, and the Great Majority. I have never met a group, as such, who were, in any respect, different from that swamp country school board. Oh, they may admit that the world is round; but their minds are collectively just as tightly closed against other equally obvious facts—particularly when it comes to looking at man, himself.

There was little to ease that wariness in the ambience of the time in which we were writing these letters. In the We/They atmosphere of the Eisenhower-McCarthy years, Clifton's rejection of either/or politics, if it were not actually treachery, could be understood only as idiocy. The idea that "Amuricanism" and Communism could both be at fault, or that Labor and Management did not represent automatic polarities, was largely incomprehensible, and almost entirely unpublishable, outside of SF. And in the drab self-defined "realism" of the times, the spectacle of a presumably rational intelligent adult giving credence to the existence of modes of communication and awareness unaccounted-for by existing scientific bookkeeping often called forth something like anathema.

Even among "open-minded" science fiction people, there was a fine-but-hard line drawn between speculation and acceptance. Mark explained what had seemed to me to be a certain coyness in his letters:

… Have been overly timid, but perhaps it was because of a recent experience … I mentioned a bit of my ESP to Horace in a letter. He blasted back with expletives of disgust which shocked me into realization that I had broken one of the strict rules which has governed me all through adulthood: that I, never under any circumstances, reveal myself. Painful as all hell even to tell you this much.

Horace Gold was his first science fiction editor. Mark's correspondence indicated that he was more cautious with John Campbell:

Aug. 20, 1952

You and I have gone far enough now that I don't feel the need to stick to your matrix; but others not so. John Campbell and I, for example, are trading letters back and forth with speed. Last one from him was 10 single spaced pages. But, my God, Judy, I can't see myself stepping very far out of his matrix. The man has such a long, LONG way to go before he would consider some of the things you and I say as being more than drivel. And seeing some unconsidered words could harm him greatly. I think I've already led him farther away from his matrix than he ever went before; but there's a limit. It isn't just a matter of keeping a sales avenue open (I scorn money when there's something interesting in the wind), but he does have a good mind—he is going through the self awareness exercises I used in my teens; he may learn to som! He's trying, but you have to remember the steel strong strands of cocoon which formal education spun around him to protect him from ever thinking again. Thinking is painful, searing and blasting, and he could easily retreat back into his cocoon, never to emerge again. How many ever outgrow college? No, it is disastrous to show an individual a thought trend before he's ready for it. All we can do is tease a little, coax them out a little farther and a little farther until they find to their surprise that they've grown so much they can't fit back into it again.

And of course he had to keep his science fiction lines open, because he was convinced that the only audience he really cared about was to be found there—Star Bright and her compeers, if you like—the "emergees." His letters are studded with references to the emergees, speculations on what new abilities they might have, and how they might use them, and the urgency of his own need to communicate with them—to tell them all he himself had learned and guessed —little as he felt it was.

June 24, 1952

Judy, that is why I started writing science fiction; because the emergees read it. It is the only place they are able to find thoughts to match their own ... We must not join the ranks of those who cannot bear to see something superior than they, and join in pulling it down to our own level. Who is to say that man cannot reach the stature of gods? I would not be one to deny that to the emergees simply because I could not achieve it. I wouldn't want to be that human. And neither do you; of that I'm confident.

September 9, 1952

I think perhaps we should all be comparing notes, building up this picture of the emergee pattern.

How do I know whether I am an emergee or not? We have built up no pattern of what one is. We throws the concept around too loosely ... I don't know. The emergee may not be one individual at all. The complete emergee may be a somgroup ...

June 24, 1952

I suspect that we can build that framework, that synthesis—but not from our own brilliantly warped minds. We want to build up a structure for the emergees? Then let's ask the emergees what they want! Startling revolutionary! But anyway, ask 'em. And listen. You won't like what they say. I won't like what they say. I know it. But ask them. And listen. They'll tell us. Even if it is logical, let's grit our teeth and listen anyway.

Two years later, in a period of comparative good health, he rallied his resources to attend his first science fiction convention, and wrote with unprecedented excitement:

Sept. 8, 1954

Who are these fen? I'm just positive they are, or conceal among them, the emergees; but how do you get to know them? They stand for hours just looking at you, and maybe the bolder ones will catch your eye, gulp, blush, and then ask you a carefully-prepared-well-thought-out-significant-question. But it is all in a sort of daze, and you're not really getting through.

You know, Judy, and I'm completely serious, I wonder if they're not the ones really worth exploring—more than we who are on exhibition—but how do you break through? And would it destroy something for them if you did? Hell, I don't know. I saw some awfully interesting faces among the fen, but I botched it every time ...

I'd have given any six conversations I had with other writers to have had one real conversation with one of these lads—but no luck. And, Judy, I don't have trouble getting through to people I really want to see. But I had trouble here. It was like trying to pick up mercury with the fingers.

It is appalling to me that I still do not know exactly when Mark died, or how. The last letters between us were in 1961. I am not even sure who finally failed to reply to whom. He died in 1963. I heard of it on the science fiction grapevine some time later. (How much later? I don't know.) It was a wrong time for him to die. A few more years, and he would have seen the beginning of the emergence of the young people he was waiting for: the people who have begun to turn the world around.

He missed the free university movement and the landing on the moon. He missed the ventures into biofeedback and acupuncture. He missed the antiwar movement and the ecology movement.

How much did he have to do with seeding them?

I think he got through to his emergees more than he knew.

MY FIRST SCIENCE FICTION story was published twenty-five years ago. It was called "That Only a Mother" and appeared in *Astounding Science Fiction* (now called *Analog*): It was an extremely unpleasant story about the possible (probable?) effects on one small ordinary family of life during a comparatively "clean" controlled atomic war in (what was then) the near future.

That was 1948, and a lot of us were very worried about World War III: not just about death and injury, injustice and destruction, but about the much more insidious after-effects—the cancers and leukemias that might follow years later for apparently untouched survivors; the lingering radioactivity; the sterility and mutations that might affect plants, animals, and people in the aftermath.

In 1946, 1947, and 1948, a great deal was being published about these things. One read the *Smythe Report* and *No Place to Hide* and *The Bulletin of Atomic Scientists* and World Federalist publications and the daily newspapers; and if one read the SF magazines, the total amount of information available was staggering, unarguable, and terrifying.

There has been very little change in either the extent or character of this information in the past twenty-five years—as far as atomic war is concerned. We

*Written in 1973 as author's notes
for the collection of
Survival Ship and Other Stories.*

have, of course, learned a great deal about the long-range effects of chemical and bacteriological warfare, both in the laboratory and in practice. The two significant differences now, as far as the effects of atomic wars are concerned, are 1) that the expected global holocaust has not yet occurred perhaps in part because 2) the information that was already available in 1948 is not widely understood by many people, including ordinary small families and even heads of government.

"That Only a Mother" dealt with mutation: not in broad statistical terms, and not among victims of a bombing, but as a single side effect due to casual exposure in one family in the "winning" country.

Its specific sources were two: a tiny article in the *New York Herald Tribune* announcing that the U.S. Army of Occupation in Japan had definitely established that the "rumours" of widespread infanticide due to mutations in the areas of Hiroshima and Nagasaki were unfounded (even in those days some of us automatically read certain kinds of U.S. official pronouncements backwards); and a domestic incident that brought sharply home to me how easily a mother can fail/refuse to notice a child's imperfections.

The result was a story whose horror ("I can't get this out of the office fast enough," one letter of rejection from a national woman's magazine began) was the familiar, available information which most people (in 1948) were unwilling to connect with.

Survival Ship and Other Stories, 1977.

Where do I get those crazy ideas? From the same newspapers, books, articles, broadcasts, and daily experiences everyone else has. It's all in how you put them together. The "realistic" fiction writer adds one and gets two: or perhaps more, for three. The "fantasy" writer operates with the square root of minus-one and comes up with "imaginary" results. The science fiction writer multiplies three by two, and naturally gets six (not five).

It's not the ideas that are crazy: it's the real-life ingredients that go into them that are so strange—or seem so strange because they've been put together in a different way.

Which doesn't mean that S F is "prophecy." It's "probability." If you put this and this and this together in a certain way, here's what could happen. When I wrote that story in 1947 about an armless-legless mutation, I was thinking of radioactivity, not thalidomide.

"Realistic" fiction is about things that have happened. "Fantasy" is about things we are fairly sure don't happen. S F is about things that might happen.

The first story in this collection, "Survival Ship," was originally published in 1950; in an excellent but short-lived magazine called *Worlds Beyond*. At that time the idea of a self-sustaining life-support system that would enable a two-generation trip to another star system was "crazy"—except to S F readers and a few rocket nuts.

Where do I get those crazy ideas? Sometimes they seem to beget themselves. When I started work on "Survival Ship," I was attempting a simple literary exercise: I was trying to write a story that used no personal pronouns. I couldn't do it, or perhaps I just lost interest after I found where the attempt was leading me: I wound up writing a story with almost no gender pronouns.

At the time the story was liked primarily as a "clever" trick-ending job. Remember: in 1950, everyone who was keeping up with space travel (seven years before Sputnik, about twenty years before women's liberation, and about ten years before the beginnings of the NASA promotion for the Apollo flights) knew that women were the logical choice for astronauts—if only (but not only) for reasons of size and weight.

The story was reprinted twice shortly after its appearance and then forgotten —until a few years ago, when suddenly everyone was playing the no-gender-pronouns game, and it was rediscovered by anthology editors looking for evidence that science fiction had something to say about women's lib.

Of course it said nothing at all about that, but perhaps it has something of the same effect on readers that it had on the author: because after I wrote it I began thinking seriously about a novel-to-be-written that would make use of the "survival ship" background to attempt an exploration of sexual-role behaviour. How much of what we consider "feminine" or "masculine" behaviour is cultural, how much biological? One of the SF games is psychodrama-on-paper. Set up an environment-shift or a role-switch, and see what happens.

Over a period of about ten years, I kept adding notes to a card-file outlining the "future history" of the "mother-ships" sent out by the "matriarchy" (a puritan backlash anti-war feminine oligarchy Earth Government), and in particular, the genealogy of the first "Survival Ship" and the experiences of its second generation.

The novel was never written—except for one short story, "Wish upon a Star," which appeared in 1958, eight years after the "accidental" first story, in *The Magazine of Fantasy & Science Fiction*.

I grew up in the radical 1930s. My mother had been a suffragette. It never occurred to me that the Bad Old Days of Double Standard could have anything to do with me.

The first intimation I had, actually, was when the editors of the mystery, western, and sports pulp magazine where I did my apprentice writing demanded masculine pen names. But after all these were pulps, and oriented to a masculine readership. It was only irritating: and as soon as I turned to science fiction, the problem disappeared. It didn't get serious until the end of World War II, when suddenly the working mothers' day-care centres closed, and from every quarter of society came the news that woman's place was in the home, that children who had less than constant attention from their very own mothers

Judith's short story "Survival Ship" was printed in this anthology edited by Robert A. Heinlein, called *Tomorrow The Stars*, 1952.

were doomed to misery and delinquency, and that the greatest joy available to the "natural" woman was the delight of building her man's ego. (There were not enough jobs for returning veterans, until the women went home.)

There was a lot of pressure. One worried: could it be true?

I didn't think so; neither did my returning husband. We were thirties-radical, after all, so what if it was the forties now? But I had started to write during the war, and even he found it embarrassing and uncomfortable to notice that some people thought I was becoming a good writer. Equality, yes, but possible superiority?

Bit by bit, more people began to like my work: ten years later I had much respect, a lot of good colleagues/friends (men and women) and two divorces. Complicated. One worried. And kept trying to work things out. (1973: still trying.)

"Exile from Space" was published in 1956 in *Fantastic Universe* magazine. A year later the first man-made satellites would go up, and there would be much speech-making about the space age, and "science has caught up with science fiction."

Actually, science fiction was no longer much preoccupied with space flight as such. We knew that was coming. We were more concerned with areas of lesser certainty, like the survival potential for the human race on or off Earth, the prospects for co-existence between our species and others (terrestrial or otherwise), and the possible/probable directions of our future developments, assuming we had any.

In common with a good many other S F writers, I was particularly interested in examining an area of human experience that was at that time still considered largely outside the realm of "science." Some people called it E S P, some called it "psionics"; but most of those who had any interest at all called it spiritualism. To me it seemed (and seems) to be much more closely related to those equally undefinable but fully accepted phenomena called "hunch" and "intuition" and "creativity" and "empathy" and so forth, than to any assumptions about afterlife or astral planes.

My story "Communication Completed," first published in *Universe* magazine in 1954, was one of many attempts to examine/understand/articulate something about the still only slightly understood area of human experience that is commonly called "vibes" or (ugh) "astral projection" by most young people today. I think the name I like best is the one used by Cleve Backster, the polygraph man who's been finding out how to communicate with plants. He calls it "primary communication."

Several other stories in this book, as well as a novella ("Homecalling," in the book *Daughters of Earth*) and a novel, *The Tomorrow People*, took the explorations in more complex directions. The novel, in particular, examined an idea that continues to intrigue me: that primary communication on a cellular level 1) might be responsible for many instances of "miracle cures," "stigmata," "psychosomatic" diseases, etc., and 2) might, under conscious control, allow a sentient organism

"Barrier of Dread," one of Judith's earliest S F stories to be published, appeared in *Future Science Fiction* magazine, July–August 1950.

to make much greater changes in morphology—so that, for instance, a diffuse individual might be able to exist in "empty space," utilizing radiant energy and that odd hydrogen atom.

"The Shrine of Temptation" appeared in *Fantastic Stories* in 1963, and it was my first attempt to write a story around a cover painting—one of the not uncommon practices in the heyday of the pulp magazines, when batches of four-colour covers for a whole chain of publications were often printed before the actual magazine was made up. Other pulp fields—western, detective, sports, love, war stories, for instance—could often find a story in inventory to suit the cover. But with science fiction and fantasy, where each bit of background was likely to be unique, cover stories were often assigned.

The cover in this case was a jewel-toned representation of the "gateway" in the story. Whether the story classifies as fantasy or science fiction depends, of course, on the extent to which one can accept the idea of non-magical shape-changing. But obviously, that's not what the story was about. It was written at the height of the McCarthy era (Joseph, of course) in the United States, at the time of the Oppenheimer trials, in the depths of look-alike, think-alike, blink-alike conformity-security-togetherness.

People are always saying, "Where did you get those crazy ideas?" But one time a young man said to me, "Growing up in Minnesota in the fifties, the only thing that gave me the idea anything could be different was science fiction."

The story "Peeping Tom" was first published in *Startling Stories* magazine in 1954—before Vietnam, but after Korea.

In the mid-fifties—even after Hiroshima and Nagasaki and Dulles and Joe McCarthy—it was still possible to regard one's sense of taintedness as an American as something remediable. McCarthy, after all, was finally defeated; Korea was over; the Japanese occupation was coming to an end; the International Geophysical Year was about to inaugurate the Space Age.

One could hardly visualize (or elected not to do so) that satellite-launching would become one more bawdy gambit in the Cold War—that great year of international co-operation would generate a "space race" whose competitive budgets would go up, not to look out at the stars, but to keep the "other side" on earth under surveillance—that repetitive TV-spectacular moonshots would somehow coincide with fresh bombing waves in Indochina. (As I write, there is a change for the better, I guess: Brezhnev's visit to Nixon is edging Cambodian bombing and Watergate out of the headlines.)

In any case, for a few years there, before the Bay of Pigs, and Tonkin Gulf, and the Assassinations, and other unpleasantness, it seemed as though we might start thinking, not about how to avoid destruction, but how to make use of what we had, and all the great things coming.

The step into space would (of course) bring human beings of all languages, cultures, and colours together in understanding and co-operation.

All sexes too?

In retrospect, it is both bitter and amusing to remember that when "Lady" was first published in *Venture* magazine in 1956, it appeared under the pen name Rose Sharon, because I was involved in a custody suit and was worried about my authorship of a "dirty" story being brought up in court.

Perhaps there was some reason to feel hopeful?

"Auction Pit" is both the oldest and newest piece in this book. It was written in 1946–47, before I thought of myself as a "writer." When I began publishing fiction, that still seemed a quite different thing from being a "poet." I still don't think of myself as a poet, something obviously higher and finer than just a writer. But when I came across it in a yellowed folder two years ago, I thought, if I updated a few images (charm schools, movie magazine, fur "hubbies"), it might still make sense. On second thought, I left them all: the central image, after all, is just as dated. Isn't it?

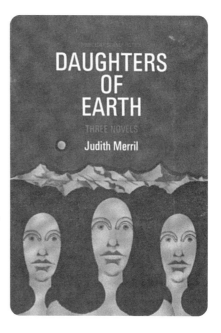

Collection of three novellas, *Daughters of Earth*, 1969.

A good deal of new science fiction in short story form is published in "book magazines" these days. The first venture of that sort in SF, I believe, was Frederik Pohl's *Star* series: "So Proudly We Hail" was written for the first of these, in 1953.

In selecting stories for this volume, I followed a general rule of eliminating anything readily available in print elsewhere (such as the three novellas in *Daughters of Earth*, and my two best-known shorts, "That Only a Mother" and "Dead Center," and then dropping everything I found embarrassing to reread, or (as will happen with SF) impossibly dated. "So Proudly" was a border-line choice.

When I wrote it, *Collier's* magazine was publishing big spreads on space travel based on live symposia at the New York Planetarium. Everyone in the little SF world was confidently awaiting the building of the first space platform. NASA and its sleek promotion campaigns had not yet soured one's simple idealism. Rereading the story in 1973, I found that the counterpoint I thought I was writing when I used the tarnished glory of the "rocket's red glare" as background for the new glory has merged into one ironic theme.

The prospect for those outgoing ships seems rather more remote now, and the question of who will or won't pass the examinations more pressing.

A LIFE FOR THE STARS by James Blish
A story of the industrial cities of space

"The Deep Down Dragon" was first published in *Galaxy* magazine in 1963. Obviously, the question of the examinations-for-space was already beginning to appear at least a little more complicated.

It is worth noting that the idea of using a projected image as the basis for the test came directly out of the happenstance that I myself was doing just that: this was another assigned story, written around a cover that depicted the opening scene of the "test."

"Whoever You Are" was first published in *Startling* in 1952; it stemmed in part from an editorial by the late editor of *Astounding/Analog*, John W. Campbell, Jr., discussing the idea of using love as a weapon. The other major ingredient came from Mark Clifton, friend and fellow author, now also dead, who wrote me the story of the little girl who threw the messages over the orphanage wall, as part of a discussion about child-raising and education.

It is probably my own favourite among the stories here.

"Death Is the Penalty" was another one of my early SF stories, published in 1949 by *Astounding*. It is also another of the borderline choices here: the political fury that generated it in the early days of "security" and "classification" has been dulled, perhaps, by familiarity—and perhaps can stand rekindling, as we move towards elimination (perhaps) of some of the weight of classification that has accumulated in the twenty-odd years since?

If it is not quite as bad in Canada as in the United States, perhaps that helps account for why many other things are also a bit more liveable north of the border.

"The Lonely" appeared first in *Worlds of Tomorrow* magazine in 1963. It was another cover assignment, based on a painting of the giant statue of a woman holding a rocket in her lap, seated on an alien-looking plateau: the whole thing fell immediately into the pattern of the matriarchy and the mother-ships background, but I had long since given up on the idea of the long novel—so this one emerged as written long after the period of the voyages.

Selecting a group of one's past stories for a book is a curious experience: all the mysteries one once set out to solve; all the conflicts one tried to resolve; all the unwritten stories one remembers in between the ones in print; all the issues one feels the years in between should somehow have settled.

There are no answers here, I guess, but perhaps what is most needed is more questions?

FIFTEEN | A POWER IN THE GHETTO: SWINGING LONDON, SOUR AMERICA, AND "FREE" CANADA

I WAS A POWER in the literary ghetto.

By the late 1960s I had been editing the SF annuals, the self-proclaimed "best of the year" in science fiction, for over a decade. For four years I had been books editor of *The Magazine of Fantasy & Science Fiction* in New York, the literary pacesetter in the North American field. After a stay in England in 1966–67 I was variously acclaimed and reviled as the American prophet of the avant-garde British New Wave movement.

I did not like being a Power. I did not like it when an author who knew I was considering his story for an annual quietly let me know that if I used it, I need not pay for it. I did not like it when another author—feeling mistreated when I failed to use his story in an annual and failed to review his short story collection—wrote me into a TV script as a vicious critic who got her jollies wrecking young writers' careers. I did not even like it much when a good young writer got a long-delayed paperback reprint right after I gave his novel a rave review. Most of all I did not like being booted upstairs out of my "family." The judge and arbiter cannot also be a confidante and drinking buddy, eh?

When I eventually immigrated to Canada, I thought it was because I could no longer accept the realpolitik of being an American citizen. No, I didn't just think so: it was the truth, and nothing but the truth. But not quite the whole truth. Another truth was that I needed to get far enough away from the centres of power to decide what to do with my uncomfortable portion of it.

❧

In 1966–67 I spent most of a year living in London, England. I found a little bedsitter a couple of blocks away from writers Hilary Bailey and Michael Moorcock, in the Notting Hill Gate area. I moved there partly because my daughter Ann was starting at a new school down in the south of England, and partly because I was fascinated with the cultural trends—including free universities—occurring in the country. I was also doing research for my anthology *England Swings SF*. I went for a few months, and wound up staying a good deal longer than I expected.

You have never read a book like this before, and the next time you read one anything like it, it won't be much like it at all. It's an action-photo, a record of procession in change, a look through the perspex porthole at the momentarily stilled bodies in a scout ship boosting fast and heading out of sight into the multiplex mystery of inner/outer space. I can't tell you where they're going, but maybe that's why I keep wanting to read what they write.

The next time someone assembles the work of the writers in this well, "school" is too formal ... and "movement" sounds pretentious ... and British "SF" is ludicrously limiting ... so let's just say the work of these writers and/or others now setting out to work in this way, it will probably have about as much resemblance to this anthology as this one does to any other collection of science fiction, social criticism, surrealism—BEM's, Beats, Beatles, what-have-you—you have ever read or heard before. Meanwhile, I think this trip should be a good one.

— Judith Merril, "Introduction," England Swings SF, *1968*

While I was in England, I wrote extensively about something new and different happening in British science fiction. It was a revolution led by J.G. Ballard and including a circle of about twelve writers. A couple of them, such as Thomas Disch and Brian Aldiss, were already established in other genres. Behind the force of this movement were young new writers, and the most dynamic of those was definitely Michael Moorcock.

It was just the time when Michael was transforming a formerly mild science fiction magazine called *Flagship* into what became known as *New Worlds*. This magazine was the publishing thermometer of the trend that was dubbed "the New Wave." In the United States the trend created an intense, incredible controversy.

In Britain people either found it of interest or they didn't, but in the States it was heresy on the one hand and wonderful revolution on the other. I was then books editor for *Fantasy & Science Fiction*, and somehow it was widely assumed that I initiated the phrase "New Wave in Science Fiction." In actual fact, I never even used the term.

The New Wave controversy became bitter. There was virtual warfare inside the SF community. While the controversy did not in any way interfere with my work options or my reputation, it was firmly plastered on my forehead. I was the heinous person who had brought the New Wave to the United States. It was a very strange sensation.

Science-fiction author Jim Ballard, circa 1965.
Courtesy of the Merril estate

Most science fiction that is considered to be distinguished nowadays would have been called New Wave back then. One example of the trend was the film *2001: A Space Odyssey* (1968), directed by Stanley Kubrick and based loosely on Arthur C. Clarke's 1950 short story "The Sentinel." I returned to New York from London when the movie was first released, and there were simultaneous previews in Washington and New York. Thousands of invitations were sent out to everyone who had anything to do with science fiction and who could make it to one of the cities. I went to the New York showing, on April 1, 1968, at which there were many special appearances simply due to the fact that so many science fiction writers lived in the city.

That original showing was about twenty minutes longer than the version that was later shown commercially, and there was even an intermission about halfway through the film. One of the biggest changes made was to shorten the initial period of pure visuals before there were any words—the "Dawn of Man." This was the part where they showed images of the early tribespeople and so forth. Another scene clipped was when the astronaut was jogging in the centrifuge. In the original the jogging went on for about twice as long, so that it became incredibly boring. You just kept watching this guy jog, and the camera angles would constantly change as the gravitational pull on the ship itself changed.

At intermission time, the audience was absolutely grim. People were saying things like, "What has Kubrick done to Clarke?" By the end of the film, those determined people who had not already escaped during the intermission were standing up, putting their coats on, and getting ready to leave. I had to get up and stand on my seat so that I could see the last few shots that showed the "star child" in the bubble in space.

That movie taught the audience two things. It showed irrevocably that life on a space station was boring. And it changed the viewer's entire perspective about what is down and what is up.

England Swings SF, 1968.

There were only about two people from the SF community who were as excited as I was by the film. One was the writer Samuel Delany, and the other was an editor named Hans Santesson. It seemed like every single other person was appalled at this business of an indeterminate ending and Kubrick's failure to follow the rules of pulp fiction.

☙

More than once, while I was living in London, I became confused by the country's cultural expectations. Hilary and Michael were my touch point whenever something was going wrong. All three of us were living just a couple of blocks from the famous Portobello Road, a tremendous outdoor market which is, among other things, known for its cheap prices.

Time and again I kept finding that the market wasn't really all that cheap for me. Eventually I realized that it was because I kept getting shortchanged. I became aware that people were deliberately unhelpful or unfriendly because I had an American accent. In fact, this was happening in London whenever I tried to get information or directions.

One time I was expecting a shipment from the States by air cargo. I'd been having a tremendous amount of difficulty getting the package. I wasn't sure what airline it had been sent on, but I knew it should have arrived. I called all the different airlines, asking for information, and nobody would help me out. In exasperation, I dragged myself over to see Michael and Hilary, and pleaded for advice. "Why can't I get any information from people?"

They looked at each other and diddled a little bit. Finally, Hilary turned to me and said, "Well, it's probably because you're rude."

"What?" I exclaimed.

"For instance," she continued. "If you want to get information about trains to East Grinstead to go see Annie, you will pick up the phone and dial the railroad. The way to get the information is to say, 'Pardon me. I hope I'm not being any trouble.' They will say, 'Oh no, no. No trouble at all.' You say, 'Well, I, I want to get some information about trains to East Grinstead.' They will say, 'Oh yes, of course. What was it you'd like to know?' You: 'Well, I don't want to be any trouble, but I wonder if you could let me know what trains there are in the morning?' Them: 'Oh, of course, it's no trouble at all …' and they'll tell you exactly what trains there are in the morning."

Hilary did this endlessly with me, in a number of different scenarios, explaining that for each question, you always start out with, "I hope I'm not taking too much time" or "I don't want to be any trouble." At first I thought she was making fun of me. It couldn't possibly be this extreme. I couldn't quite comprehend that even though a person is speaking to you for the purpose of answering your questions, you had to go through this elaborate process. The whole system of politeness was quite different than it was in the United States.

In the States, if you want to be polite, you say, "Excuse me. I wonder if you can tell me about the fares and schedules for East Grinstead?" But in England, you had to take everything one step at a time, and each new question had to be introduced with, "I don't want to be any trouble."

When she was done explaining, I felt miserable, but picked up her phone to try it out. I called one of the airlines and said, "Excuse me, I don't want to be any trouble."

The woman answered, "Oh, no no. You're no trouble at all."

I said, "I know this is stupid of me, but I'm not certain if a package for me was sent on your airline. They didn't tell me what line they sent it on ..."

British science-fiction author and friend Michael Moorcock, London, circa 1967.
Courtesy of the Merril estate

I went through the whole conversation being every bit as extreme as Hilary had been, and the woman gave me all the information I needed.

Hilary drilled all this home for me, and she didn't stop right there. She continued: "If you're at someone's house, you just stopped in for a visit, and they say, 'Oh, would you like a cup of tea then?' you must say, 'Oh, no, no, no. I don't want to be any trouble.' They say, 'Oh, well do have a cup of tea!' And you must refuse three times. If at the end of the three times, they don't offer it again, they're really glad not to have to make your tea. But if they really want to make something for you, then that's when you can say, 'Oh, well, if it isn't going to be too much trouble.'"

She informed me that I must also say thank you and please at every single opportunity. In the States, people hardly ever say thank you or please. It's indicated with a smile, or a tone of voice. My problems stemmed from the fact that when I first got to England, I was treating the people there like they were American.

Once Hilary explained the politeness markers to me, I realized that it wasn't just my American accent that was causing problems. Still, it did cause trouble for me. I stood out like a sore thumb. My pride was smarting all the time because in the United States I had been sure that I was accentless.

So I began to study the way British people formed their words. I watched their faces and discovered that the big difference between how Americans and Brits spoke was the energetic use of the tongue, lips, and teeth. That made all the difference in sound.

I began speaking energetically when I dealt with people in shops. It was a hoot. My accent didn't resemble any known English accent, but it clearly was not American. People started saying things to me like, "Well, are you from the West Country, then? Or perhaps Ireland?"

I found that when I was trying to buy things at Portobello Market, three things were going on. One was the difference in markers of politeness, another was my American accent, and the third was on the level of cultural context. For example, in the United States or Canada, if you want a quarter-pound of something, you ask for "a quarter-pound." In England you just say "a quarter." I would say "I want a quarter-pound of beef," and they wouldn't understand, they just heard "pound."

☙

Both the American and British codes of politeness, I was to learn, are different from the Canadian code. Canada was halfway between the two extremes. I could get along either way, by negotiating the balancing act carefully. Proper Ontario people still found me a little bit brash if I didn't use the right "thank you" and "please" phrases. The biggest problem in Canada is appearing to be pushy. People found my American manner brash, because I was blunt and stated outright opinions.

In a way, I was lucky to have had the time in England (and to have learned from my mistakes) before I went to Japan a few years later. Everything that is true of the politeness system in England is even more true in Japan. By the time I got to Japan, it was easy for me to make this adjustment. The Japanese have dozens of ways of saying "excuse me" and "thank you." They say "please" with everything. They use these modifiers almost as a way of marking the beginning of a new statement.

One major difference in politeness between Japan and England, however, is that in Japan they always serve you without asking first. They never ask, "Would you like a cup of tea?" It is more like, "Here's the tea."

Little changes that I made in my everyday communication, like learning the politeness rules, made life in England and Japan possible. I realized that formal politeness is much easier to negotiate than the code I had learned in the United States, which is a kind of tightrope act in which you never use formal words but have to be gracious at all times.

Meanwhile, the news about Vietnam was getting worse and worse. My British friends kept saying to me, "Now that you Americans have taken over the world and we don't have to worry about it any more, what are you going to do with it?"

I had been very much aware of the wickedness of my country for a long time. This was not a sudden discovery on my part. The Vietnam War brought it to a whole new quantitative level. There was something telling in the fact that the particular group of people I knew in Britain were all terribly relieved they were no longer running the world. I was not a bit happy about the idea that my country was now running it, and doing a miserable job. At some point I realized I had to go home and see if there was a revolution I could join. If there wasn't one, I felt strongly that I couldn't go on being an American citizen.

So I went home and ardently looked for a revolution. I kept searching until the Chicago Democratic Convention in 1968. I went to Chicago partly to seek out a revolution, if there was one happening, and partly because my seventeen-year-old daughter Ann and her friends Peter and Martha wanted to go. In New York the kids were the backroom squad with paint stains, the "McCarthy Art Department" who had been silkscreening all the campaign posters and visual propaganda for would-be Democratic presidential nominee Eugene McCarthy.

By then, I was shaken up. I hadn't been able to do any work since getting back home from England. I decided to drive the kids out to Chicago in my station wagon of medium vintage so they could bring their silkscreen equipment. About four or five of them went with me. I was also interested in going because Paul Krastner, editor of *The Realist*, had reported a few issues earlier that the hippies planned to put LSD in the Chicago reservoirs during the convention. I thought, "My god, if that actually happens, I want to be there."

Daley City, they're calling it, Fort Chicago, and now Prague West. Barbed wire and security checkpoints. Chemical Mace and police clubs; sequin-spangled Humphrey Girls—street-scene Yippies, sleepless, beaded, bandaged, bearded— V-signing clean-for-Geners, earnest smiles and angry eyes; incongruously baby blue bright helmets of Chicago's Finest, and the long slow convoys of army-drab Guards on Lake Shore Drive.

The kids I drove out here are a backroom squad, not-so-clean Geners, doing their thing here the way they were doing it in New York, with silkscreen and paint stains, but working on cloth now, block-letter STOP THE WAR posters for delegates to smuggle, folded, into The Hall.

The buses and taxis are on strike. The kids tell me, wear your McCarthy button, and any McCarthy-stickered car will stop. What will they do when the miracle doesn't occur? If they get through the plank battle today, nominations will happen tonight, and the mood here is more and more mortuary—a growing feeling that they may even Dump the Hump tonight and Draft Byrdman— if the Kennedy Heir Presumptive doesn't come forward: whoever it is, it won't be McCarthy.

If he agrees to a fourth party, they'll get some sleep and get back to work, I guess; and if he doesn't—the SDS is waiting on the corners, and the police make the Yippies look better all the time. Black Chicago growls and glowers and grins in the ghettoes (except for the watchers patrolling the Loop: "Go home, sister—no black blood spilled here tonight."), but what happens if the next reporter the cops club down and Mace spray on the ground is Black?

From here and now, the batch of books I brought out to review seems remote and pallid.

This was the Democratic Convention at which Lyndon (Byrdman) Johnson handed over the reins of power to Hubert (the Hump) Humphrey, and the Chicago police clubbed down anti-Vietnam War kids in the streets: Yippies (radicalized hippies), SDS (Students for a Democratic Society), and Eugene McCarthy's (clean-for-Gene) supporters. THE WHOLE WORLD IS WATCHING, the kids shouted into the lenses of the TV camera, and they were close to correct. Nobody who watched it will ever forget it, but decades later only the ones who were in the middle of it still remember the acronyms, the slang, the jokes, and the terror.

I still have my red, silkscreened cloth banner that says "STOP THE WAR," which my kids made with their silkscreen press. These banners were unfurled in the balcony of the convention because the Democratic committee was not allowing McCarthy's people to bring in any literature, or posters. This was their prize item. There was this one marvellous moment on television when all these young people stood up in the middle of the convention, opened up their banners, and sang "We shall overcome." But that was the only three minutes of the entire week that was anything other than completely horrifying.

I wrote the Daley City piece holed up in a friend's apartment in South Chicago, where I was watching TV in between attempts to do my book review column. When I saw tanks rolling down the streets on the screen, I forgot it was the same day that the Russians were invading Czechoslovakia. I stopped trying to write.

In the end my book review column began:

Milford, Pa., September:

Too remote. The peace plank was defeated, the kids' cloth STOP THE WAR *posters made some prime* TV *time, and all the savagery of the streets up to that point seemed nothing at all beside the film clips the networks (finally aroused) began showing alternately with the Amphitheater Nominations coverage that Wednesday night. The whole world is watching, they chanted in the streets, while Delegates' Ladies aimed cocktail glasses from the windows of the Conrad Hilton at the cops below. Next morning, I phoned Ed Ferman in New York, warned him there'd be no column from me, packed up the typewriter and drove up to Lincoln Park. Later, I drove a Medic team between the hospital station at St. Chris' church on the near North Side, and Michigan Avenue. ("Don't mind her, she's a good kid," the med student said when the student nurse screamed at him: "She's just been gassed. It makes them irritable.")*

I had reached such a level of despair that my conscience demanded I either find a revolution to join NOW, or I would have to get out of the United States—back to Swinging London, maybe. My review column continued:

For two days, I interviewed medics and patients, and took names and addresses of people there was no time to talk to on the spot. (But no one who wasn't there wants to believe it the way it was; some of the publishers I approached said they'd be glad to do a new science fiction anthology.) And here I am, with the same stack of books, and some more. Some of them are pretty good reading, too. But almost all of them are—remote.

At the end of the Convention week, the taste of America was sour in all our mouths. I had not found any revolution to join, but I had seen a copy of the *Toronto Anti-Draft Manual*, which was telling people how to come to Canada. I had also learned a great deal about the anti-draft program. We decided to drive back to Milford by way of Toronto—we figured we'd drive home in a free country.

When we came across the border into Windsor, we were elated. If we had been wearing hats we would have been tossing them up and shouting, "Yippee! We're free!"

☙

I phoned an old friend who was living in Toronto, a mathematics professor named Chandler Davis. He had been teaching at the University of Toronto since he got banned from all U.S. universities because he wouldn't sign the loyalty oath. He was happy to hear from me and said, "Sure, come along, all of you. We can put you up."

We stopped to see him and he was eager for news of what had been going on in Chicago and New York. He invited a friend of his to come over, and the friend turned out to be poet Dennis Lee, who was then very much embroiled in starting Rochdale College. Dennis told me all about the plans for Rochdale.

Suddenly I realized, "This is where people who have even more urgent need than I do to leave the States are coming. I should be here too, because I can be of use."

So I signed up with Dennis as a resource person for Rochdale, went home and packed up all my goodies. Shortly after that, I wrote to him.

Nov. 17, 1968
Milford

Dear Dennis:
I think the last delay is now past. I was foolish enough to drive on the Long Island Expressway in a storm, thereby losing car (not that much damage, busted radiator, but unbelievable situation whereby it costs more than the value of the car—unless virtually new—to get towed off the highway for repairs!) which complicated all arrangements. Now have definite arrangements, reservations, etc. Will leave here 6 pm Friday evening, with local friend driving hired trailer. Depending on customs delay, should arrive in Toronto any time after 3 am on Saturday.

If you have not already done so (Chan was going to try to phone you after I phoned him last night), can you send me a formal/proper sort of letter of a sufficiently pompous nature to reassure the customs/immigration people that I am entering Canada as a (staff? faculty? resident?) member of the College, so as to make sure I don't flunk out on your immigration point system? I think anything giving the impression I am Honorably Employed and with Assured Residence will do ... ???

Sending copy of this to Chan so whatever message you leave there will not need any explaining. See you Saturday—or whenever you get back from wherever you are then—
Best, Judy Merril

I returned to Toronto as a landed immigrant. I left the repression in the United States and came to the freedom of Rochdale. Of course, it was months later when I paused to think and realized that truly, in my heart, I had immigrated to Canada.

Rochdale, and Toronto at that particular time, meant different things for different people. I think the best illustration I can give of what it meant for me is something that occurred when I was living in the first apartment I had in Rochdale, which was on the third floor, overlooking Bloor Street.

I had been there only two or three weeks when I got a phone call from Peter Turner (who had been Ann's boyfriend in New York—Ann was, she thought, on her way back to England to register for a psychiatric nursing course. As it turned out, she stayed in Toronto to start the first youth clinic in the city.) He told me he had just gotten his draft notice and wanted to leave the States. He asked if I had room for him. I told him I did.

The day he arrived he was sitting in the living room of the apartment, looking out the window. I was in the back of the living room, and out of the corner of my eye I saw him suddenly jump back, away from the window.

I was surprised, and then I realized what was going on. The taxis in Toronto, or at least the most frequent taxis on Bloor Street, were the same colour and appearance as cop cars in New York. A whole string of them would park or cruise along the street in front of Rochdale. The first couple of days I was in that apartment I did exactly the same thing, because I had taken the precaution of going downstairs, standing out in the street, and realized it was possible to see up into my window.

We had gotten that kind of consciousness in New York, where you would notice what was supposed to be an electric company van parked across the street for several days, and you knew that there was a listening device in there. So every time something that looked like a cop car drove by, I jumped back out of sight of the window, and now Peter was doing it.

I started laughing and said, "Peter, they're taxis."

He sighed with relief.

That situation was, in distilled form, the essence of the difference I felt between the Toronto of 1969 and where I had come from; this felt like a free country.

In 1992 I was asked to write an Afterword for a new anthology of Canadian science fiction, *Ark of Ice*:

Once upon a time, in the shining years of the youth movements, the time of turning on and tuning in, the days of draft dodgers and deserters and Fuller domes, first moon landings, and Whole Earth Catalogues, there was a high rise building in Toronto called Rochdale College: a "free university," student-owned and run, dedicated to a concept of education that had everything to do with learning and almost nothing to do with teaching. The elder members, like me— anyone over 35 was an elder—were not Professors, but "Resource Persons." It was a good place to be, for a while; and of course it lasted only a short while. But for a few years, Rochdale was a moiling boiling collective center for people —artists, social scientists, planners, politicos—trying to create (yes!) a truly new world order, to carve the future to a shape and in a substance better suited to the planet and its humans than the painful present we were experiencing, let alone what we knew of the past.

Most of the people at Rochdale read science fiction. I came to Rochdale in 1968 from a fairly cushy spot in the world of U.S. science fiction—a world that was just then in the process of exploding out of a dirty-little-genre ghetto into both literary and commercial respectability. I came to Rochdale, and for that matter to Canada, for the same reason I have invested the largest part of my adult life in speculative fiction: I wanted to change the world.

SIXTEEN | ROCHDALE COLLEGE: A "WHAT IF" TIME

DO YOU KNOW HOW hard it is to write about sex? Or love? If you try to describe either one (whether as pornography or in an artsy/erotic mode) you—well I, at least—just make yourself (myself) sound ridiculous. Writing about Rochdale College after the fact is much the same. There have been five or six books about it, and at least two TV documentaries. I'm not the only one who has failed foolishly.

Yet I must try … Some of it is clear and simple: Rochdale College came into being as a Noble Experiment initiated by idealistic academics at a time when "free universities" were in. This one was an eighteen-storey high-rise co-op near the University of Toronto. It combined a residence with experiments in restructuring education. Administration, finances, housekeeping, and education were all under the total control of the student body: that is to say, almost everybody in charge was under the age of twenty-five. There were a number of "Affiliates," substructures inside or connected to Rochdale, several of which outlasted the college: the Indian Institute, one of the earliest Native cultural organizations in Canada; a film series run by Reg Hartt, specializing in classic surrealism and cartoons; an experimental theatre group known as Theatre Passe Muraille; a new small independent publisher, the House of Anansi (one of the co-founders was Dennis Lee; its office was on nearby Spadina); and the Coach House Press, located in a back alley off Huron Street, just behind the college.

I came there as a Resource Person in Writing and Publishing. My salary was my room and board. When asked what exactly a Resource Person did, I usually answered, "Learn to be resourceful enough to live in Rochdale." I loved it.

The year I lived there, and the two more I participated from outside, turned my life and psyche around. It was truly a place, a time, an experience that was far better to have loved and lost than never to have lived at all. I can't describe it any better than I might describe a twenty-five-years-ago loving act of sex, but two things I wrote at the time get some of the feeling.

One was in a letter, dated June 29, 1969:

Judith, after moving to Toronto.
Courtesy of the Merril estate

I am too much involved with Rochdale to be able or willing to give the sort of simplistic semi-descriptions *Newsweek*, or other such sources, offer. Yes, we are a "dormitory for U. of T(oronto)"—or so thought about 500 U. of T. students who lived here till last month [...] Yes, we are the Drug Palace of North America—or so think hundreds of speed freaks and dealers who come pushing in, and are pushed out. Yes, we are a "free school," "experimental university," "intentional community," "co-operative," student-activist and/or draft-resistance centre. Yes, we have free love, happy families, virgins, homosexuals, you-name-it. No, we don't have classes in Black Power. Most of the kind of things we do are listed in the Catalogue [...]

The 1969 Rochdale Spring Catalogue was a seventeen-by-twenty-two foldout sheet published by Coach House. I wrote it.

THE ROCHDALE CURRICULUM: *Nobody knows exactly how many Education Things are going on here. Seminars come and go before anyone has thought to write them up [...] Quantitative measurements will get you nowhere, and all descriptions are on their way to being out of date [...]*

Still, a college catalogue has to have a curriculum: the catalogue listed seminars in everything from Greek philosophers to revolution, the activities available through the affiliates, and a variety of workshops (chess, and sculpturing, for instance), but the best space went to our specialty, the "Living Laboratories." These included two projects of mine, The Pub(lishing Centre) and the Spaced Out Library. But the central gems of the catalogue were the descriptions of the Governing Council and the Maintenance Squad:

GOVERNMENTAL AND SOCIETAL DYNAMICS: *Mon, Wed, Fri, 3:30, Room 202; alternate Wednesdays, 8:30, main lounge. Attendance, 10–100, usually including a quorum (6 out of 12) of the Rochdale Governing Council. (Non-Council members are all, in theory, auditors.) The planned curriculum includes: Fiscal management; Intercorporate relationships; Government by General Manager; Government by discussion; Tourism and immigration; Population dynamics; The microcosm as a state. Spring semester extras, to date: Public Health (making a clinic, & corridor cat-shit control); Donation acceptance techniques (making a library); Security: crime control, police control, firearms control, theft control, vigilante control; Penology in the unstructured society (Is banishment the ultimate punishment or the only available one?); The media— making overexposure pay; Inter-institutional relations—making sociology surveys pay; N-dimensional space-time allocation.*

HOTEL AND BUILDING MANAGEMENT: *Andrew Raney, craftsman/ designer in metal work, and brewmaster extraordinary, Director. A continuous seminar and laboratory course with 12 student/instructors under the supervision of Property Manager Raney, plus an indefinite number of specialist, part-time, and temporary participants. An 18-storey high-rise building in downtown Toronto with a hyper-active shifting 24-hour population of 1000 or more has been secured for laboratory facilities. Typical projects include: The Otis Trip—elevator and overworked computer maintenance; Garbage compression and chute clearance; Locksmithing and master key control in an individualistic society; Bulletin board theory and practice; Plumbing for overcrowded Ashrams; Fire alarm suppression; Supplies: theory, distribution, and control—furnishings, cleaning equipment, linens, light-bulbs, etc.; Property management in the co-op and/or communal and/or chaotic society. This course has had notable success with vocational training of philosophy, poli-sci, art, and poetry students.*

Or, summing up—

EDUCATION AT TOCHDALE IS—

—happening, in flux, multi-level, unpredictable, dynamic, continuing, many-sided. You discover tomorrow what you learned yesterday. Nothing is extra-curricular.

—yours to make, take, find, give, design, improvise. If that sounds like free-dom, remember it's also the heaviest load of responsibility you've ever carried. You have to start by learning what it is you want to learn: you may be surprised at the answer. A lot of us have been.

Right away, given my position of Resource Person in Publishing and Writing, I decided to start things moving by establishing a learning space. We used two rooms on the second floor of the building which we called the "Pub," short for "Publishing." The Pub contained typewriters, mimeograph equipment, and various pieces of low-tech equipment that could be used for getting whatever was in your head out on paper. Anyone in the building was welcome to use the Pub's resources, which included any knowledge contained in the heads of my-self and another resident, poet Victor Coleman. There were also a couple other people who made themselves available.

The first summer at Rochdale was the summer of the first moon landing. It was the perfect time to open up the first version of a science fiction library, which we called the Spaced Out Library. The Rochdale library was nothing more than a collection of books owned by people in the building who were pre-pared to lend them out knowing that they were going to lose some. The books weren't actually donated to Rochdale. It was understood that they were to be temporary donations. I think I put in the largest number of books, but a lot of other people contributed. The Toronto Public Library System (Harry Campbell was then chief librarian) helped us establish the library by lending us display shelves and giving us information about how to catalogue publications.

The little library opened spectacularly during the first Rochdale Summer Festival in July 1969, held specifically to coincide with the landing on the moon. The festival featured a group of science fiction writers and literary figures who had travelled to Toronto from various places around the world. One of the most notable personalities was Ed Emshwiller, an artist and filmmaker. It was a big event on the night of the moon landing, and it occurred fairly late so as to happen simultaneously with the actual event. Leading up to it we held a seminar with four science fiction writers and four astronomers from the University of Toronto. They discussed the moon landing and its predicted ramifications.

This was a "what if?" time in history. A time of complete change, when fiction —especially science fiction—had an important role to play in questioning the existing social structures. People were rejecting values that had been enforced on them by society or their parents, and were now searching for new values. Young people were travelling across the continent and around the world looking for other ways to live. Rochdale was one of the places they came to from all over North America, Europe, and South America.

The first time any long-haired kid who entered Toronto saw another long-haired kid they would ask, "Where can I crash?"

The answer would always be, "Rochdale."

It was built to accommodate 850 people, and at any one time there were about 650 who were paying rent. By Christmas of the first year we had a population of two thousand, most of them just crashing temporarily. People were even sleeping in closets. There were a lot of problems to deal with, and the people who had to deal with them were the same ones who were living there, trying to sort out their own lives. Of the two thousand people who lived there, only about twenty of us were over the age of thirty-five.

❧

Rochdale had more Michaels than God, but there were four Michaels who were mine: Goldstein, Phillips, Price, and MacDonald. At one time I shared a large apartment with two of them and another person. At another time I shared a smaller apartment with one of the Michaels. In fact, there's only one Michael I never shared an apartment with, and I shared a library with him.

Michael Goldstein was the genius of the maintenance squad at Rochdale. He was about sixteen or seventeen at the time, and a really brilliant kid, totally competent at all things mechanical or electrical. He had not waited to get his draft notice before coming up from the States. His family had backed him entirely—they agreed it was better if he didn't have to run, either psychologically or physically, when the time came. So he came to Rochdale and joined the maintenance squad.

Mike Goldstein was the New York Jewish whiz-kid of Rochdale, and there was something incredibly sweet and innocent about him. This stocky, sturdy sweetness has somehow survived to this day. I don't think he has ever done anything unkind to anybody. Since the Rochdale years, Goldstein has moved out to Vancouver, married a quite interesting young Japanese woman, and had some kids. He became a soil chemist, and removes toxic soil for various companies. He's also into computers in a big way—owns numbers of them, far more than what he needs for his business, and evangelizes them to people.

Mike Goldstein, Mike Phillips, and I shared one of Rochdale's large suites, which were called Zeus suites. The middle-sized ones were called Aphrodites, and the small ones were not suites, they were communal living arrangements.

Phillips was slim, dark, and intense. He came to Rochdale from Montreal when he was nineteen years old. While he lived there he was rental manager for the entire building, and somehow managed to juggle the incredibly complex rental situation. Somewhere after the middle of the first year, Phillips suddenly decided to leave. His departure from Rochdale was so abrupt that he only had about a week to put down on paper everything that he had been holding in his head. This was essential, so that someone else could take the reigns and the building could continue to operate smoothly.

There was a tremendous sense of betrayal from the community. I don't recall the reasons he left (if I ever even knew them), but I do know that Phillips had a kind of double agenda in life. I don't think he discovered this until he was at Rochdale. He was fascinated by performance, in particular dance, at the same time as he was seriously interested in medicine and psychiatry. For some years after he left Rochdale, Phillips alternated these interests. He would do a year of university and then take six months off and join a dance company. Then he would do another year of university, and take six months off and go abroad somewhere to do some performance. He kept on doing this right through medical school, and eventually become a psychiatrist.

When I saw him last, in the early 1990s, he was on a short trip home from China, where he had spent six or seven years working in a psychiatric institute. Before that he worked at a geriatric/psychiatric facility in Vancouver. When I saw him he had a fairly newly acquired wife and a baby. There was still somehow a kind of purity in this man—the sense of someone who had found a way to live his own life with integrity in a totally corrupt and polluted world.

D.M. (Michael) Price, my third Michael, was a poet and artist. During that Rochdale year he was a little older than the first two Michaels, maybe in his early twenties. He had no money, no job. He was crashing on a mattress in the large cupboard of someone's Zeus suite rent-free. This was fairly common; many people used the cupboards as free bedrooms.

When we decided to open the library there, Price, a devoted reader of science fiction, volunteered to start organizing the collection. We found enough money in the so-called "education budget" to give him free meals at a restaurant that was part of Rochdale, and put him to work. Later on we also gave him a bed in one of the Ashram facilities.

For six months he read his way through all the science fiction books and catalogued them. After that we found a small stipend for him, which was perhaps $50 or $100 a month on top of food and board, to work in the library. Then, because he had incredible sums of money to buy records, go to plays occasionally, and date girls, he wasn't nearly as efficient a librarian as he had been before.

Later he too moved out to Vancouver. I don't think he's even writing poetry anymore. For quite some time his preferred two jobs were working in a bookstore and in child-care facilities. He's in a bookstore now on a fairly steady basis. He has also become a fanatical birder.

Mike MacDonald (Mike number four) was certainly not sweet and innocent.

He was considerably older than the others, and not part of the same scene at all. He was originally from New Brunswick, and had maybe one-eighth Native blood. He and I shared an Aphrodite for part of the time I was at Rochdale. MacDonald worked for the Addiction Research Foundation as a sort of undercover man in Rochdale. (He wasn't really undercover because everyone knew what he did, but his job was not at all high-level or visible.) He collected samples of all the street dope, and took it back to Addiction Research for tests, so they could find out what was toxic. Then he would tell the results to people in the drug trade, who came in and out of Rochdale. He also let the Rochdale people know what they shouldn't be fooling with. Mike basically kept Addiction Research, which hardly ever dealt directly with street people, in touch with the street drug scene.

Eventually Mike MacDonald also went out to Vancouver, and he became involved with the Native scene there. Once, when I was out in British Columbia doing a reading tour that took me all over the province, we travelled together throughout the northern part of the province. I cashed in the air tickets the Canada Council had bought for me and dedicated the money to gas, because Mike had a car and wanted to go up to the same places. We went to Hazelton and Terrace, Prince Rupert and the Queen Charlottes. We covered a lot of territory.

Mike knew Native people in all these places, so it was a really exciting trip. We went to the Haida community in the Charlottes, and it was salmon-smoking time. We went to a cultural centre in Hazelton, where they were doing some work with totem poles. In Terrace he had a close friend named Dora Fitzgerald, who was living there at the time. She was also involved with Native affairs. The three of us spent a fabulous evening at the local bar patronized by mostly Natives, listening to Native country music, and dancing. Mike had total entry wherever we went—he had become accomplished in video work and made a lot of videotapes for Native groups for political purposes.

So those are my four Michaels. Mike MacDonald has by now just about disappeared from my life; when I go out west I can never find him. But when I talk about loves that are lost, the first three Michaels were only ever lost by distance.

❧

At the time (1969), many places called themselves free universities. In most cases this simply meant that students didn't have to pay to go, and that they, rather than a faculty of academics, determined governing policies and educational modes. In the case of Rochdale, the concept was carried even further: various people had combined their talents to put up a high-rise building in which all of this could happen (for a variety of reasons—not all pure and holy).

The fact that we had a dedicated building was wonderful, and Rochdale was one of the more successful attempts at operating an experimental school. But, as in any experimental institution, major problems will arise. There are only two things that can happen with such a large-scale experiment.

First, it can get co-opted by the conventional system. In this case, the main-stream pronounces it "successful," as soon as it stops being an experiment and starts being the status quo. Second, it can fall apart after a little while, because it doesn't have the infrastructure necessary for growth, maybe even survival.

This second situation is indeed what happened with Rochdale: partly because there was confusion in everyone's mind about whether Rochdale was an intentional community, or whether it was a school. I believe it was an effective school, but once you had reached the point where you knew what you wanted to do, and had started to train yourself in it, you had to get out of Rochdale, because you could no longer function there.

After a year or so, I moved into a shared house down on Beverley Street with five or six people, and kept doing some stuff with Rochdale from a distance. By that time I was also active in a group that we had formed specifically to help people who had come up from the States get settled and make their way into Canadian life. We worked directly with, or after, Toronto Anti-Draft, which helped people get up here in the first place.

The Rochdale experiment didn't last so long—after much tribulation it was finally shut down in 1975. The Rochdale building is now a senior citizens' residence, and I, for one, am now a senior citizen. The Space Race fell off the pop charts long before the U.S.–U.S.S.R. war games (and the Soviet Union itself) collapsed, and the liberation generation students of the 1960s and 1970s are now mostly struggling with middle-age middle-class mortgages and migraines. The new youth are addicted to nostalgia instead of novelty, and prefer medieval fantasy to speculative future fiction. The future seems to be on hold.

People here have some pride in where they live!
  — *Kevin Israel MacDonald*

KEVIN IS NINE years old. He lives in Philadelphia. He was talking about Toronto.

He's my grandson. It was the third day of his first visit to Toronto. He had been to "the Ex" (the CNE—the Canadian National Exhibition, held annually in August). He had been to the Island and the Ontario Science Centre and Honest Ed's discount shopping emporium, to Peter's Restaurant, to a grocery store and a laundromat and a branch of the Toronto Public Library. He had been on the ferry, the subway, buses and streetcars, in a taxi, for a walk on Bloor between Manning and Spadina, and in the back of a truck from Bloor to Palmerston, where I was living.

Can you have pride in your home and not know it? If you live in Toronto ...

**From a typescript written around 1973; source unknown. It appears to be a draft essay prepared for a proposed book in which Judith Merril, as an American, would be the "token immigrant."*

181

Gentle reader, if you are not from Toronto there is no way I can describe City Hall and have you believe it.
— *Duncan Macpherson, 1970*

Duncan Macpherson is a great political cartoonist. Great cartoonists are symptomatic of highly complex, sophisticated cultures. *The Toronto Star*, which publishes Macpherson's cartoons, is almost as simplistic/anachronistic as Toronto City Hall (cast and direction, not stage or setting). It is the total-surround of Toronto that produced Macpherson. ("Total-surround" is a well-known contemporary communications phrase that also came out of Toronto.)

Gentle reader, if you are Toronto-born-and-bred, there is no way I can describe Toronto and have you believe it.
— *Judith Merril, Token Immigrant*

Toronto is a city of foreigners and immigrants. And students. Like all great cities. (Well, I warned you, this quota status wouldn't be so bad if I could get out of character. This kiss-the-soil-of-the-promised-land enthusiasm is just as embarrassing to me as it is to you, dear Toronto.)

Toronto is one of the great cities of the world. It is cosmopolitan, corrupt, mannerly, creative, historic, innovative, multivalent, gentle, bold, concerned, and exciting. It is Toronto the Good and also Hogtown. It is probably the most active centre of intellectual, artistic, political, educational, and communications ferment in North America today.

Well, I did warn you. I've had a few dismal glimpses into what it used to be like here and what most Canadians still seem to think it's like now. Maybe only us immigrants (and students) know the city I can't tear myself away from. I promised myself I'd never live in a city again, but I'm rediscovering why cities were invented. It begins to make sense to try to clean the place up instead of throwing it away. In Toronto, I even imagine it might be possible. (I was born in New York, so I was born knowing You Can't Fight City Hall. But in Toronto … ?)

I wasn't born here. I came by choice.

☞

My Toronto is small. It looks something like an egg inside an amoeba.

Depending on the day, the mood, weather, and company, the amoeba contracts or spreads itself out. In an average state of consciousness, the pseudopodia are probably about as far out as they show here. The whole thing exists inside a vast expanse of flat grey housing tracts punctuated by vertical grey-and-glass slabs. The egg (or cell nucleus) changes shape and size only very slowly, and always in the same direction—out—though sometimes irregularly. As shown here, it is about 2.5 miles long and 1.5 miles at its widest point.

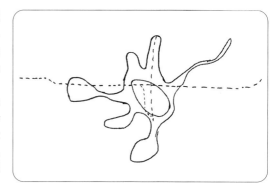

If you're better than I am at figuring out the areas of eggs and cities, you now know just how small it is. If not, the dotted subway lines might help. The astonishing thing is how much, or many, it contains (not just the properties—the people and processes).

I don't know how to get official population figures for egg-shaped territories, but they'd probably only confuse the issue, since many people who live in the egg sleep somewhere else, officially. But I'd guess at perhaps a quarter of a million, effective population—not including the thousands and thousands who work in the office buildings, department stores, banks, restaurants, etc., but carry on their real lives in Don Mills or Etobicoke or Mimico or Willowdale.

A simple, if esoteric, calculation would be to take the total number of hotels, hospitals, university residences, ashrams, student co-ops, communes, over-the-store flats, hostels, and missions; add the St. James Town and Ontario Housing Corporation properties; subtract the total space occupied by office buildings, parking lots, department stores, garages, restaurants, government buildings; throw in an unknown factor for museums, lecture halls, laboratories, seminar spaces, research foundations, experimental theatres, boutiques, charitable organizations, churches (since there's no way to tell which ones people work at and which ones they live in); and then remember the side-street and back-alley pockets, everywhere, of five- or eight- or twelve-room houses; consider the combined registration of the University of Toronto, Ryerson Polytechnic, the Ontario College of Education, the Ontario College of Art, and the Ontario Institute for Studies in Education; add Rochdale College. What do you get?

The important thing is not the figure, which could be one hundred thousand, or five hundred thousand for that matter, but the percentages: in this part of town, almost everyone is a student, and probably no less than 75 per cent are immigrants.

The immigrants may be from no further away than Orangeville—or East York. Readjustments from Scarborough are sometimes are difficult as from Singapore. The students may be studying philosophy or barbering or medicine or theatre or shorthand or welding or theory of communications (with Marshall McLuhan himself, or at night-school English classes) or just Canada. But most people move out of the nucleus when they stop studying something.

SEPTEMBER 3, 1968

We drove into Toronto in deepening twilight, en route "home" to Pennsylvania (but not at all sure where home was) after that Very Bad Week in Chicago. There were three embittered young radicals who had been "Clean-for-Gene" McCarthy-liberals a week before, and me. We came off the 401 and drove down into the top of the Yonge Street pseudopod, watching for St. Clair, according to instructions: on our way to talk to an old friend about the idea of moving to Toronto.

We saw gardened parks that seemed to have been designed to draw us in off the street. We couldn't really tell if how good it felt was Toronto or just thank-god-not-Chicago! But—strangers, looking for a strange place—what we noticed most of all were clearly legible lit-up street signs—with house number indicators on them yet. Our questions were half-answered already. This was a city for people to live in.

Just inside the southernmost point on the shell of my egg is the Toronto-Dominion Centre: the veritable symbol of the faceless commerce-warren, endlessly cubicled into office, display, and sales space by day; brilliant, mysterious, and endlessly rewarding after dark. The view from the top at dusk is more than you bargain for: after sunset, when you can bring yourself to look closer at things, you find yourself at every turn revolving in space/time between glass-enclosed inner-case displays of Eskimo sculpture and glassed-in outer-brace frames for white man structures. Gleaming polished sandstone seals inside: shine-surfaced bright-light highways outside.

The block I used to live on, contained by Phoebe, Beverley, Sullivan, and Huron streets, consists of a large parking lot, two and a half streets of co-ops and communes, the Huron Street Hall, and the Toronto RCMP headquarters. On Beverley, all the neat Canada Trust fence-rails were taken down by mutual consent, so that the whole row now shares a long narrow backyard-park. The RCMP headquarters is about to move. When it does, another big development deal will go up in the dust of the Hall along with the stained-glass windows—unless the "counter-culture" types turn out to be more stubborn than the Chinese families and welfare people who lived there until Canada Trust took over the properties in 1969, painted them all clean grey, repaired the floor-boards, and raised the rents $100 a month.

What remains of the Chinese residential area runs north and south of Dundas to Spadina: bright red-painted houses with tiny front gardens brilliant from spring to fall, lavishly tended and lovingly arranged. Cornflakes and jasmine tea crowd the shelves of the small corner grocery stores; children on errands buy ginger root and Popsicles and Chinese cabbage.

The eggshell curves around Kensington Market: Toronto's inevitable cross-breed of London's Portobello Road and New York's Delancey Street—plus some. It's the "Jewish Market" to one generation of Torontonians and the "Portuguese Market" to another—where you can buy West Indian fruits and vegetables, Romanian candy, Spanish rolls, Dutch cheese, Italian wine grapes, German sausage, fresh Ontario eggs, and fish and poultry. The Portuguese gardens on Augusta are just as lush as the Chinese yards, but more in vegetables than flowers.

The old synagogue at Bellevue Square has been for sale since I first saw it. So is Bathurst United Church, maybe. There's a difference of opinion, as I write, between the "regular" and "experimental" congregations. The building has been functioning for a couple of years now as a community centre and theatre centre. Even the critics have begun to notice that Toronto is a "theatre town," and periodically pay cautious acknowledgement to Toronto Workshop Productions, Factory Theatre Lab, and Theatre Passe Muraille for accomplishments recognized in London or New York by the filmmakers. Eventually, perhaps they will notice how many young talents from New York and London are coming to work with these theatres, and with other groups not yet respectabilized in Toronto, like THOG, at Bathurst United.

Try this on for size: Toronto is where things happen for the first time nowadays. One minor item, probably a world's first, is the special science fiction collection maintained by the municipal public library system. Spaced Out Library (SOL) marks the tip of the Toronto egg for me in so many ways it's hard for me to write about it at all. Too much of dream-come-true, and too much of the paper-concretization of a quarter-century of my own life and work on the shelves and in the file drawers there, and one more old-house-soon-to-be-torn-down.

I have an office in the library. When we were first sorting things out and getting the place set up, during my third year in Toronto, I took a place on Bloor, halfway between SOL and Honest Ed's. Tetsu Yano, a friend from Japan (we translated Japanese science fiction stories into English together), was coming to visit me there, and in preparation I sent him a long letter full of practical and other information. Some places mentioned, like my own apartment, have since changed hands: the area has a lot of mobility, but this is how it was in the summer of 1971:

When you walk down the street from the library to Honest Ed's, you see people from about four feet tall to six-foot-six—Swedish blond to African purple—speaking in every conceivable accent, and a few completely inconceivable languages, in every style of dress (and undress). Barefoot students in jeans and shorts—the boys as often as not without tops; "WASP" Canadian ladies in dresses to just-below-the-knees and stockings and hats even in August;

Indian ladies in saris; the occasional older Korean lady in long pleated skirt and short jacket; young Canadian and American girls in African or Amerindian or just "old-fashioned" costumes—or in hot pants or miniskirts. The Greek men tend to be very sleek and trim in tight-fitting trousers and open-necked fitted shirts; the West Indians often in bright-striped cotton slacks or tailored lacy shirts.

(The word "ethnic" fascinated me: Canadians—well, Torontonians, at least—seem to use it so wonderfully impartially to grace all manifestations of non-Anglo-Saxon-non-French culture—but one senses so much more of envy than of patronage in its use—as if they think English/French/"Canadian" means acultural—non-ethos?)

I read somewhere that there are fifty-four foreign-language newspapers published in Toronto, in twenty-eight different alphabets. I think every one of them is read by someone within three blocks of Bloor and Bathurst. I think if you stood on the corner there long enough, you might hear every language of the world spoken.

It's the way I used to think of London and Tokyo. I still think of Hong Kong this way: I haven't been there. Washington D.C. has just as many languages and nationalities (or New York), but everyone tries to look and sound all-American.

I also warned Mr. Yano about the high cost of alcohol and tobacco here, and of books and magazines (astronomical by Japanese standards): 10 to 50 per cent higher than the United States. But entertainment is very cheap—I don't really think about it as a "budget item" at all, because there is always more going on (theatre, films, lectures, galleries, happenings, everything) that I want to go to that is free or just nominal-charge, than I have time for. Except when I get a spell of listening to a lot of jazz, and then the cost is basically just doing a lot more eating-and-drinking than usual.

☙

I was trying to pre-see the city through Tetsu Yano's eyes. When he got here, early in September, I re-saw a lot, and saw some other things for the first time. It happened when my grandsons came too, but of course Mr. Yano's eyes were more-different.

One: The Ex is really great. I had been there the year before with Toronto friends who steered me past the kitsch to the worthwhile things. Now Mr. Yano and I just wandered and got more and more euphoric. Never mind the ridiculous exhibits—it was the life, the colour, the colours and the people. Maybe the greatest County Fair on Earth? It was his first night here. "I am a Torontonian forever," he kept saying in the sleepy Bathurst streetcar afterwards.

Two: The reason why I do so little eating-and-drinking-out (except when gripped by my cyclic music addiction): the sad fact is, with liquor licences so hard for restaurants to get, you need a sky-high budget to have wine or beer with good food; very few places that serve drink take any trouble with the quality of their food.

Three: The reasons why I do eat out a lot: the really phenomenal number and variety of excellent restaurants in the two to three dollar dinner class. (Mr. Yano learned to say "thank you" in at least eight or nine languages before he left.)

Four: The wedding parties in High Park. Pink, red, violet, green, yellow, orange and blue parties of bridesmaids floating alongside black and frosted bride and groom along the paths and bridges of the formal gardens. (It just happened I had never been to High Park on a summer Saturday afternoon before.)

Five: "Welcome to Canada!" is almost a Toronto reflex: at least in smiles and small friendly acts, and usually in just those words. In all the encounters in restaurants, subways, parks, museums, everywhere (fifty? eighty? two hundred?) where my friend's desire to learn made him explain that he was newly-from-Japan, I recall only one (shocking! by that time) instance in which there was no immediate welcoming response.

Of course, this had happened to me, too: but I had somewhat forgotten, and never did get quite as much response; neither the people I met, nor I myself, were as aware of my new-foreign-ness.

Six: No two people in Toronto seem to speak in exactly the same accent, whether "ethnics" or "Canadians." Welcome to Canada! comes in every shape and colour.

The first time I went to England, I discovered quickly the wisdom of (whoever) first said the "British and Americans are divided by a common language." (At one point, I was going to compile a U.K.–U.S./U.S.–U.K. dictionary.) The problem is even more complex here, because even if the Americans are not, the British are very conscious of the differences. But Canadians—"nationalist" types even more than others—seem convinced it's just the same here as below the border (except of course less glamorous, poorer, and much more mannerly) and Americans coming up (myself once too) tend to believe they're in Cleveland-North. The dislocation in the first few weeks here is considerable—and for most of us a disorientation of pure delight. But some are so geared to uptight, the only answer is to go back. (Or to Montreal.)

JULY 1971

The Immigrant (me; this time not Token) is being interviewed for a CBC program on "intellectual refugees." The interviewer is a brilliant and perceptive man, warm, easy to talk to. I use up a lot of tape. I get a bit lyrical.

[...] I can remember when I was a kid in high school in New York—more than thirty years ago—feeling great swells of pride and patriotism and—and joy. I remember thinking (it was true then): New York is the cleanest big city in the world, and I remember saying contemptuous snobbish things like, about South America: Well you know the way they change presidents is by assassinating them! And the awareness—the absolute thrilling awareness of living in a country, which I lost and which I am now regaining. I feel this way in Canada ... in Toronto. I don't know Canada. I don't think it feels the same in Quebec.

Later, the interviewer said, laughing (but I'm not so sure how serious he wasn't): "Watch out, Judy. If you don't learn to be a little bit more critical, we might not let you become a citizen."

Well, I am critical, of course. I came here to Rochdale, not Rosedale. I was critical of Rochdale, too: and totally, enthusiastically, immoderately committed to it. I like to think of this apparent contradiction as "romantic realism"; but not everybody understands the concept of Pollyanna as Revolutionary. I was a "resource person" at Rochdale for ten months and two weeks. I wouldn't have missed it for anything in the world. I couldn't have stayed another week: the commitment was just too much for flesh and bone.

I'm still a member of Rochdale. More extraordinary, I still live in Toronto. I moved out of New York twenty years ago, when it was just beginning to go bad, and after that the longest time I spent in any city larger than five thousand, until I came here, was nine months (in London, you understand, where you can breathe again).

I get a lot of questions about Toronto. The word is getting around here and there (I mean, there: outside of Canada, of course) that Toronto is were it's at. People who don't like where they're at, want to know more. It's not easy to know what to tell them. Except a few, a certain kind of writer/artist/thinker/scientist/explorer/world-citizen, for whom Toronto is exactly where it's at, all considerations of economics, politics, or circumstances notwithstanding. There are no jobs, of course: but for anyone with the resources to qualify for immigration without a job, life in the fertile egg can be very inexpensive. Students and artists and poets and musicians and dreamers in the Beverley and Sullivan area are sharing nine-ten-eleven-room houses at a basic monthly room and board cost of $50 to $100 each. And the combination of intellectual resources, artistic ferment, cosmopolitan colour, psychic freedom, communications, and contact is unique. (You can go by foot anywhere inside the egg—it's so together.)

Clockwise eastward along the eggshell: a wave to Casa Loma in the first northward extension of the amoeba, where I now live—but is the fresher air really worth being so far up? Then just above the "border," the Toronto Free Clinic at Spadina and Dupont. Another old house, which served as a student co-op/commune and "external Rochdale" unit in between commercial life as a funeral parlour and public service use as the clinic.

We honestly didn't know, when we put out that Rochdale Spring Catalogue, whether there would be a Rochdale for people to come to in the fall. As I write, no one knows if it will be there by the time this book is published. But the important thing was, and is, the fact that it happened at all. It couldn't have happened anyplace else: not for the first time. Not anywhere in the United States, or in England, Sweden, Denmark, Switzerland, or Japan. Not in Montreal, Vancouver, Ottawa, Calgary, Fredericton, St John's, Halifax …

And one intriguing question continues to be: how much of the rest of where it's at in Toronto is Rochdale spin-off? People drawn to Rochdale who couldn't get it together there, but found a few others to work with and rented a house somewhere? People who came to Rochdale in formlessness or desperation or freakout, found out what they wanted, and went off to it?

Or, how much of what's happening now is simply coming out of the same nexus, matrix, atmosphere, vibes, that also produced the potential for Rochdale? (The theatre groups … the church happenings … the Ontario College of Art … Environment-environment … A Space … Toronto Dance Workshop … Stop Spadina … the Huron Street Hall … the Baldwin Photo Gallery … the U. of T. Daycare Centre … Toronto Free Clinic … The Electric Gallery … *Guerilla* and *Cabal* … New Press … the new jazz renaissance … the Spaced Out Library … Vulture Press … SEED alternative high school … CBC's "Bringing Back the Future" … St. Lawrence Centre Town Hall's public affairs meetings. Some of these began at Rochdale, some were/are staffed by Rochdale dropouts, some seemed to arise independently, around the same time.)

Which came first, the Rochdale chicken or my egg?

Almost across the street from Rochdale there's a complete inversion: the Ontario Institute for Studies in Education (OISE)—beautiful spaces, wall-to-wall secretaries, even the janitors (they say) are Ph.D.s. I am inclined to dismiss it. But maybe the parallel is not just incidental? Counterpart manifestations, perhaps, of the same (however reluctant) new fertility?

If you think about it, where else is so much tax money so well wasted? The *Bonaventure* aircraft carrier? Chemical warfare? Scarborough expressway?

Try to figure out how to educate kids for a future not one of us can anticipate and for which the schools today offer little better preparation than my own did. Where do you start? At OISE, as at Rochdale, ninety-nine starts out of a hundred are false ones. At OISE, of course, they have to keep records of all that money, so they know what they've tried that didn't work, and maybe why, and maybe what to try next. At Rochdale, they have to keep trying the same inexpensive things over and over, because they have no money and no records—and sometimes something works after a while. Which way is worse?

☞

Draw a line of tennis ball stitching down my egg: call it yin/yang. Try to figure out what to put where as you go through the massive egg-within-an-egg that is the University of Toronto complex.

Maybe U. of T. is not remarkable at all. Maybe the handful of genuinely bright creative students I know who think they're learning something there are duplicated in other multiversities, or are just deluded. James Eayrs, whom I respect, and who should know better than I, says the environmental aesthetic/intellectual experience is not to be found there. But I look at the little blacked-in building blocks on my map, and remember: a Sonny Greenwich concert at Hart House ... the Chicago Seven lawyer Bill Kunstler pouring a pitcher of water on someone's head at Convocation Hall ... the old Red White and Black office in the Student Activity Centre (SAC) building basement at 44 St. George Street ... the lab where I saw how they analyse the moon-dust ... Vosnesensky reading his poetry in the Medical Arts Building, and Auden showing up to read a translation ... the philosophy prof on the Interdisciplinary Studies Committee, explaining the relationships of physics, sound, and thought with the hand-crafted clockwork mechanisms and souped-up electronic organ in his office ... the Daycare Centre Occupation ... the Madness Conference being planned as I write ... and all the rest of the complex, which multiplies itself through interaction with the university ... Carl Sagan talking about extra-terrestrial life in the old grey Ontario College of Education ... Buckminster Fuller and Marshall McLuhan celebrating Irish Arts (!!) at St Mike's ... the Clarke Institute of Psychiatry ... the Royal Ontario Museum ... Metro Reference Library ... the Planetarium ... the rock benefit one lovely summer day on the green circle in front of Hart House ... talking science fiction with priests at St Mike's in front of a fireplace in a panelled room ... the Festival of Underground Theatre in 1970 ...

St. Joseph's College School cafeteria: endless coffees with Sister Bede Sullivan (talking filmmaking) and the writer/broadcaster Stanley Burke (talking politics) and Muñoz and Mike Malone and Dave Dexter (not talking, dreaming music), after the sunrise memorial service outside the legislative building at Queen's Park for the four students killed at Kent State College …

SEED School: maybe it could have happened without the time and space university people made available the first year to high-school students who wanted to learn something—maybe—or—

Maybe what happens in and around the university generates some of all the rest: maybe, again, it is just further manifestation of the Toronto ferment.

APRIL 1970

A street corner barely inside French Montreal, waiting for the friend I drove down with. He's late, when you're driving in Montreal, you're usually late, unless you're a Montreal driver.

The snow has been melting, first real thaw. All the litter of last November lies on the streets, soaked and redried, sooted and crumpled. I open a fresh pack of cigarettes, remove the cellophane, look around for a receptacle, see none, crumple film and foil into my pocket to dispose of later. And realize—

I have become a Torontonian.

In New York, Boston, Philadelphia, San Francisco, Los Angeles, Chicago, Cleveland, Orlando, Newark, Washington, Denver, Austin, St. Louis, London, Paris, Brussels, I might have looked for the trash can; in many smaller towns, I might have even held onto the wad till I found one. But in Toronto, where no one (outside of Rochdale) had ever told me not to litter, and no signs matter, public trash bins are few and far between—in sixteen months in Toronto, I had somehow become a person who put the cellophane in my pocket to throw out at home.

The trip to Montreal was my first visit away from Toronto since I arrived with fresh immigrant status, eight thousand books and magazines, fifteen file drawers of jumbled junk and value, a couple of mattresses, sheets and blankets, pots and dishes, in November 1968. Driving back into Toronto this time, we left the 401 at Yonge and laughed in unison—home again!—as we took our place in the minuet of stately traffic merging south.

For some reason, most of the people I've come to know in Toronto who live any distance outside the nucleus are either in the pseudopod that reaches due west to enclose High Park and Gothic Avenue, or in the one that runs north along Yonge and Avenue Road to Eglinton, the thick base of which includes Yonge and Bay, Yorkville, the galleries and filmmakers of Hazelton and Avenue Road. A little farther north, there's the pop radio station CHUM, and overall, a significant portion of my church connections in Toronto—which constitute an overwhelmingly significant portion of my church connections anywhere.

The main reasons for this rises from the complex of motives that brought me driving down Yonge Street, watching the lit-up street signs for St. Clair, that first time in September 1968. When I decided to leave what had been my country, I was in no danger of enforced military or penal service, but rather of taking up arms myself against the enforcers. I will never know with absolute certainly whether some Greater Ethic might not have been served by doing just that. I only know that from the instant of awareness of gleeful relish at the prospect of cop-killing, I could no longer live with myself in the United States.

One of the many reasons for Toronto in particular was the large number of young war resisters coming here: the idea that it might be less "copping-out" if I went where I could be of some use to others alienated for the same basic reasons, but with less resources or options than I had. In this connection, Rochdale was an inadvertent perfect choice that first year, when the street grapevines all led to 341 Bloor West.

When Rochdale's hospitality became strained, Red White and Black was organized late in 1969, as a reception and reorientation service, to provide for immediate physical necessities and an anchor through that first period of dislocation, the time of discovering that it is another country. Through RW&B, and later CARM (Committee to Aid Refugees from Militarism), I came into close contact with more church people than I'd known even casually in all my life before.

—Meetings with Canon Maurice Wilkinson, Gordon Stewart, and Gerald Loweth at the Canadian Council of Churches office on St. Clair Avenue: the always somehow unexpected juxtapositions of compassion, practicality, and high humour.

—More meetings (the Interfaith Committee for Draft-Age Immigrants) at Jim Young's Glebe Road Church: and the monstrous Christmas dinner mounted there one year by the Voice of Women.

—Rabbi Abraham Feinberg—again and again—whenever we needed someone.

—The whole roster of Toronto denominations who turned out for the Queen's Park Memorial Service after Kent State: the passion and human dignity of those who spoke.

But not all the sudden clergy in my life came out of one bag. Edgar Bull (who also came to Queen's Park) I met first in his church, St. Thomas' Anglican, on Huron behind Rochdale. Someone had told me, "It's a good place to be when things are too uptight—good vibes—and the door's always open." Not only that, but when the pastor saw me coming in, he made sure to welcome me, without pressing me to worship.

St Thomas', Trinity, Avenue Road, Bathurst, the Fred Victor Mission, the Unitarians —all of these have opened themselves to the people of the city, in different ways, but as one in not demanding a farthing of ideological repayment.

These are the places I happen to know. I am sure there are many other, in Toronto. I am almost as sure they exist in other cities—the churches are changing, along with the rest of society. But my experience of church people like this, before Toronto, was measured on less than the fingers of one hand.

Ann Pohl, Judith's second daughter, at age eighteen, shortly after they arrived in Toronto. 1968.
Courtesy of the Merril estate

FEB. 14, 1970

My daughter's wedding at the Unitarian Church ... everyone gets a balloon ... the music is a tape pre-pared by an audio-freak of theirs, the music they like ... the ceremony is one they wrote themselves, saying only what they mean to say to each other and the world ... guests in their party-best, everything from morning coat to dayglo orange plastic overalls ... Alan's grandfather has come from his midwest farm-house to be at his deserter-son's wedding! Neither Ann nor Alan belong to any church, but the minister is a man they know and care for, Al Fowlie, whose aid and advice from his position on the staff of Addiction Research Foundation helped form and foster the Rochdale Clinic, where Ann and Alan met each other. A happy wedding. A happy place to have it.

MAY 4, 1970

A camp forty miles outside Toronto, at the conference called to form the Interfaith Committee for Draft-Age Immigrants. This is my first meeting with many of the people I will be calling upon time after time for aid.

Red White and Black, together with a mixed bag of young Canadian "street" and "youth" workers, is trying to find a good place for a reception, infor-mation, and activities centre for transient youth—Canadian and immigrant. We've found a cheap rundown hall on Huron, a perfect place, but Canada Trust is doubtful about renting to us: maybe some Respectable Church backing can help. They seem interested.

About five, we break up and start back to town, and get our first outside news of the day. Four students have been killed at a state college in Ohio.

There is going to be a lot of work for the new committee.

MAY 9, 1970: "CITY IS FOR PEOPLE DAY" IN TORONTO

A day of booths and music and communication in Nathan Phillips Square had been officially proclaimed by Mayor William Dennison weeks earlier as a final compromise between the campaigners for a "Leave Your Car at Home Week" (with a downtown mall closed to traffic) and the appalled response of City

Hall's Old Guard. A bad bargain, but we were getting set to make the most of it—except that May 4 came before May 9.

There's a solid mass of flesh jammed onto the sidewalk in front of the U.S. Consulate—hands linked, some smiling, a line of Metro police prevents them from spreading out into the street ... occasionally the mass opens up a crack, we can distinguish arm-banded May Fourth Movement students, shiny-eyed Maoists. The mixture under compression is an explosion waiting to happen.

Across the street, the Vietnam Mobilization marshals a highly disciplined picket line on the east sidewalk, behind another linked-hands line of Metro cops, not only smiling, but joking. Plenty of space there, placards parading in an endless oval, a good Torontonian demonstration—five hundred people or more.

Some forty-five hundred more people are either packed into the mob on the Consulate sidewalk or with us on the median. The traffic flows freely up and down the Avenue.

On the median, there is a Sunday spring parade mood. We walk up and down, find friends, join small groups singing folk songs on the grass, watch left and right, the orderly procession to the east, the even tighter-packed crowd to the west. A flag is burned, cops charge in, put the fire out, red ink is splashed— who? Can't see the faces. We look nervously for reassurances from each other.

We are Americans, exiles, dodgers, deserters, political/cultural/social/psychological/ethical refugees ... traitors? We are not alone on the median, there are Canadians too, quiet sympathizers, angry humans, who feel the same need to be in this place at this time—but no desire—maybe an anti-need—to join the "activists" on the west sidewalk, and for us, a somehow un-invited feeling about the picket line on the east.

We are the aid-group members, writers of letters to editors, anti-war joiners, the nucleus, receivers of midnight phone calls—I just got in from Detroit, someone gave me your number in Buffalo, is there a place to crash? Bill just got busted, we're getting evicted, I took Al down to the Clarke, can you give them some groceries? Tom is freaking out, can you ... Almost all of "us" are there.

Four students have been killed by the Ohio National Guard at Kent State. Six students have been killed in a free-fire zone by Mississippi storm-troopers at Jackson State. We all knew it was coming: since Chicago, since the Panther shootout in L.A., since the Pentagon, from the beginning, the growing grim awareness that it would come to this. What now? What are we doing here?

Walking on the mall. Politely staying off the streets. Traffic keeps flowing, the roads roll. We're no longer Americans, not yet Canadians, roots torn, futures unknown, not in the mob, not the ordered picket line, greeting each other with glances left and right. We who have formed a habit of the word revolution, make little jokes, hum songs, grow sad, swap gossip, look again nervously to left and right …

Is killing a pig better than killing a commie? Basically, "we" are the ones who couldn't kill for peace. Now we climb on the ledge bordering the brilliant blossoming tulips to see what's going on across the southbound traffic strip. The roads keep rolling. Something is happening—deep crowd-throat noises!

They're burning a flag. For an instant, I see faces that I know—Canadian student-activists. Why do they want to burn that flag? I want to, but I lost my right to such symbolic fire when I crossed the border north. American flags should be burned in America, by Americans.

I wanted a vigil at the Consulate, with armbands of black, not red, inside, during work hours, mourning Americans come to the piece of ground inside Toronto that is America, to heap our ashes of grief and shame. These student-warriors should be at Queen's Park or in Ottawa, telling their government to stop: stop the magnesium and nickel, the oil and water, message-passing, piously neutral aid that keeps the slaughter-machine going. Stop! Before it happens here.

It won't happen here. I teeter on the inside ledge of the flower bed, not quite wide enough to stand on securely, straining to see over heads balanced on tiptoe on the further ledge. Something is happening. The traffic's stopped. Happening here? What? I can't see …

I have to see—and then it hits me, as I look back and forth along the tulip bed: we are all straining to see, and yet (Oh Canada! Oh Toronto-the-Good!) all teetering on the ledges, the spaced tulips perfectly intact and undisturbed between our two ledge-fulls … It can't happen here …

The horses!

Can't happen here? It did. But it didn't. Ninety-three arrests, no injuries reported. Two serious aftermaths:

1) *The tulips*. No editorial rehash failed to mention the battered tulips. But none of them explained what happened: maybe no one noticed, because the reporters and photographers were all concentrating on the action with the horses—just like us. The tulips were still okay until the horses rode up on the sidewalk in front of the Consulate to push people off into the street. That's when we forgot to tiptoe and pushed forward: right afterwards, the horses pushed the people who had been on the sidewalk off the street onto the median—that's when they jumped up on the ledges without thinking about the tulips. The horses were marvellously well trained: I watched a hoof start to come down on someone's foot and lift it again before it could do any injury. The tulips on University Avenue died because hundreds of miles away, police and militia were killing children—and the well-mannered police of Toronto

used their well-trained horses to keep the street clear for traffic while protecting the Consulate of the child-killers.

2) *The mayor.* The newspapers of Monday, May 11, described it as "Anti-War Riot … The Fury of Dissent … Clash with Police … Three Hours of Violence … Downtown Toronto Chase … " Most of this was reaction to, or justifiable by, the run through downtown streets after the demo was broken up, where several hundreds each of athletic exhilarated kids and motorcycle cops between them succeeded in smashing a bunch of windows and heads, and overturning a lot of ashcans and ideas. Eleven days after the event, Mayor William Dennison told a dinner meeting of the Engineering Institute of Canada, "I have been trying to educate American hippies and others in the etiquette of big-city life here." What he actually taught us was something entirely new to Americans who had grown up knowing that "You can't fight City Hall" was not only tried-and-true, but also included every vested authority right up through the White House.

We found out, in Canada, that you could do it legally and quite non-violently.

❧

By Tuesday, May 12, we began to think the worst was over. The first court hearings had been held; bail money had been raised; fifteen lawyers had formed a volunteer defence team; apparently there had been no serious injuries. Ron Haggart wrote the first of several columns in the *Toronto Telegram* that began to set the public record of reportage straight. Police Chief Harold Adamson issued a statement withdrawing his own earlier imputations—promptly picked up by Mayor Dennison—of "instigation" by U.S. organizers. Only thirteen of the ninety-three arrested turned out to be U.S. citizens, and almost all of those were landed immigrants. The "mystery buses" parked near City Hall turned out to be regular Saturday sightseeing tours from Buffalo. (One load of Eastern Star ladies was doing City Hall through the excitement.) "U.S. citizens in Toronto," said the police chief, "do not appear to be the leaders who caused the problem Saturday."

All week the papers were full of retractions and modifications of the absurd riot-expanding first coverage. The only thing we were still worried about, in Toronto, aside from a couple of possible deportations, was the unhappy potential of the new confrontation-seeking May Fourth Movement group to create difficulties for new immigrants through a false identification with the anti-war movement.

So right. And so wrong. Early next week, back to business, I went to see the rental manager about the Huron Street Hall (now likely to be more needed than ever). No more reservations: flat-out negative. They couldn't possibly rent to a group connected with "violent demonstrations." He understood RW&B had not promoted the "riot," but after all he had the newspapers and the mayor to consider—something about "corporate image."

Canon Wilkinson said he would phone Canada Trust. It might have helped, but the next day the *Star* had a banner headline in red splashed across page 1: "Dennison Warns U.S. Deserters against Violent Protests."

The Globe and Mail was more restrained: "Keep Your Pet Hates away from Canada, Mayor Tells U.S. Exiles" was the page 5 head. The *Telly* dredged up a weekend item: "Student-Imported Riots Criticized by Stanfield," which continued, "Young Americans should not import violent methods of dissent to Canada or try to form a sort of government here, Conservative leader Robert Stanfield said."

It was no longer a question of such comparative luxuries as a reception centre. People who had offered housing and help to newcomers in the past were getting uneasy. Simple survival was at issue now: slated for goats, we could no longer try to play at sheep.

We called a press conference for the next day. The St. Lawrence Centre gave us the time normally slotted for its Town Hall meetings. We asked the mayor—he was busy. The media newspeople came; and afterwards the mayor phoned and asked us to a meeting at his office.

We went to call on Mr. Dennison and spent an hour of mutual non-communication. The reporters waited outside eagerly. Next day the mayor issued a statement backing down—sort of—and made another speech. The *Star* had an item, "Mayor Steps down on Draft Dodgers," and the following morning's *Globe* said: "Welfare Brings Hippies from U.S., Mayor Says." That was the one where he explained he was trying to educate the American hippies. But it didn't matter. The letters to the editor had been piling up. The press had made a complete switch. We had been able to present a strong case forcefully, with evidence and reason on our side—and the press and public had listened.

Canada Trust decided to rent us the hall.

When Ontario's premier Bill Davis stopped the Spadina Expressway from being built through the heart of the city, after a vigorous urban grassroots protest movement against the highway, the only surprise was who did it, and the style he did it with: I knew by then that Toronto was the place where short-sighted self-interest and bureaucratic death wish can be stopped.

When ten thousand students converged on the U.S. Consulate in November 1971 to protest nuclear testing at Amchitka in the Aleutian Islands, there were no arrests, there was no undue police action, and University Avenue was closed to traffic.

Gentle reader, if none of this seems at all extraordinary to you—you must have grown up in Toronto. Can a person have pride in her home and not know it?

I keep hearing about the "Canadian identity." Most of what I hear sounds like some kind of treasure hunt: if we invest everything we've got in the search, maybe we can inherit someone else's lost or abandoned gold. It's a con-game, friend, and a particularly dangerous one. "Ethnicity" is one of the identifiable Canadian traits, a kind of hanging-loose that most hung-up cultures envy.

I remember a little item in the paper: a school trustee in a Toronto suburb—I wish I remembered who and where, to honour him—indignantly rejected a proposal for a daily salute to the flag in the public schools, pointing out that the two countries he knew of where that type of patriotism was common—Nazi Germany and the United States—were not examples to be followed.

"Identity" is not a uniform, or even necessary-uniformity. It's what you are. From outside, it's what you show: the characteristics that identify. Does Trudeau have an identity? Diefenbaker? Montreal? Eskimos? Calgary? Banff? Victoria? The Prairies? The RCMP? CBC?

If I were in the middle of, let's say, the Indian Ocean, with no program title or announcer's name or station-break to guide me, I believe I could tell a CBC radio broadcast from any British, U.S., Australian, or probably other Canadian offering, no matter which accent the CBC program happened to have. CBC-Radio has a distinctive and unmistakable personality: it hangs loose. If I say non-commercial or non-professional, probably no one will understand that I mean to praise: so I'm back to people. CBC voices may sound British- or French-accented or U.S. or Maritime or Albertan or Upper Canada College: but they sound like people, instead of announcers or experts or entertainers, or other kinds of media-machines.

I have this notion that anyone in Canada—in Yellowknife in the far North or Cabbagetown in Toronto—if they have something they want to say badly enough, can get to say it on the CBC. CBC-Radio is open: in style, structure, and subject. Maybe CBC-Radio is the "Canadian identity" …

One reason I want to be a Canadian citizen is that it seems the closest I can come, in a foolish world, to being a world citizen. Perhaps the reason I put up with Toronto's foul climate, smelly air, unshovelled snow, grey flatness, is that it comes as close as I can get to a World City, and that, for me, perhaps more than any other part of Canada, it represents the national open and hang-loose and people images.

EIGHTEEN | LIVING AND WORKING IN THE TORONTO CULTURAL SCENE

I CAME TO CANADA with the draft dodgers because I could no longer be a U.S. citizen. As for hopes and dreams, I had none. When I arrived, I had no intention of staying forever, Toronto was to be the "in-between" place where I would figure out what I really wanted to do with my new, un-American life.

Due to the political situation in the United States, several public figures had recently left and outwardly renounced their citizenship. The most outstanding example was a guy named Garry Davis, who declared himself the first Citizen of the World and invited other people to join him. Basically, that's what I wanted to do.

Garry Davis was profoundly influenced by his experience as a U.S. bomber pilot over Europe in World War II. His father was Myer Davis, the society band leader, so before the war Garry grew up expecting to be a song and dance man, and he did indeed become a Broadway actor. After the war he heard about an American who went back to Europe to help rebuild after the destruction, and he decided to go to France to help out.

In France in 1948, at age twenty-six and within a few months of his arrival, he renounced his U.S. citizenship. He was objecting to a world that, he said, in the absence of an international government, was "a naked anarchy." In a "statement of renunciation," he declared, "I no longer find it compatible with my inner convictions to contribute to this anarchy, and thus be a party to the inevitable annihilation of our civilization, by remaining solely loyal to one of these sovereign nation-states."

At the time the United Nations was about to hold a session in Paris and the president of France declared the land around the meeting place, the Palais de Chaillot, to be, at least temporarily, "international territory." When Garry hit Paris after coming north from the small town where he had carried out his act of renunciation, he was left with no papers of any kind—a citizen of nowhere.

So Garry went and sat on the steps of the Palais and declared himself a citizen of the world. He demanded that the United Nations convene a constitutional convention and establish a world government so that he could have a citizenship. This stand garnered enormous public response, and worldwide media attention focused on Garry. Strangers set up a little pup tent for him and restaurants sent food. Prominent personalities, including Albert Einstein, Albert Camus, Albert Schweitzer, and Richard Wright, gave him their support. Eventually the French government got nervous and grabbed Garry off the steps of the Palais and took him back "to France" and threw him in jail. A big crowd followed them to the jail and demanded his release. Eventually he was. For the rest of his time in France, Garry went around wearing his worn-out old U.S. air force uniform. If he had to have it cleaned, he didn't go out. That was his identity. He was trained for the stage, so he carried this whole thing off very well.

In the United States we heard about Garry Davis, but it was through mocking newspapers articles. In Europe, and every other part of the world that had suffered serious damage in the war, the story was of greater significance. Garry started getting thousands of pieces of mail and postcards from Europe, Asia, and Africa. People wanted to join what he was doing, and his response was always: "I am not a leader. I have no organization for you to join. If you like what I'm doing, figure out what you should be doing."

In 1949, though, Garry founded the International Registry of World Citizens in Paris. Over 750,000 individuals in 150 countries signed up for world citizenship. After a year and a couple of months in France, he returned to the United States—still without a passport and official status. It seemed to me he somewhat compromised his principles by allowing himself to get into the United States in an underhanded way—the authorities temporarily cleared the airport's customs hall and walked him through.

I was very excited about this guy, and when I eventually met up with him at a science fiction convention he was somewhere in between Garry Davis the Icon and Garry Davis the Song and Dance Man. I saw him flip several times between the two personalities, as if he were possessed. When he became the icon he would grow about two inches in size, and his entire personality was different. But during the period when I associated most closely with him he was definitely back in the song and dance man phase. He appeared on Broadway in "Bless You All" (1951) and "Stalag 17" (1953–54). He wanted to write a book about his experiences in Europe, to be based on books of clippings—articles published about him—and statements he had written. He asked me to work with him on it, and I was curious about the job.

Judith and the dragon, during the CBC Radio and TVP years, Toronto, circa 1982.
Courtesy of the Merril estate

But I was interested in writing a book about the idea of world citizen, and Garry wanted it to be a book about an adventurer, something that he thought would make good reading and sell. Our collaboration lasted only a few weeks.

In the meantime we were in New York one afternoon, along with the writer Richard McKenna, who had done some science fiction before he wrote *The Sand Pebbles*, for which he is best known. Garry was telling us about some of his experiences, and when we made a trip downtown to the 42nd Street area he said, "I can show you photographs of what happened."

He led us to the offices of World Wide Photos, which was part of some larger media conglomerate. When we inquired about the accessibility of the material he wanted he was told he would have to make an appointment to view them. Something about the pieces of paper and bureaucratic procedures triggered Garry. McKenna and I watched him grow two inches, turn around, and walk back out the office door. He waved to us, turned a corner, and walked down to the end of the corridor, where he found another door and went through it. We followed and found ourselves in the file room. Two women working there came over, looked at him for a moment, and said, "Yes? What can we do for you?"

They dug out all the pictures of him that they had on file. We looked at them and Garry pondered the matter of getting copies made. We left. Garry retreated his two inches. It was a startling experience. How did he know where to go? How did these women know that they should give him whatever he wanted? Had I been alone with Gary, I would have misdoubted what I saw and heard, but McKenna saw and heard the same things I did.

Anyhow, it was a rich and agonizing experience trying to work with him. After that period he decided to establish an increasingly bureaucratic World Government, and the organization he founded in 1954, the World Service Authority, still exists. His book was eventually published, in 1961: *The World Is My Country* (for some reason the title of the U.K. edition is different: *My Country Is the World: The Adventures of a World Citizen*). Garry also printed passports and money. None of it was illegal, it said exactly what it was, and everything was signed by Garry as First Secretary of The World Government of World Citizens.

The last time I saw him, he had become a guy who was living his own legend entirely—selling passports and handing out World Money—but he could no longer grow two inches.

In 1968 I also thought that what I wanted was to become a World Citizen. In order to do that, I had to locate myself somewhere I didn't mind staying, because once I renounced my U.S. citizenship I would no longer have a passport or any other legal documents. I wouldn't be allowed to travel anymore. While I was still in the United States I thought there was no city in North America that was liveable, and that I would have to tramp back to Europe to find myself a city I could actually live in.

My daughters were grown up enough to be on their own, and I wasn't married … so many possibilities! I love cities, and I gradually realized that Toronto was a city I could actually live in. The realization happened slowly, over the first year I was here. At first, I was totally involved with Rochdale, and wasn't thinking about the future at all.

After a little while I discovered that I was irritated at not being able to vote. This was exciting, because for several years in the States I had been absolutely unwilling to vote. At one point I thought to myself, "I guess that means I have to get Canadian citizenship and a passport."

It was about as close as I could get to being a Citizen of the World without having to make that the focus of my entire life. Meanwhile, I could do a lot in Toronto that would make my time worthwhile.

Artistically, in 1968–69, I was not doing anything in particular. I had been editing anthologies for about twelve years, and was really tired of doing them. I thought I wanted to open up more time for writing fiction, but when I did open it up, I wasn't writing. It took me a surprising number of years to realize that I didn't really want to write fiction anymore.

I got involved quite early on writing documentaries for CBC-Radio, and discovered that I absolutely loved writing for radio. For the first time in my life I could incorporate all the "what if?" questions I wanted into my work. All my speculations could be made into direct statements. I know that I could do this partly because I was working in Canada rather than the United States, but mostly I think it was that during the conservatism of the 1940s and 1950s, direct dissonance was simply not possible. For example, in the earlier years, when science fiction writers were dealing with issues like telepathy and special abilities, writing about them directly (as I did at one time in a magazine editorial) was to exclaim to the world, "I am a crackpot." Speculating about them in fiction, however, excited a huge amount of interest. This was true about any idea that was not conservative and conventional at that time.

During the 1960s there was a change in our cultural environment. It was liberating to suddenly discover that I did not have to dress up my ideas in costumes and put them on stage sets behind the guise of fictional stories. People would listen if I just presented my ideas by saying, "This is what could happen. This is how things might be."

Like everything else that ever happened to me (my first pulp story, my first science fiction story, my first anthology, the anthology series …) the CBC opportunity arose because someone came to me and asked, "Will you do this?" And then they wouldn't let my inexperience answer for me. In this case, sometime around 1971, a writer named Robert Zend, a very unusual man, called me to ask if I would do a segment on an *Ideas* radio program he was producing. The show was about contemporary myths, which I had already written about. I found the subject intriguing. He wanted a twenty-minute segment from me in which I would connect familiar, conventional myths with modern experiences. (For instance, twisting the old myth about twenty-league boots to make it a metaphor for air travel.)

Through that initial Zend experience, I met some of the people involved with *Ideas*, and after that first show, I kept being invited to do more. The first shows I actually did on my own were for *Kaleidoscope*, a children's program, which had some overlap in personnel. After a while I started getting assignments that were mostly speculative in nature. It was through doing those documentaries for *Ideas* that it finally dawned on me that I really didn't want to write fiction any more.

The *Ideas* department, at that particular time, was an exciting place to hang out. They didn't really have an executive producer—poet Phyllis Webb filled that role from 1967 to 1969, but she had since returned to the West Coast. The whole department worked very much as a co-operative. The *Ideas* office was like a twenty-four-hour-a-day seminar. People would drop in and pitch program topics, or talk about the show they were working on, and everybody contributed to everybody else's concepts. It was like a constant jam session. I was completely and utterly involved in it for a period of about three years.

I did one five-hour series, which we eventually cut down to four, called "How to Face Doomsday without Really Dying." It was about ecology, overpopulation, pollution, and the whole host of problems that people were talking about at the time. It happened that at the time I was doing the series, Toronto was planning to have a World Science Fiction Convention (WorldCon). There were going to be a lot of science fiction people in town, so I had been asked to plan a program for the convention.

A whole afternoon was set aside for a major seminar including Isaac Asimov, John Brunner, Fred Pohl, Katherine MacLean, and somebody else (maybe me). Each writer took one aspect of the ecology issue, made predictions and discussed the subject, and then there was a panel discussion afterwards. The seminar ended up being about three hours long. We taped the entire thing, and it formed the starting point for the Doomsday series. Later we taped interviews with some of the authors in groups of two or three. Then other authors, including Samuel Delany, listened to the tapes and commented on them.

One of the most curiously interesting things I learned during that process was something Richard Rohmer said to me. At the time he was a right-wing writer who had just published his first science fiction novel, *Ultimatum* (1973). I asked him if he thought we were moving towards a world government. He responded, "Yes. It has already started. The multinational corporations are already organizing a world government that has nothing to do with national governments at all."

Each show in the Doomsday series hit on a different topic. For example, the last one was called: "Is There Intelligent Life on Earth?" I used different kinds of music in each one — a lot of Beatles stuff, mainly from "Sergeant Pepper" and a little bit from "Yellow Submarine."

☙

A little later, the idea of doing follow-up commentaries for *Dr. Who* episodes came from a TVOntario producer who was stuck with putting out the show. She taught some part-time courses at a community college and had been around TVO for quite a while. *Dr. Who* was probably TVO's lowest-budget item, but because it got the rights from the BBC the channel needed to add an extra element to it so that they could fill out a half-hour time slot. BBC content was usually a little shorter than TVO's because, although BBC didn't have commercials either, the British didn't operate on the precise time constraints of North American television. There was anywhere from three to eight minutes left over to fill.

At the time, TVO was promoting itself as the educational television channel. Before me, they had another guy, who was a futurist, doing little extros during which he talked about whatever the show had been about. This allowed them to say, "Another learning experience from TVO" at the end of each episode. However, my predecessor suddenly decided to move back to Hawaii, where he had come from. The producer phoned to ask me if I would take over at the beginning of the summer, just when I was packing to go off to teach at Wesleyan University in Connecticut for the season.

I responded, "You mean you want an audition?"

She answered, "No. I've already seen you on talk shows, and I know you're good. I know all about your work. You can do it. You know everything that you need to know. I want you to do these extros."

I said, "Well, I've never worked for television before."

"That's all right. Nothing to it."

I said, "But I'm going to be away all summer."

"That's okay," she said. "I'm going to be away in August, too. We'll start production right after Labour Day. In the meantime, I'll send the twenty-six shows to your office so that when you get back in the middle of August, you can take a look at them. When I get back, we'll figure out what we're going to do. Don't worry, the season doesn't start until the third week of September."

Fred visiting Toronto in 1978. From left: Ann, Tobias, Fred, and Judy. *Walter Weary*

She offered me a sum of money that sounded like a lot at the time. It was, in fact, peanuts for television. But compared to the freelance writer's life and CBC-Radio payments, it seemed like a pretty good deal.

I watched all the shows, and learned how to write and produce the mini-documentaries under pressure for a month and a half at the beginning of the season. We had a mobile unit and together we would decide where to film, depending on the nature of the show—on a street, in a warehouse, etc. It was a lot of fun.

We had a ball that first year, and for most of the second year. Then during the second year my producer left and I got a different producer, and the third year yet another. This third producer, instead of being one of the old trusting types (all of whom they were easing out), was a young untrusting one whom they were easing in. He was very ambitious, and decided we needed a studio setup. He made us use ChromaKey, wanted me to dress up in costumes, and edited all our scripts to the exact second.

We did a few good shows that year, but it was a lot more work. I decided I would need to get a hell of a lot more money to keep doing it the way he wanted. They responded, "You're absolutely right. You should be getting twice as much, but we just had another budget cut. I think we'll do without the extros altogether."

That was that for my career as a *Dr. Who* specialist.

A year or so after the Spaced Out Library began at Rochdale College, maybe even less than that, the library was closed. Rochdale had run out of education money. There never was much, but the financial situation eventually became desperate. By that time I had moved out (I was still active in Rochdale but I was no longer living there), and I wound up having to reclaim and find a place for those of my things that were still there. I was sharing a house with five or six other people. When I brought all my books home, my tiny room was completely filled with them. They were climbing the walls up to the ceiling all around me. I fell asleep at night waiting for the books to topple onto me. I figured I should sell them, but it seemed wrong to sell them off one by one, so I tried to find a place that would buy them as a collection. The offers I got were so ridiculously small compared to my estimation of the collection's value that I didn't even want to consider them.

Then Harry Campbell of the Toronto Public Library came along. He had heard I wanted to dispose of my collection, and suggested I give them to the library system so that they could start a special science fiction collection. It seemed the perfect solution. In 1970 the Spaced Out Library became an official part of the Toronto Public Library with my donation of some five thousand books and periodicals. In return Harry wrote into the deed of gift that I was to have office space in the collection for my entire life. Over the years this has surely added up to more value than I could ever possibly have gotten from selling them. And in the city's hands the Spaced Out Library grew to become, in John Robert Colombo's words, "the world's largest public collection of such literature." Its mandate is to collect everything published in its subject areas. By 1987 the holdings totalled 35,146, and growing. Later, in 1992, the library changed the name of the collection, against my wishes, to the Merril Collection of Science Fiction, Speculation and Fantasy.

This addition to the public library system suited me fine. The decision to donate my books was, I thought, a wise and practical move, in the spirit of its tiny Rochdale incarnation. Some years later, I found myself forced to fight against the stripping-down and cutting back politics of the times and stand up for free library privileges. An article I wrote on the issue was published in 1994 in *Quill & Quire*, the Canadian book industry magazine.

HERE'S THE BEEF: WHERE'S THE BOOK?

An alarming erosion of Free Public Library services is taking place across Canada. This is of course fuelled by municipal budget-cutting; but it is shaped by the kind of thinking that is replacing the job of "Chief Librarian" with a "C.E.O.," while schools of Library science are renamed "Information Sciences." Meantime, Library Boards are installing user fees, but finding money in their curtailed budgets to hire Management Consultants to teach them Marketing Strategies for dealing with "customers" who used to be "borrowers" or "patrons."

The concept of the free library in North America began about a hundred and twenty years ago with private charitable ventures. Today most free libraries are in public systems controlled by office-holders and bureaucrats; and all too many vote-hungry politicians have fallen prey to a mindless "downsizing" frenzy that cannot distinguish between a budget deficit and imminent cultural/social bankruptcy.

The Big Business response to economic recession is to increase profits by automation—replacing employees with electronics. "Customer service," for instance, becomes pre-taped answers to a limited number of questions accessible only from push-button telephones. This may make some kind of short-sighted sense for companies interested in increasing immediate profits at any cost.

Photo of Judith cut out and pasted against an old futuristic cityscape, as part of an article entitled "Future Woman," circa 1982. *Origin unknown, courtesy of the Merril estate*

But libraries?

Take Toronto. (Not because it's unique; I live here, it's the system I know best.) In 1991, the full-time staff in the Toronto Public Library's (TPL) branches numbered about 400. It has now been cut (by attrition, they will assure you, not layoffs) to 326. Part-time staff reductions are as great or greater. I believe they hope to lose another 20 full-timers by the end of 1995 through early retirements and at least that much again by "voluntary separations" (departures with not-so-golden handshakes).

The TPL Board is now studying a "Strategic Agenda" for the next ten years; its main goal is set forth as the provision of "cost-effective, convenient access to accurate, in-depth information and library materials—through implementation of the electronic library and continuous innovation in delivery service."

Did you hear the word BOOKS anywhere there?

TPL apparently dislikes old books, and they feel their two internationally acclaimed specialty collections—the Osborne (rare children's books) and the Merril (science fiction and fantasy)—are "growing too fast." They've been talking about restricting purchases to new books and limiting donations. They want all acquisitions to be made through one central department.

The Writers' Union of Canada is concerned. The health of a literary community is inextricably linked to the health of public library systems. It was in local public libraries that most of us, readers, writers and publishers and editors as well, first experienced the full spell of the magic of books. And we think free public libraries should be as much about literature as about information.

Most writers use computers and we think public access to the info-net is a good thing. I happen to be a science fiction writer, and I think the info-net is *great! But I also know that the highly sophisticated kind of artificial intelligence needed to replace a good librarian is (if ever possible) many years in the future. Replacing librarians with keyboards today or ten years from now is not going to lead to healthy libraries, increased literacy, or a good prognosis for Canadian culture. It is going to lead to shorter hours, less programming, fewer books— and less publishing, because without library sales, very few companies will be able to print anything but best-sellers.*

"Freedom to Read" means more than just no-censorship. Free public libraries are not the place to trim municipal deficits.

In the interests of cultural-environment protection, the Writers' Union has established a national Libraries Committee, charged with surveying the extent of the damage so far (across the country, not just in Toronto), and determining the best means of preventing further erosion.

The Writers' Union hopes other concerned organizations will join us in this effort …

One of the significant things about Rochdale, and indeed that whole period of time in history, was the "do-your-own-thing" aspect of the institution and political scene. People were following their own stars, as it were. This had a great effect on me and my notion of what a utopian social reality might be like.

The people I found most interesting were, by and large, the ones who were doing things—whether it was getting into heavier drugs, more postmodern art, or intense Canadian nationalism—that I would never consider getting involved with. It was great to be there with them, rubbing up against all the energy. For example, it was fashionable at the time for people like Margaret Atwood (I use her symbolically, I'm really talking about a whole bunch of writers) to put forth the idea that Canadian nationalism was not anti-Americanism. Throughout the entire decades of the 1970s it was a popular thing to be a nationalist and to explore the Canadian identity through one's art.

I did not want to be a Canadian nationalist, I did not even want to see nationalism increase in Canada. I feel that, to the extent that I am a Canadian nationalist, I am so because of my anti-American tendencies. Interestingly, that sentiment is the same one that keeps me from being a whole-hearted Canadian nationalist. When I left the United States, nationalism had reached the status of religion. I would even say that nationalism had become the new American religion.

My anti-nationalist sentiment extended to "Canadian" science fiction. I have never specifically been interested in what might be called Canadian science fiction, except maybe in connection with the Spaced Out Library, the Writers' Union of Canada, and my extreme pleasure at being a "free" citizen when I first emigrated here. But much later, in 1985, Ellen Godfrey at Press Porcépic asked me if I would do an anthology of Canadian science fiction. Although I had quit doing anthologies some years earlier, at that particular point in time I felt compelled to pull one together.

I also thought it would be an opportune moment to start an incarnation of the Hydra North club because there were just enough exciting people around, and just enough happening. I suppose there was a bit of a nationalist motivation, or at least something similar to it in the sense that I was eager to see more stuff being done here. I felt that the anthology *Tesseracts* would encourage that. I expected that we were going to have to look backwards to move forward and involve established writers like Margaret Laurence and Marian Engel to help sell it. It turned out, much to my surprise, that we didn't need them as far as content went, and we didn't even need them to help sell the collection.

The Spaced Out Library's first home on St. George Street, Toronto. From left: Doris Mehegan, Judith, and David Aylward, Toronto, circa 1971. *Courtesy of the Merril estate*

To be completely honest, there is little "Canadian science fiction." There are a lot of Canadian science fiction writers, and a lot of them are good, but almost all of them are trying to be as American as possible, because that's where the money is.

Science fiction has become a money field. There are individual authors who are still writing in the genre because they like exciting ideas, and there are individuals who write it from one political view or another. But most of what is labelled science fiction, which includes fantasy and horror, doesn't interest me at all. Some of it I find appalling. A large number of people who might have been good writers are corrupted by the relatively easy money, which is what happens whenever large sums of money are available.

This commercialization of the genre is not something I wish to rail against. I would never discourage writers from cashing in on the benefits of their writing, unless I think he or she is a really fine writer whose work is about to be undermined. Even then my advice would be: "Be aware that the financial temptation is strong, and make your mind up about whether or not you want to succumb to it."

NINETEEN | **JRPAN FUTURE PROBABLE**

DURING MY EARLY YEARS in Toronto, one of the most memorable things that happened to me was the time I spent in Japan. I went there for the first time on an invitation to participate in the International Science Fiction Symposium, which was to be held as part of the 1970 World Expo. SF people were attending from the States, Canada, England, and the Soviet Union. The initial attraction was that I could imagine no other likelihood of meeting Soviet writers.

Originally they expected the symposium to be part of the World Fair, and to get some funding from it. However, that particular year's Expo wasn't making any money, so the symposium organizers wound up doing everything themselves. They held the first two days in Tokyo, the next day in Nagoya, and the last day at a resort near Kyoto. There were sessions in the morning and afternoon, and then in the early evening, one Japanese, one Russian, and one English-speaking person would each make a prepared speech.

There were interpreters, but they were not high-class interpreters. The best ones were all tied up at Expo, and the symposium's interpreters were the leftovers. They had no problem when a Japanese person made a formal speech—they could translate it into English and Russian without much difficulty. They had hardly any problems when either Russian or English speakers made formal speeches—they could translate fluidly into the other two languages. However, as soon as the speeches were over and general discussion began, particularly when the Japanese people spoke, a tremendous argument would go on at the interpreters' table. Finding adequate translations was a difficult process. Sometimes the speaker would get involved, and chastise them for being wrong.

This was fascinating. The Japanese translators made up a large portion of the people who were attending the symposium, so I started to strike up conversations about the process. I became interested in how the language a person speaks influences how they think. We all started to hang out regularly—they all spoke some English—in local bars and restaurants.

Bit by bit, I began to get clues as to what was going on. The Japanese had no written language until about fifteen hundred years ago. They borrowed, or adopted, the Chinese characters, made some changes to them, and began using them for Japanese. Therefore, each character had an underlying Chinese meaning, and a Chinese sound. Anybody who reads Cantonese, Mandarin, or Japanese can read all of those languages. They can't pronounce the characters, except in their own language, but all of the written information is there.

The Japanese sound that went with a character meant something entirely different. The result was that every character acquired a double meaning. The more formal written language had an enormous amount of portmanteau words, puns, and double meanings that were layered on top of each other. The more literary or literate a person is, the more levels of meaning they will incorporate into their written language.

☞

As a result of my increasing fascination with the language, I wound up going back to Japan two years later, in 1972, to do some team translation.

We were working out a method of translating from Japanese to English that would keep the cultural subtexts. It was complicated process. I did not know any Japanese, but learned to read simple characters. I'm good at learning syntax, and within a short time I understood how the Japanese language was put together. I'm not nearly as good at learning vocabulary, but I could generally figure out a great deal by looking at the larger context of a story.

Since I knew comparatively little of their language, the translators had to explain, one by one, the meaning of things such as the more complex Chinese characters. One translator explained these characters to me by comparing them to a Feroshki, a piece of cloth that was folded on the diagonal, turned into a sack bag, and used to carry things. Each stroke in the characters has its own meaning; you unwrapped the characters stroke by stroke and thus arrived at its total meaning. They were painstakingly unwrapping these Feroshki for me, and explaining all the overtones. This linguistic structure seemed much more complex than the linearity of an alphabetic language.

The way you write the strokes has meaning too, like a signature. Calligraphy is arguably the most significant way in which Japanese people express their individuality. Each person's way of making characters is absolutely unique, and can be very much admired by other people. However, this uniqueness doesn't change the actual meaning of the word.

I had a Kanji (Chinese character) dictionary, which demonstrated that characters were composed of radicals, like roots. Each stroke in a character has a meaning that may or may not be its central meaning. The central one is surrounded by others of lesser importance. In any given character, a stroke may just be a little corner of the character, and the amount of weight on it varies with the shape of the character.

Our team translated four Japanese science fiction stories into English. Our process represented an attempt to avoid the way translation was almost always done before: a native Japanese speaker who knew English would write a draft, and then a native English speaker would rewrite it. After those two completely distinct steps, the original Japanese story would have been reformulated into an unrecognizably westernized story. The translators read English sensitively, but they could not write it as well. When they did it with me, for instance, they would provide a direct translation for something and it would almost always contain at least one wrong word that would throw off my understanding of the text. In order to avoid these problems, our team developed a complicated process. We were trying to avoid the misuse of English. Together we created a draft English version of a section. Then I would rewrite it so that it expressed what I thought the original text was saying, and after that I would show the result to the translators. They would read my draft and tell me where the meaning was not exactly right. When they wanted something changed, we would have an entire discussion about why it wasn't right, but they wouldn't try to tell me how to rewrite it. Each draft got better and better, and in this way, we got some really good translations.

Unfortunately, our elaborate technique was not commercially practical because of the length of time it took to do each story. It was a start, though. What ended up happening after I left was that a number of English-speaking people who knew Japanese started working with the original team. They used a modified system of translation, which meant that the process went faster, but they were still getting good translations. However, these faster translation were still done directly, not through the multi-stage process we developed.

During that second visit to Japan, I also did a lot of interviews with New Left students, linguists, and assorted interesting people. I had set up a contract with *Ideas* to do a program before heading off. The CBC didn't specify how long it should be so I ended up putting together a ten-hour series that I called "Japan Future Probable." The title of my *Ideas* show came from the fact that in the Japanese language there is no future indicative tense.

What English translators of Japanese call the Japanese future tense is really a subjunctive. You cannot directly say that something will happen. You can say it should happen, you will make it happen, or it will probably happen—depending on the context in which you use the verb. The only way to be definite about the occurrence of an event is to use the past tense alongside the word tomorrow. Basically, in Japanese, in order to express an event that will happen in the future, you must use the present or even past tense (that is, this happens tomorrow or even this happened tomorrow). In this way people know that the event will definitely occur.

Japanese locates time with adverbs, and the verb tenses simply indicate the relative probability of an event's occurrence. The whole idea that there is no future certainty in the culture fascinated me. It seemed to me that everything about the actual, pragmatic culture, and the physical realities of day-to-day life, reflected this cultural facet, including the crowdedness and the incredibly uncertain climate in which tornadoes, typhoons, and earthquakes are expected. I'm talking about real Japanese people's culture, not the Americanized stuff you hear about like temples, shrines, and Zen. These social factors are inseparable from the language itself.

Another example of how the culture influences the language appears in the many different ways of saying thank you. You can say "*aregato,*" which simply means "thank you." But rarely do people just say that. They say "*domo aregato,*" which means "thanks a lot." People also sometimes just say "*domo,*" even though the literal translation is "a lot." To indicate informality, you might say "*domo, domo.*" And if you are being quite formal and want to express serious thanks, as in "I thank you," in Japanese you would say "*aregato mash*"—where you add an honorific verb of moderate intensity. If you want to go all out and say "thank you so much," you would say "*aregato gotsei mashta,*" because "*mashta*" is past tense, and "*gotsei*" is the honorific root. Therefore, the very strongest possible thank you is "*domo aregato gotsei mashta.*"

Also, the slower you say something, the more emphasis you're giving the statement. When people speak casually among friends, they tend to speak

Japanese very fast. This is called "rude conversation." That is not meant to be a criticism, as it would have been in England; it is a way of describing how you talk to friends.

When I was learning the syntax, my knowledge confirmed what I had already suspected. Japanese was a matrix, as opposed to linear, language. I got so excited about this discovery because I had been doing a lot of thinking about the transition our Western society was undergoing in the change from what I had identified as a kind of linearity to a matrix-layered thinking process.

TWENTY | THE WHOLE WORLD IS WATCHING: CONSIDERING THE NOTIONS OF PRIVACY AND PUBLICY*

There comes a time in the affairs of human beings when it becomes necessary to reconsider conceptual basics and redefine terms of reference.

We are living in such a time. Big Brother HAL sees all, knows all, studies lip movements, thought movements, REMS, student movements, bowel movements everywhere: spins them through computer relays to map presidential campaigns, market analyses, and Buckminster Fuller's "World Game."

A "classical age," as Samuel Delany describes it: a time of myth-making. Or like the commercials would say, a New Dimension of Living.

Some of the new words and concepts are already familiar: global, pluralistic, multimedia, mosaic, planetary, interdisciplinary, relativity, quantum-leap, ecology, synergy, matrix, multiplex, and lots more. That's not to say the words are meaningful to most of us yet. (Maybe a lot of them aren't meaningful at all, except to describe transitory quanta.) But we are, perhaps, approaching reformations by exercising new semantic structures.

I want to put forward another (hopefully) quantum-jumping word: publicy.

Publicy is a quality/quantity roughly opposite to privacy.

The whole world is watching!

You watch.

*An early draft of an unpublished essay written around 1975.

215

Beyond the Barriers of Space and Time, an anthology edited by Judith in 1954. It was released the same year in the U.K. under the title *Human?*.

You watched Chicago '68, Biafra, Vietnam. You watched Nixon in China and maybe (how old are you?) Oppenheimer in D.C. (1954). You watched Jackie Kennedy mourn, and *This Is Your Life* and Mamie Van Doren and *Laugh-In* and the Moon landings. You saw Lee Harvey Oswald and Bobby Kennedy die, and students riot, and Bengalis starve. You've watched breakfasts and birthdays and floods and heat waves and typhoons and tea parties.

Publicy also has to do with such contemporary phenomena as computer credit information, traffic jams, housing developments, the "welfare state," the "population explosion," communes, nudity, the drug culture, religious revivals, TV, holography, automated libraries, universal literacy, Public Information Officers, Public Relations Experts, advertising and market analysis, "corporate public image," promotion campaigns, international money crises, balance-of-trade figures, environment-and-pollution control, weather satellites, atomic testing, PCB and Strontium-90 percentages—and lots more. If you can extract the common essence of these phenomena, you know roughly what I'm talking about.

Who's watching you? (Have you ever watched yourself, watching yourself?)

How important do you have to get to start being watched?

In 1952 the U.S. government had a dossier on me because I was the author of a science fiction novel about atomic warfare, and I lived in a "sensitive" area where Joe McCarthy was doing a lot of investigating.

When Arthur H. Bremer was arrested for shooting George Wallace, it turned out the Canadian police had a photo of him because he'd been standing in the wrong part of a public gathering when Dick Nixon went calling on Pierre Trudeau in Ottawa.

Crime prevention? Security? Invasion of privacy? Well … It is routine humanism/liberalism nowadays to deplore, or actively oppose, the collection and computerization (other kinds of storage systems don't seem to upset liberal ethics as much) of biographical data and personal (financial, sexual, political, etc.) information for commercial or political purposes.

The motives for this opposition are many and varied and mostly honourable —but not always well-considered. Take, for instance, the objection that much of the "information" is misinformation, hastily secured by ill-trained or corrupt investigators. The same people who protest misinformation in the computer files usually object even more vigorously to any increase in surveillance efficiency.

If you don't happen to think that national security or credit card systems or even law-n-order are good enough reasons for being watched and weighed into the computer, what about heroin control, automobile licensing, gun registration? What do you think about the prevention of airplane hijackings, assassination attempts, political kidnappings? How about Medicare, weather prediction and modification, famine prevention, flood control and pollution warnings?

One or more of these you'd probably like to see handled intelligently and efficiently. And at the present level of population and realpolitik, the only way to handle any of them is through publicy-oriented policies of information-gathering, storage, and dissemination.

(Am I in favour of public snooping into private lives? What difference does that make? I've been living with it for a long time. So have you.)

In European and North American society, the privacy mystique provides a major indicator for the more subtle gradations of the social snobbery scale. If you came from a certain sort of "background," you never open a closed door without knocking; and you pause in discussing last night's bed-adventure with your best friend while the waitress is setting down the coffee cups. Chances are, even with the bed-adventure confidante, you don't discuss family finances.

On some other social levels, prices and money may be discussed in detail, and continuously, but bed is verbally completely taboo. The combinations may vary, not just on economic class lines, but also by sex, age, region, and sometimes occupation, among other possibilities. Within any definable social grouping they are (or have been) as rigid as they are distinctive.

Aside to women's liberation: 1) "Never ask a lady her age"; 2) It seems to be part of the unwritten law—in the United States, at least—that a certain margin or perjury is permitted a lady to "protect her chastity," that is, to maintain the privacy of her sex life. But please note I said "lady." I doubt the privilege applies to prostitutes, hippies, yippies, zippies, bra-burners, strip-artists, sun-and-nature nudists, or anyone else who has already publicly violated privacy.

Privacy/publicy is not a simplistic linear polarity. It is not truly susceptible to quantitative gradient measurements. It is not quite an orthodox dialectical thesis-antithesis formation. It is rather a spectrum of coloration running through all planes of behaviour, experience, and consciousness.

On any familiar plane (like politics, literature, sex) it may manifest itself as a duality or polarity or synthesis, but it is more fruitful to consider it in matrix or gestalt or ecological terms. With this kind of conception, it is easier to recognize that a distortion or modification of the spectrum on any one plane will be reflected on, or resonate to, all other planes—sometimes in almost unrecognizable forms, and on a number of levels of consciousness and experience we have not yet learned to identify clearly through definition or measurement.

I cannot provide a sharp, tight definition for the concept as a whole. The ideas expressed here have come together very slowly in my mind over the past two or three years. The fact is, much of the concept is still outside my own present frame of reference. I am just beginning to learn how to handle multiplex, pluralistic/relativistic perceptions and concepts.

J.G. Ballard talks about "three levels of characterization" in his work. "Subjective" and "objective" are familiar to everyone. He describes the third level as being, for one thing, a character "displayed on an enormous billboard as a figment in some vast CinemaScope epic" or again "the world of public events, Cape Kennedy and Vietnam mimetized on billboards." Billboards. Media. "Admass" in England. "Mass-comm" in Japan. "Public image."

What killed Marilyn Monroe? What is "astronaut's syndrome"? Why do movie stars and heads of state, baseball heroes and generals and chess masters, all seem to get wackier and wackier? Is it just that they can't hide behind a false front with cameras poking in the bathroom windows? Or do the cameras make them crazier? What's it like to know a million or a hundred million pairs of eyes are watching you? (Desiring, despairing, admiring, envying, hating, cursing, even loving you?) How do you learn to live with it?

We're all going to have to learn. A little bit more all the time.

.

In the years after I arrived in Canada I slowly discovered that I was not as I had been in the United States: a very large frog in a very tiny pond—a big name in science fiction, but totally unknown elsewhere. It was not unusual for mainstream Canadian writers to know some SF, and indeed to write some themselves, so a good many of the leading Canadian authors turned out to have read my work. Three extraordinarily good writers who became close friends were Margaret Laurence, Marian Engel, and Gwendolyn MacEwen.

Among them, the most extraordinary, I think, was MacEwen, but on a certain level it is hard to say who beats whom. In each case we shared so many ideas, so much intellectual property, and so much identity as women that the friendships established were easily, readily formed and had a quality as intense as the friendships expressed in my long correspondences with men during the earlier period of my life.

Judith, getting older, but still loving life fiercely, Toronto, circa 1993.
Courtesy of the Merril estate

Jan. 22, 1979

Dear Judy,

Funny I was thinking about the house and what I would do when I got back to it and I thought of the big round table and you were at it. Gosh, it will be good to see you again. You are remembered here with affection.

I guess you're through at Centennial [a community college in Toronto]. I just cleaned my desk and found an invite from them. How the hell can I find words to apologize for a five-month delay in answering? Fall was hell, Will in dreadful shape and me learning how to teach and do PR for *Glassy Sea*, the crits of which were so bad. But things are more fun now: a few social things are happening and Will is going off his drugs and getting much nicer. But there is something that is not me about Edmonton and I'll be glad to get home. It's about 100 per cent short of loose people, that's it. I keep pondering the purchase of a parrot.

Have been reading Maureen Duffy's erotic world of faery which ends up discussing SF. Fun if you like Freudians.
Keep the flame alight, baby
love, Marian

Jan. 29, 1979

Dear Marian—
Nope, Centennial is still on—the full year, except not doing it right now for two reasons—

I am just emerging from convalescent period following Horrible Illness in December. I thought I was food poisoned—turned out to be an abscess in the intestine, due (probably, they say) to a perforated appendix that walled itself. The three weeks in hosp, days on IV, lots of drama. Scary but interesting. Part has been slow convalescence slush/snow weather.

So—now I'm ready to start getting back into commitments, the Ontario Community College support staffs have all gone on strike. So far it has been impossible even to reach people on tangled switch boards to discuss ways and means of functioning without crossing picket lines!!!

So I have time to answer letters.

Do thou likewise. (Depending on what happens with the strike of course … I think Jack David would still like to have you come this spring.

Lessee—what's happening here? Or has been? I've been out of things pretty much. From the moment I got back from Connecticut at the end of August till the end of November, I was working nonstop on performer-educating for TVO's *Dr. Who* series, with time out only for twice-weekly treks to Scarborough and that piece for *Chatelaine*.

One of the things that happened in the 1980s was that I fell in love with Jamaica—and the people there. For a decade or so, until my health wouldn't allow me to go back there any longer, I spent three or four winter months there. The following article appeared in *Departures* magazine, spring/summer 1981.

JAMAICA: A VIEW FROM THE BEACH

You must bathe in the sea at seven in the morning—then the whole day will be good.

This is accepted Jamaica wisdom. The first time I heard it was from the wise-and-kindly marimba player in the calypso trio at my first Montego Bay hotel. When I tried, the seven-o'clockers explained that it is only in the morning before the wind comes up that the beach water has a full concentration of ocean salts and minerals.

My day in Jamaica this past winter began early and ended late, at the beach. The tourist-area beach strip in MoBay runs about two miles roughly northward from the centre of town, a mixture of public and private areas, sand beaches interspersed with woodsy and rocky stretches. There's the big, new (free, public) Fletcher Beach; the famous old (private) Doctor's cave and a dozen other favourite spots. My place is the tiny perfect cove the old-timers still call Sunset Beach. Most of the newcomers call it Carlyle, for the hotel across the street.

At seven, in February, the sun is still behind the top floor of the hotel. The beach is in the shade, yet for some reason the water is warmer than at any time later in the day; and quiet—no wind yet, just the gently lapping tide of a barrier-reef bay. The street is quiet too, but the morning regulars are already gathering on the beach: a handful of hardy tourists and perhaps two dozen Jamaican locals. Rastas are off to one side, washing vigorously, and singing.

When I got back to my beach in late morning, after my last-day shopping downtown, one sailboat was out on the horizon. Jim, from Toronto, was giving his first windsurfing lesson of the day. "Just Lee," the all-day patty-and-beer pushcart man, had just been joined by "Sir Morris," operating the lunch cart with roast beef sandwiches and ackee-and-saltfish and sour sop drinks. The beach was lined with fruitwomen (their head-baskets set out on display) and the "higglers" selling black coral, wood carvings, straw goods, and peanuts. White, pink, red, tan, bronze, brown, and black bodies were moving in and out of the water, stretched out on towels, examining wares, playing backgammon, drinking Red Stripe beer.

Usually, it rains at night. That afternoon, it rained. It was a long rain for MoBay —twenty minutes. I went back in for a swim, then spent the hot part of the afternoon over fruit punch at the shaded bar, picked up jerk chicken at the Pork Pit, and climbed back to my guesthouse to watch the sunset as I ate on the terrace.

☙

Jan. 21, 1983—60 years filled!

Dear Marian—
This birthday letter can only be to you, because at least you were here, you have some image of my surround; you met Zach, however briefly—
    What instincts that man has!
    Where to start? With horror story, I guess, from—what? 8–9 days ago. The Nights, rather. I had gone to bed early, for some reason totally exhausted, and was apparently sleeping very deeply indeed, in some involved dream which I do not remember, when I heard—in the dream, I thought—a rushing sound, which seems to be the sound the field rats make when they rush over the roof of my room at night (once just after dark, once just before dark—where do they migrate at night?). This result (dissolved?) in the dream, to a sensation of tiny feet rushing over me. The rats? My pad my pad—platform was still down on the floor, I leapt up (stark naked) and DD used (forgive clichés, there is no other expression so apt) in horror at the sheet where, in moonlight coming through the windows slats, I saw small shapes on the bed. Migod! Not rats, giant cock-roaches! Divebombing?
    Gradually became aware that an urgent whisper from the window was saying, "It's all right, it's Zachariah—it's Zach—don't make noise—open the door—it's Zach—Judy, it's Zach, open the door. Don't make in the noise—it's Zach."
    Trembling, in total shock, still not connecting the two events, I grabbed my robe, turned on the light, saw that what the bed was full of was peb-bles, opened the door and let him in, in muddled combination of terror, delight, disgust, desire, surprise, and (most of all still I guess) shock, which is quite beyond me to describe.

The man slipped in, put down his shoes, reached for me, bragging happily about how successfully he had sneaked in through the yard, and said in dismay: "You didn't have any clothes on before."

He was already starting to take his off. I was totally incapable of speech—with the exception, I found, of two words, which were essentially all I spoke for the next half-hour:

"No, man!"

It got through to him everything was not cool.

(Jamaican exchange, standard greetings: hey, man wha' hoppen? … Everyting cool man, everyting cool.)

I did manage to get out a few words about pebbles, rats, and roaches—not coherently, but enough to slow him down. Also, there was a burst of lights and laughter through the hole in my closet as the teachers prepared for bed.

(Digression—one of how many to come? Is this a letter to you or the pretentious Jamaican journal I never did start? The big fat trunk with my fridge, my pots, my Underwood noiseless, the rest of my priceless supplies of whiskey, toilet paper, etc., was to have arrived about Jan. 10. The latest of three calls to the custom-brokers in Kingston said they believed the ship was on the way, probably due to arrive this weekend, but had not received the documents, so not sure my trunk was on it. Call back Thursday. I figured that meant call today, Friday. Maybe they will give me a birthday present too—a call to Kingston is J$3.80. That means 38 "10-centses"—I spent two days trying to make the first call before I found a phone that worked and their line disengaged. Then the phone wouldn't take my coins—it was too full. Now have arranged a deposit-against-the-bill system with little white-goateed retired watchmaker and his warm plump wife, Iris, who somehow maintain a chirpy English-tooting style menage Studies in their retirement cottage just off the beach.)

So: man says, "Turn on the tape?" At midnight, I thought aghast and said—you guessed it—"No, man!" (Recognizing in split sec after refusing that it would have surprised, upset, unsettled, awakened no one to hear music suddenly spill out at midnight.)

Impassioned pleas about the way we feel about each other, the some-thing "special" between us, life is to be lived, stop denying myself, etc. He came because he knew I was waiting for him. (True, even in the state of shock, I knew that was true, did not say no, man—for days he had been making love with eyes and gestures during every brief meeting, on the street, in the bar, etc., and I had been, yes, waiting.) Impassioned explanations: "This is Jamaica, man!" He knows how things work, everything will be cool, it is not natural or expected that a woman will stay alone all the time, he knows what he's doing, this is Jamaica. This room is my own, I can do what I want.

No, man, no, man, no, man ...

But by the time he left I was very pleased indeed. (That could be misleading.) It was, no, man, all the way. He never got his clothes off. Finally said, okay, it was all up to me now. Let him know when I was ready. I was very pleased.

Lay awake and thought. He was right, obviously, about everything except throwing pebbles in my bed. (An old Jamaican rite, I now understand.) Next morning I sought out my friend Jeannie in a quiet moment, and invited a bit of gossip. Background—A local school teacher of high repute, Dell Gibbs, who is a close friend of the household (and another expert on herbal healing) had just separated from her husband when I got here. He brought another woman to their house; she moved out to their older, smaller house, on the same lot (Jamaican: "in their yard"). During the long holiday here she spent most of her time in this yard, doing washing, kitchen work, eating here, playing games with the kids, and also conversing in the bar. I had the idea she was also spending most of the nights with Patrick, the other boarder. So I broached it with Jeannie. (It's none of my business but I'm curious ...) And sure enough, she and Patrick were having it on, with the knowledge of the whole household. (So: risking the children knowing about something is no problem.) (A teacher in their school, frkrissake, not just a nutty foreigner!) Jeannie proved eager to go into details, was obviously enjoying (a) the situation itself and (b) my interest in it. I got a strong impression she also understood why I was asking, and was telling me, go ahead. [...]

So I thought a bit more, and went over to Zach's and found him alone, and said, I have to explain something about the other night. Made clear what had happened about rats and roaches. So, two things. One, I have to get my bed up off the ground, because I can't sleep down there. Two, you were absolutely right about everything except the way you came. I have to know beforehand. Okay?

Amused: "You me to have to make it date?" Serious: will find you some cement blocks.

That day my bed got hoisted. Next day he got hold of the windshield-less truck he shares with a friend (or three?) ("The next man has it now") and took me to the lumber yard to get the way to attach my desk-section. Monday he brought the carpenter around to saw it up and bang it together. One way or another he showed up somewhere every day, loving

Judith, returning to Toronto after
wintering in Jamaica, circa 1982.
Courtesy of the Merril estate

eyes, helping hand, murmured intimacies, but always the "runnings" were
not right for that night. Soon. When the runnings were cool.

Yesterday noon he stepped through the empty bar to the back, saw no
one around, found my door with my improvised latchstring, broke it, and
stepped in, waking me from a light nap, and stepped right out again,
because the window slats were open and Blossom (resident poor relation)
who was washing in the side yard, could see right in. (Rooms are very private. You will recall all the visiting was on the verandahs.) No one was
home at his place; he wanted me to come over. I went to the beach.

I guess he figured that was notice enough.

I guess it was, at that. When he called through the window about
11:30 last night, I was sleeping, and had smoked-up a little before I went
to sleep. I entered my 60th birthday feeling young and tender and good all
over and very grateful.

(Wow! He was really disappointed when I sent him home at one a.m.!
I explained I was a bit rusty from disuse, and had to get into practice for
more athletic bouts. He smiled and went half-asleep in my chair, playing
footsies with his bare feet, we waited for Manley and friends to abandon
the backyard.)
XOXO Judy

Feb. 1, 1983
70 Marchmount Road, Toronto

Dear Judy,

It's shrink day and tonight I went down and started cleaning the front room of the basement. It amuses me when I do something that instinctive and it does my heart good to throw out old bicycle inner tubes nobody got around to fixing and bits of wood with pieces gouged out of them, the kinds of things other people keep in one's basement because they might come in handy. Well, if next week someone comes and says the plumbing can be repaired only with an old bicycle inner tube I guess I'll feel like shooting myself, but right now I'm durned glad to get rid of all that junk.

The boy moved out last week. Earlier than we planned, but he'd blew a gasket and messed up Char's room [Charlotte, her daughter] and beheaded all my plants so we said enough was enough. It's good, he's got a room on Dovercourt in a house where another ex-patient of Phil's lives; it's a zoo but the rate isn't too bad and I've lent him money against his grandmother's inheritance, for first and last month's rent, etc. After that nothing, though I'll pay Phil until his 18th birthday. [...] I've had a bad week, the shade of my mother in my dreams talking about castrating tom cats, but I'm coming through it.

I've dreamed a lot about Jamaica, too and lollipop black lovers, so the visit didn't do me badly, did it!

This letter is therefore to confirm that you can stay here for a while when you're home. [...] I gave your address to the Women's Press, who wanted to do a written interview. They were incensed when I tried to get them to pay you. Fuck them.

I'm reading in Vancouver next week and then going to Victoria for a couple of days. I'm going to stay at the Empress if I can ... me with no bloody income. But I figure I can get a short story out of it and need a couple of days' depaysement after all this uproar. Desina will stay with Char. So I've got that, and then a Union translators' Conference March 11 while you're at the house, then Edmonton on the 18th March ($500 yummy) and then two readings in April because Randy's raised my prices and I'm selling! Not often, but a couple of people are coming through.

So you'll have a bed here when you want it. I'm painting the room a nice pale grey and getting the old bedstead up from the basement. I know you like the floor but the bugs do too; and this bed is as hard as iron.

Then no—income bit he says worrying as the outgo continues; but I am working hard on the book. Gosh, I wish I was down there right now. It's a

mild winter, but a gloomy one. Much love now and take care. Regards to Jeannie and brudder, love,
Marian

Thursday … Yours in the mail this morning … unbelievable: brudder and the dancing cockroaches, what a story. Happy 60th indeed. Will I get anything as good for my 50th? Some things have happened already, Will left after a minor blow up, but on good terms. The two of us lived like mice again, happily. Some bits of the book are good though I fear my agent doesn't think so. She hasn't called. I have to write a story about Mobay to claim my expenses on the income tax. Mary Abbott pretending she is a poached egg in deep blue sea, I guess. And meeting whom? A man who looks like a baby in a plush jump suit?

What news? Marker is still good and mad, damn her, my neighbour Willie streaking on booze, getting himself good and beaten up. Good thing I don't keep anything in the house. He put the shower and dishwasher in okay, though. If I paint that room myself I'll get paid on the broadloom. Our reading at London in March, going up with Austin and dining with the West Indians afterwards. Going to Van and then Vic on the 15th, staying with Aritha and then in the Empress hotel which is only $33 a night.

Gotta go write the Van. People to meet my plane. Much love. I'm glad you're repaying the loan: I'd forgotten about it until yesterday. […] Must buzz love and happy returns and lots of papaya and all those good things.
Marian

[n.d., probably March 1983]
Dear Judith—
Thank you for reminding me that there is more to be written, and that perhaps something has been written …
Gwendolyn

April 3, 1983

PLEASE KEEP THE STACK OF OLD GLOBES FOR ME. I NEED THE BILL FRENCH COLUMNS. THEY COULD GO IN MY OFFICE.
Judy: welcome, in case I am not here. You're the first to arrive and ought to know that David Hunter at No. 63 and Mary McDonald at No. 33 have keys to the house, to look after pipe and cats. Perhaps you could tell them you have taken up residence.

Please take my room. The bed is as clean as I can make it this morning, i.e. I am about to look for another clean bottom sheet and the pillow cases are fresh. I haven't washed the duvet cover but I take a lot of baths.

Char arrives 10 April; give her a hug for me and tell her to phone either my sister Helen (844–6711) or the hospital to find out where I am. Hunters have said they will keep an eye on her! Please take the cats over from Mary. Sophie gets one can a day, Bennie half a can, There's oceans of cat food but you have to make sure Sophie lets Bennie eat his. Please do not shut Sophie away from the kittens for any length of time. She likes to go out for 2 hours only, so if you're going out for half a day, push her away from the door.

[...] Sheets and towels are in the wooden trunk in my room. The basement's a bit of a mess, I had to get J's bed out and couldn't put it back in order. On the bulletin board are operating instructions for the house. Give me a call and meanwhile enjoy, enjoy. My surgery is scheduled for the 7th, if there's to be some, and I'll be in the General. Best phone my sister, tell her who you are, and get the details.

Kitchen light is behind fridge.

Use office and typewriter. If you can pick me up some new Coronamatic black nylon ribbons please do; I'll pay you back.

This is all I can think of!

Lots of love
ME

Sept. 5, 1983

To: TWUC [Writers' Union of Canada]—The Inner Circle
I recently received a request for permission to reprint several of my poems in an anthology in preparation entitled "Canadian Women Writers Anthology." The letter was from one of a group of six graduate students working under the supervision of a professor; it described the work as "a comprehensive anthology of Canadian women writers," which would run to around 650 pages and include about 100 authors.

I wrote back, saying that I would prefer delaying my decision to grant permission until they had found a publisher for the book, and added that I also wanted to think a little about the anthology, because (and I quote from my letter):

"I confess to having a certain bewilderment about its nature and intent. Writing is the property of both sexes; surely it is not your intention to suggest that women are a breed apart?—or that we have been so suppressed in writing (which we haven't) that we need a whole anthology of our own to set matters straight? What would a book entitled "Canadian Men Writers Anthology" look like?"

Hmmm?
Gwendolyn MacEwen
cc. Judith Merril

Feb. 13, 1985
JUDITH MERRIL WSBEACH

MARIAN VERY CRITICAL BUT NOTHING ANYONE CAN DO IN PERSON
PHONE ANY ONE OF US FOR UP TO DATE DETAILS
GWENDOLYN [MACEWEN]
COLL LT

Feb. 16, 1985
JUDITH MERRIL WHITESANDS

VERY SORRY MARIAN DIED FRIDAY NIGHT FAMILY FUNERAL MONDAY AFTER-
NOON MEMORIAL SERVICE ABOUT A WEEK LATER ORGANIZED BY DAVID
YOUNG HOPE YOU ARE OKAY
GWEN & BEVERLY

Feb. 19, 1985

Dear Judy—
I just returned from the funeral and thought to write you. Learned about your appendectomy from David, and phoned the hospital half an hour ago; they said you were comfortable. (Had a bad connection and couldn't get more out of them.) Hope you'll phone one of us soon and let us know how you are. So PHONE SOMEBODY when you can!!!

The week of agony with Marian is over, blessedly, for her. Hard on us, but no longer on her, is how I see it. She looked so bad when I last saw her (and spoke to her though I doubt she even heard) that I prayed for her sake she wouldn't come out of it if it meant a prolonged period of further torment. We still don't know what caused the seizures and what was the specific reason for the deterioration. As ever, everything was linked to everything else, and one can get bogged down in medical jargon.

Thought you'd like to see these obits (at least I hope you'll like to have them, didn't want to send them if they would depress you). A marvellous thing that I heard this week was when the sister Helen was talking to Charlotte about heaven (or something) and Char said: "Mom knows all about heaven and she doesn't want to go there." (!) Bless her for that, and Marian, who would get a kick out of it too.

DO WRITE OR PHONE.

love, Gwen

P.S. Memorial service at 7:00 on Feb. 28—don't yet know where.

THIS LETTER MAY GET TO YOU BEFORE THE OTHER, BECAUSE REGISTERED
Feb. 27, 1985

Dear Judy—

Ann phoned to say you were out of the hospital and OK. Good! It must have been rotten for you, and even worse being down there alone with the grief of Marian's death. I told Ann I had sent some clippings, etc. (this is one time you might appreciate my insanely methodical nature)—and am enclosing more things now.

The memorial service is tomorrow, and in a way, this letter will help me organize my thoughts on what to say. (By the way, it is extraordinary that Marian also underwent an appendectomy when they did an exploratory operation a few days before the end.)

I think I'm going to say that Marian and I were light years apart as writers —I was never a great reader of fiction, and she didn't quite understand my poetry—so it was wonderful—we didn't have to be literary! Also, some recent memories, including you and I with her in the hospital room last summer with the awful hamburger and the laughter and us talking about what we might have been if we hadn't become writers.

Also—she brought me a marble egg from Paris (something magical for Gwen, she had written on her shopping list)—and me visiting her at home about a week before the end saying Marian, let me do something USEFUL— so she suggested I straighten the books on the shelves (perfect job for me) and I came across the children's classic *At the Back of the North Wind* [by George MacDonald], which she said I should take. Marian, I said, do you realize you're always giving me children's books? Oh, Oh, I should watch that, she said, taking a long drag on her cigarette and giving me that sideways grin. You read me so well, I told her.

Also—an amazing conversation about a month before when she said she was thinking again of finding her twin sister, but she didn't really want to … and I said (God help me) Marian, I think the sister you're looking for and don't want to meet is your celestial twin, your spiritual twin, your ka, your soul … Another long puff on the cigarette, then, with absolutely no malice or sarcasm—Oh Gwen, you're so smart.

Then I guess I'll end my piece tomorrow night with the poem (enclosed) and hope to hell all I've said will hit the right note, the right tone, and be a proper tribute to our brilliant and gutsy and much-to-be-missed friend.

What else can I say? I know if you were here you'd make a far better job of it than I will … but I thought you'd like to know that I'll mention you in the course of things, and I know you'll be there in spirit.

Take care, write if you can or want to—I guess it won't be long til you're back.
Love, Gwen

[December 1985]
THE YEAR OF THE EARRING, 1985
—for Judith Merril—

This was the year it all hung out, Judy—life, death, everything.
Our best friend died, and I transferred half of her garden
To half of my garden
Where some of it still blooms in the cold thrill of the autumn.
This was the year we got rid of our appendages,
Including your appendix which got removed in some Jamaican hospital
And various lovers who rode off into their respective horizons.
This was the year when earrings were the currency, the gelt,
The coinage of the realm, pure fantasy.
People had so many earrings they were coming out of their ears.
They had cruise missiles hanging from their ears.
This was the year both of our books came out, but I knew
Something was wrong when I found myself facing Barbara Frum
On the Journal, and she said: All right, Gwendolyn, I want
To talk earrings.
I didn't worry when I saw you walking down College Street
With the rings of Saturn hanging from your ears—why?
Because we both knew we were living in Interesting Times
It was some year, and we danced our way down University Avenue

With Caribana, and the street was a sea of sweat and laughter
And earrings. But I began to worry, Judy, when you wore nothing
In your ears, and you feared for my sanity when you saw me
In High Park with this great Zero hanging from my left ear.
God, it was some year.
And things reached their head when we got a free week at 21 McGill
And were turned away at the door because they said:
We don't like your earrings. And things were going too far
When I stopped giving poetry readings because none of the earrings
Matched my shoes, and now none of my earrings match my thoughts
And I am temporarily in hiding until I can set things straight.
But this was the year when everything was possible,
And we let it all hang out—life, death, everything.
But now our interviewers are no longer asking us about our latest books
But our latest earrings, and our plans for future earrings.
So you'd better head for Jamaica and get away from it all.
    —Gwen

Jan. 17, 1986
White Sands Beach, Jamaica

Dearring Gwendolyn—
Yesterday, for the first time in these 6 weeks (see enclosure at leisure) I got
to the library with enough time to suss out books I wanted instead of grabbing the first two possibles from the just-returned rack, and came home
with, for one, Wilson Harris' *The Age of the Rainmakers*—which I commend
to you (probably) along with other "companion" titles. He's dealing with
Arawak myth in a somewhat-parallel to what you were doing in *Noman's
Land*—which I have with me, and began rereading in snatches this morning.

One of the things that I find suspect in myself—syntax don't work,
though that's the wording I wanted—well, then, sometimes wonder about
myself is whether I love the people I do love AS people or as wordifiers (primarily). Anyhow—

Today I love and miss you very much, and as it happens—

Tomorrow a friend of a friend is returning to TO and will carry letters
up, so I have a sense of immediacy in writing to you that is impossible with
the usual anticipation of two weeks or so delay in delivery.

I have been wanting to write to you not only since I arrived here, but
since the last evening I saw you—when you came to pick up the stereo—

which you may not remember too clearly, because you were (not uncharmingly, but) very drunk at the time.

Are you still reading? Please, I hope so.

I had in fact been wondering, from various familiar signs, whether you were back on the booze again, but was disinclined to ask about it, because I know how you feel people are always watching/waiting to see you Fall From Grace. Well, I don't give a shit about Grace, but I do about you, and that night you were not only acting, but smelling, drunk. So I had my answer, but it took me a while to figure out just what business I had saying anything to you about it—not to mention getting clear in my head exactly what I meant to say.

Okay, with luck, I've waited long enough so you have things under control again, and all that follows is unnecessary. If so, please file this letter for next time it starts to get bad enough for you to reach for a bottle, because I might never be in just this space to say it again.

So *Rainmakers/Noman's* has made that clear—while renewing ponderings about myself and the nature of my affections. In your case, right now, you know, I love you dearly. I love your wild chatter and space-people humour and the serious giggling we do together, and having someone with whom to share some (sane? mad? irrelevant) parallax-making visions of the mad? sane? surround. I don't want to lose all that—especially so soon after Marian.

Of course I don't have all that when you're drunk anyhow (brace yourself, this is Straight-Arrow Judy on the computer now) because (this is what I meant above, see word "familiar") you start repeating the same joke over and over and can't hear what I'M saying (DEADLY sin!). So if you drink enough to kill yourself, I lose a friend who matters a lot to me—and if you just drink enough to keep the pain fogged out, I lose most of it.

(Note I'm not talking about what you lose, because that's YOUR choice, of course, and how the fuck do I know if you're losing or gaining more, in YOUR experience?) But what I realized this morning was something (more important? silly word—anyhow)—

Flashback: I had another friend I loved very dearly indeed, and indeed still do, though I have little contact with him now, because he too is a writer whose work I also love—sometimes—and what I found out eventually with him was that the work I most want to see from him gets written ONLY WHEN HE'S DRINKING—and the person I want to be with is at home, so to speak, only when he's not. Okay, this guy has an incredible constitution, and at almost-75, after 40–45 years of getting on and off the juice, he's still relatively healthy. Maybe that could work out for you, if necessary—

NECESSARY? That's what I've been getting around to. I THINK *Noman's* and the new poems were written sober. If indeed they were written drunk, the hell with my personal loss—just keep drinking, baby, because my loss is the world's gain—and also my own. But if that IS the case, try and bear in mind that whether you've been seeing me or not, any time the booze starts to threaten your physical well-being and your ability to write, if you holler I will come and try and get you back on your feet. I mean, in your chair, at the desk.

BUT if my first guess was right, and you had not started secret tippling when you were doing that work,

(This rotten machine, for which I did NOT get extra memory chips before coming down, chose this point to flash MEMORY FULL. So I had to print out this far, and hope to hell MY memory will carry me through the paragraf.)

... so—if you did that writing on water and coffee (fkrissake, Pepsi or even PERRIER!), and if you ARE still boozing now—

Pick up the phone NOW and get hold of your friend Mack and ask him to get the hell over and help you get out of it. AND/OR

Pick up the phone next time you wake up relatively sober and phone 809 952 5096, where (if it is morning) you will almost surely find me home, and if I'm not and anyone else answers, just leave word for me to call Gwendolyn. (We now have a phone extension from the landlady's flat upstairs in our place so sometimes you get Peter or Janetta upstairs, but two stations are cheaper than one personal.)

Latest hot news since writing the 6-weeks report is that our little dream house may still be available. I am to go and see Miss E tomorrow morning. But we'll still be here at least till the end of the month. (PO address will stay the same in any case.)

Hey, maybe you'd phone even if you don't need me, just to let me know you're still speaking to me? Or send a night-letter? Or anyhow write? Much love, dammit!
Judy

March 13, 1986
TO JUDY MERRIL CARE WHITESANDSBEACHPO, JAMAICA

THANKS FOR LETTER. RIGHT ON WAS SICK. BUT HAVE RECOVERED THANKS TO JOYCE, MAC, AND TWO DAYS HOSPITAL. SEE YOU SOON
GWEN

TWENTY-TWO | **THE CRAZIES ARE DYING***

I DON'T THINK I'm really crazy enough. I don't know if I can handle it all. I have always thought of myself as a survivor but I'm getting old and honoured and of course that makes it much tougher. Plus, it's hard to be crazy enough when you're crying.

Milton is gone. First it was Marian, then Robert, and now Milton.

The crazies are dying.

Never mind Borges, Calvino, Dali. Never mind Herbert, Hubbard, and Sturgeon. These are the Proper Crazies, kooks from the down-home Krazylands: Argentina, Italy, Spain, and U.S. science fiction. It's easy to be a crazy some places and there are always more coming up to fill the ranks. But—Canada?

I mean, I'm not talking about mean-crazy, hide-in-a-hole crazy, catatonic crazy. I'm talking moon-mad and sunstruck; I'm talking flaunt it and shake it. I'm talking fiery-eyed and magic-mouthed. I mean true far out flamboyant Crazy.

Like Milton. Like me, I guess, when I came to Toronto. And from the time I came (to Rochdale, first), people kept telling us about each other.

You mean you've never met?

Originally published in NOW (Toronto), 1986.

Milton Acorn, the People's Poet—I'll tell you how we finally met.

It was in Thunder Bay, maybe eight to ten years after I came north from Pennsylvania, a lot more than that since he came east from Prince Edward Island. The library people began apologizing as soon as they met me: the audience for my reading might be small because Milton Acorn was reading at the university. We try to avoid conflicts but we didn't know ... Milton Acorn!

I didn't mind small readings, I told them. I just wanted to meet Milton.

What? You mean you've never met?

We figured the university reading would go later than the library one, so we raced over as soon as I was done and tramped through empty corridors until somebody said: Okay, I know where Milton's got to be.

It was an enormous beer hall. There were three rooms, each about the size of the main hall at Toronto's Union Station, filled with large round tables, the kind of table in Chinese restaurants that takes eight, ten, twelve people.

In the first room, all the tables were taken except one, right in front of the (loud) speaker. Nobody saw Milton anywhere. Half of us sat down, and the rest went to scout the other rooms. A waitress came and loaded the table with beers. I didn't take any; I was coming down fast from the performance high, starting to feel cranky, and where was Milton anyhow?

So this Neanderthal-looking type, with untied running shoes and sagging cotton work pants and some bare belly between the pants and rumpled shirt, and a scraggly beard and the craziest blue eyes in the world came over and swayed a little, standing over me, and smiled a big lopsided smile around his cigar and said—shouted—YOU'RE JUDITH MERRIL!

Then you've got to be Milton Acorn. I told him we had been looking for him all over, but how did he know who I was?

Those crazy eyes! he said.

We found out we were living just a couple of blocks from each other, near College and Spadina, and for a while we saw a lot of each other. In those days Milton was living at the Waverley Hotel on Spadina and hanging out just down the street at the Crest Grill. When you walked by the restaurant you could look in through the windows and see who was sitting in the booths. If he was there I went in, and if I was there he went in.

But let me detitillate: we were never lovers, in the flesh; in fact, we hardly ever visited each other's rooms. Just for that time we sought each other's spaces, confided, quarrelled, roared with laughter, argued, anticipated, every bit as lovers might.

Then Milton moved out of the Waverley and did his cafe-sitting elsewhere and we found others, closer, to confide in and confess to. When we bumped into each other, our conversations were mostly about politics and outer space. Milton was an addicted reader of science fiction magazines—much more so than I was.

He would tell me what to look at in the new issues and spin out marvellous plots for SF stories he was going to write. But more than science fiction itself, it was the sensibility of free-ranging through cosmic space and time that we shared: ultimate adventurers reaching out from the corner of College and Spadina.

Of course we shared a lot of other, vital, heart's-blood things. (Or people would not have kept saying, all those years—You mean you've never met?)

Somehow it is hard to write about this. I don't mind talking about sex, which is important, or personal love, much more important, or love for space and adventure, which many people think is childish or "escapist" or even "reactionary"; but I am oddly shy about proclaiming that love for humanity and passionate social anger that is called idealist ideology. This is what we shared most deeply.

Frederik Pohl, Elizabeth Anne Hull (his wife), and Judith discussing the state of the world at Emily's dining room table, Toronto, 1995.
Emily Pohl-Weary

(Milton was once given an award by other poets, who felt it was his proletarian politics that had kept him from getting the Governor General's Award for Poetry. They gave him a medal that said he was The People's Poet, and he wore it around his neck, under his clothing, and never took it off.)

We both had this passion, then, for quaint notions with embarrassing names like democracy and freedom and justice-for-all, a sort of perverted taste for things not only proletarian but lumpen, and a wistful desire to be as underdog as possible. And of course that's what our mightiest battles were about: fierce unbending fights that stemmed from crucial, often trivial differences about social ills and their remedies.

Mostly these quarrels ended with one of us walking away grim and tight-lipped, making sure that his notorious physical anger did not explode to ruin everything for good. Next time we bumped into each other we would start fresh, talking about his latest multidimensional or space/time idea, but more and more often drifting again into battle.

The last few times I saw him before he went off to Prince Edward Island he was heavy into Islam and anti-abortion. I was not sorry to see him go, but I never expected him to stay on his Island. I only saw him twice after that.

He was in Toronto for a reading, and had a heart attack. I went to the hospital to see him. He sat on the side of the bed, a greying man in a grey hospital bathrobe with stubbly grey on his cheeks and his eyes all greyed out. He had nothing to talk about, and everything I thought of seemed unkind to mention. The Crazies —my Crazies—had already started dying, and I had been very sick once myself, and I was scared, and couldn't stand it. I kept promising myself I would go back, but I didn't, and I was relieved when I heard he was back on the Island.

Life, by its nature, is full of unfinished business: incomplete expressions, untidy pauses, unrounded sentences. Stuff you're going to get around to tomorrow or next week or next decade. Or never. If you die in the middle—of anything—you're forgiven, of course. But if your friend dies, how do you forgive (yourself or your friend) for the unfinished business?

I had to cope with that, in different ways, when Marian Engel died, when Robert Zend died, when Ted Sturgeon and Elizabeth Smart died. In the nature of things, it would have been that way when Milton died, but it wasn't.

When the Poet's League met in Toronto in June 1986 I crashed their Saturday night dance, and the first person I saw was Milton, spruce and spry and red-cheeked, with his eyes on fire again. We talked and laughed and when the music started we danced. Milton was a lousy dancer; he sort of wanted to polka to everything. We had a wonderful dance. At the end he was dripping sweat and panting. He went up to his room to rest and someone told me he was still having heart problems. But the dance didn't kill him. It was good. No unfinished business between us. Just all the unfinished business of the vanishing Crazies: the people who will shout what they think needs to be heard, and flail away at any windmill that needs flailing.

Well, hell, I know I'm not the only one left, but we seem to be an endangered species, and I think I have let my flail get rusty, and every time another one dies there's that much more crazed the rest of us have to be. And it's really hard to be the right kind of Crazy when you're crying.

June 21, 1990

PRESS RELEASE

For immediate release:
The House of Commons and the Summer Solstice

The Writers' Union of Canada, frustrated in the conventional avenues with the imposition of the impending Goods and Services Tax on READING, the postal subsidy cutbacks, and the lack of democratic political leadership in the management of changes to Canada's Constitution, calls on all politicians to become statesmen and stateswomen of the highest rank. To assist them in this endeavour, The Writers' Union of Canada today enacts, at the time of the summer solstice, an honoured date for the aboriginal peoples and witches, a ceremony of exorcism. This ceremony, performed by Robin Skelton, Judith Merril, and a Wiccan Witch, is to dispel all evil spirits lurking in the corridors and chambers

*The press release was issued by the Writers' Union of Canada; the speech that follows was delivered at an exorcism on Parliament Hill in Ottawa, 1990.

of power. Thus enabling honest, forthright, considered and creative thinking to prevail and deliver us from these dark times.

The Writers' Union of Canada is a national organization of professional trade book writers.

For further information contact:
Trevor Ferguson, Chairman (Montreal)
Jo Anne Williams Bennett, National Council Representative (Ottawa)
Penny Dickens, Executive Director

☙

I AM A CRONE, and I speak for Gaia.

A crone is a granny, an old woman who has outlived the years of traditional female service, and has earned the right to be rude, and the rudeness to be forthright. Crones are assumed to have acquired a certain amount of—usually disagreeable—wisdom. We are sometimes suspected of being witches and often thought to have certain powers of prophecy.

Because I have thought and written about the future for many years, I will accept the role of seer. It needs no mystic magic to foresee the disasters that lie ahead on the suicidal paths most of our decision-makers are pursuing—crises, confusion, and catastrophes for nations, cities, towns, and villages—for the seas and the continents—for farmland, water, and the very air we breathe—for our families and the individual men and women who compose them—and above all else for the children whom our families, religions, and social and political institutions are meant to nurture and protect.

Our leaders seem to be impervious to common sense and reason. So now, on this solstice day of power—the longest day of the year in Ottawa, the day of absolute balance between dark and light at the equator, the day the sun never rises at the South Pole, and never sets at Canada's North Pole—on this day, as futurist and as woman, I call upon whatever powers of magic I may have acquired to speak for our children, and our children's children.

I speak in the name of Gaia—the ancient name of our planet, Earth—a name now revived to mean the LIVING PLANET, the fertile mother of all life on Earth, the dust from which we come, and to which, one day, we all return. I do not speak on BEHALF of Gaia. She does not need my pleading. She will survive, in some form, whatever foolishness or malice we, her creatures, may commit—but her survival will not necessarily guarantee our own.

There is a tide in the affairs of people and of planets which, taken at its flood, leads on to fortune, peace, and plenty and the fulfilment of human aspirations. Throughout our history, power-blinded empires have failed to seize this flood tide—and perished. We live today at a time of power and of danger unprecedented in all the millennia of human history. For centuries we have multiplied our numbers, and with each multiplication we have sought more and greater tools to compel the environment, the planet, to yield up to us greater and ever greater resources to support our growing numbers.

Our ancestors learned to till the soil, make fire, mine metals, and manufacture tools. When their growing clans, tribes, and nations needed more tillable land, more water, more metals, our forbears learned to turn their tools into weapons to rob, by conquest, the resources of neighbouring clans, towns, and nations.

When humankind was thinly enough spread across the Earth, and our engines of destruction were no more than spears and torches, our leaders began to learn the lessons of cruelty, conquest, and control, of power-posturing and political gamesmanship. Skill in these crafts became the criterion for successful leadership.

In recent decades our technology has multiplied

Judith arguing onstage during the tribute to her life at Harbourfront Centre, Toronto, 1992. She spent several days shopping to get this particular look.
<www.readings.org>

even more rapidly than our population. Today we can cut down the forests too fast for the trees to regrow. We can burn the fuels too fast for them to replenish or for the air to recover. We can eradicate vast areas of farmland and of habitation in minutes. But the old habits of chest-beating and stick-whirling are still in practice.

The governments in which we trust to restrain, indeed, retrain us and guide us to new patterns that can make use of our astonishing technology, not for destruction, but to enable both the people and the planet to survive in harmony and comfort—these governments are caught in the old patterns of pride and place even more ruinously than the individuals they claim to govern.

I now call upon the power of Gaia, imminent in every spark of sentience on this planet, to say to the minds and spirits that inhabit this house of governance:

In Gaia's name, I beseech you—Pull yourselves out of the tawdry trappings of yesterday's dreams and address the urgent needs of today, and the hopes and demands of tomorrow—the world we will leave to our children and their children's children.

In Gaia's name, I require of you—Put aside, from this moment on, the perilous politics of pride and power, preening, position, patriarchy and prestige, personal profit and patronage.

In Gaia's name, I command you—From this moment forward, invest your high office with the intelligence and the awareness that you MUST summon to resolve the true crisis that confronts humanity today: to find the ways to feed the hungry, house the homeless, free the oppressed—not only of one province, culture, nation, but also of the world.

If you, the chosen leaders of a uniquely fortunate country, fail to find a way to deal with domestic shortfalls and shortcomings so as to achieve decency and dignity for all—not just for the most populous, most prosperous, or most politically astute groupings—then there is small hope for this same process on a planetary scale—and we shall, indeed, all perish in our pride.

TWENTY-FOUR | GROWING OLD IN THE 1990S: DEAR FRIENDS

IN 1990 I MOVED to the Performing Arts Lodge (PAL), a wonderful co-operative housing community for mostly retired but still incredibly active members of ACTRA (Alliance of Canadian Cinema, Television and Radio Artists). PAL is a breath away from the Toronto lakeshore, and close to the downtown St. Lawrence Market. Since its inception, the building has been filled with colourful people who share the space in happy disharmony.

I moved in like a storm, settled, and became active in the community, the board, the newsletter, and the daily Coffee Klatch. The co-operative aspect of the place was its greatest strength. Here's the statement I wrote the time they tried to get me to sit on the board.

Statement for PAL Board Elections from Judith Merril

If enough of you want me on the Board, I'll serve, but I'm not sure it's a good idea.
I'm often disturbed about (a) the inadequate communication we get from the Board and from Community Relations, and (b) the frequently autocratic/ bureaucratic management style of Park Property.

I'm an experienced shit-disturber, and so far I have been able to make some of my (and others') dissatisfactions heard. I think people like me are often more useful outside the power structure.

(Like: look at our Premier, Bob Rae!)
Judy Merril.

One of the things I worked on was the idea of a "monthly supplement" to the new *PAL Insider* newsletter. In February 1996 I sent a memo and a "draft/suggested copy" of the column to fellow board member Sharon Dyer:

To Sharon Dyer

Draft/suggested copy herewith. Maybe in March newsletter? Maybe solicit a few real items to replace the "frinstance"? You can redesign/rewrite or give me needed info and suggestions.
JM

Announcing:
THE PAL TENANT'S ASSOCIATION INSIDE/OUTSIDE
A monthly supplement to the new PAL Insider

PAL has got to be the most public private place in Canada. People who live here are appearing on television every day. We're in the movies, on the stage—but most of the time we don't know when to watch or where to go to see our friends and neighbours do what we do best.

Inside/Outside will keep you informed about your neighbours' public appearances, and let you keep your neighbours informed about your own.

When you get hired to act, sing, dance, direct, opinionate or just spear-carry on stage, screen, TV or at a public event, just tell Inside/Outside, and Inside/Outside will tell the (PAL) world.

Inside/Outside will be a regular feature of the new Tenants' Association newsletter, the Insider; in the months between issues of the Insider it will be posted on lobby bulletin boards and distributed to members of the Tenants' Association. But you don't have to be a member to get listed: you just have to live in PAL and give us the information.

TO SUBMIT: (UNDER YOUR DOOR, SHARON? A BOX IN THE GREEN ROOM? WHAT?) Give us the information any time. It will appear in the next Inside/Outside.

KEEP IT SHORT: Frinstance—
Janie Doe and Dickie Joe will be featured on a commercial for Ruff-Ruff-Rufie's Dishy Dogfood starting (date).

Patti Prime is doing her stand-up comic routine at Kuy-Kuy's (address) for three nights, July 14/15/16. Showtime 11 PM, $5 cover.

John Q. Jingle will play the role of Puck in A Midwinter's Night Dream at the skating pool at Toronto City Hall. 8 PM nightly, March 15–31. Free.

☛

Meanwhile, I tried to keep friends up to date through letters.

Aug. 22, 1991

An open letter to friends, colleagues, well-wishers—
This is a cheap, scurvy, inadequate way to acknowledge the heart-warming, health-hoping notes, cards, messages, letters, and books with which so many of you have blessed me over the last ten months of extended gestation for my rebirth into borrowed time. On the other hand it is surely overkill for those of you who have simply been waiting for a reply to correspondence that had nothing at all to do with my travails. But any other method of trying to wade through the stack on my desk would probably mean some of you would be waiting most of another year.

I thought the invalid life would give me lots of time (and boredom to spur me on) to answer letters. Time and boredom were plentiful; motivation, and often simple intelligence, were lacking. Between October 1 and, I guess, about midsummer I seemed to need all my meagre energies to work at the onerous business of daily life and the urgent business of healing. All this was overlaid with what I'd like to think was a realistic, and not just morbid, awareness of mortality—so that almost the only mail I could make myself attend to was what was necessary (financially, etc.) to keep things from being unbearably messy for my heirs.

The last month or so I have been joyously/painfully picking up the pieces of a life that now seems to promise (note the caution—"promises, promises!") a bit of usable future. I have renewed subscriptions, paid (cannily) delayed annual dues, begun a bit of work again on memoir projects—and am, herewith, cheating my way to an empty in-basket.

Double-cheat, I guess: I'm not writing most of this (letter?) new, but compiling it out of one (THE one) I actually did complete during the Bad Days, and another one that more or less broke the logjam in July.

P.S.: Just because I send it is no reason you have to read it. For most of you, there is probably far more here than you want to know, and probably some you already know—but I haven't yet learned how to program my computer to give me coded sections to individualize for each recipient—and how could I tell anyhow who actually LIKES medical detail? So just heft-and-riffle if you like, as long as you credit my correspondence-debt Paid. Fact is, there was nothing to write about all this time except How I Spent a Year's Vacation In and Out of Hospitals. The NEW news, just about to start, is that I will be Writer in Res at U. of T. this year—a fine genteel job for a senior re-entrant.

March 12, 1991:
So yet another day I came in to the office; I have been doing this on all but the most impossibly bitter days (when I dared not venture out), sitting down at the computer and waiting to see if I could summon up the energy/will/optimism to write some vastly overdue letters.

This grim effort was not aided by the demon in the boiler room, or more accurately in the airflow system. My office is in a library building; I was gifted with the space when I donated my personal SF collection to start a special branch of the Toronto Library—til recently the Spaced Out Library, now, embarrassingly, the Merril Collection. The building contains, as well, a notable collection of rare children's books, and rare items in the specialty collections have been crumbling for years due to inadequate climate control; land has recently been purchased (after ten years of site-hunting) for a new modern building, but the ground is not yet broken; meantime the library system is reluctant to do any repairs, and the heating/cooling system gets worse and worse. In the winter heavy-heating time, MY office, at the end of the line (a bridge with an adjoining building) is alternately at C30 above or C15 below, with occasional deviations toward the centre. I have not really been aware of the problem before, because for the last twelve years I've always been away during the serious winter.

(Today, it is about C18 above in the office, which means I can work for a bit—but not likely long enough to finish what must be a very long letter.)

My pattern for some years has been to spend three or four winter months in Jamaica, swimming, walking, thinking, dancing, some years doing some writing—relatively isolated, unplugged-in—then come home in time to do my income tax, try to catch up on accumulated mail and jump back into all the in-plugs (Writers' Union of Canada, the new Spec Writers Assoc. of Can., family, politics, etc.). It used to be when I came back up, I would be healthy and energetic and really ready for the hectic life, but over the last few years I have been disintegrating. Eyes and ears slowly fading; acute arthritic flare-up in one knee a few years ago; needing to be more careful about diet, blah blah, otherwise known as getting old.

Reason for unwonted presence in the cold is an infarction I suffered on

October 1. Recovery has been slowed by a Catch 68 (Do you too have to stop to marvel at your age?) which has to do with vigorous exercise being needed, and the difficulty of (arthritically) walking even one block on ice-paved surfaces. I'd have been better off in the south, except that (a) the IMF et al. have taken their toll on Jamaican medical services; (b) even if there were a doctor or hospital I could trust in emergency, the place I stay (and can afford to stay) is at the top of a hill on a bad road, where taxis will not drive in, and I (this year) would have trouble walking in and out even if (relatively) healthy; and (c) they have STILL— after three years—not been able to get a telephone at the house.

Dinner celebration after Ann Pohl's wedding to Juan Miranda. From left: Emily Pohl-Weary, Oscar Miranda, Judith Merril, Ann Pohl, Juan Miranda, Tobias Pohl-Weary, Toronto, 1984.
Courtesy of the Merril estate

Well, then, the Heart Attack (with some digressions into associated matters such as descendants, archives, memoirs, travels, jazz): Last year, I did a trip from Jamaica to a science fiction convention in San Francisco, with stopovers in NYC and Philadelphia. (In S.F. I stayed a few extra days to visit with Fritz Leiber, one of the few Important Old Friends who is not already dead; in Philly I spent our joint birthday with my then one-year-old great-granddaughter Kelli Nicole MacDonald!). The previous year, I had come to the startling realization that I not only WASN'T writing any fiction, but that I didn't WANT to. Took me quite a while to believe this. COULD you stop wanting to? Once I got used to the idea, I realized what I really did want to do was write about my own life.

Not an autobio. Just the interesting parts. While I was in N.Y., I read Chip Delany's book of memoirs and decided to get started by doing short pieces on special people, times, events. Started researching my old letter files (closest thing I have to a journal).

My papers are in the National Archives in Ottawa. I went up and sorted out a bunch of stuff; began reading, remembering, writing connective stuff. Meanwhile, it was a big year in the busy-stuff departments. Readings, workshops, stuff about Native writers; a political exorcism (of the House of Commons); Toronto's first annual Book and Mag Fair; and blah some more blah.

September was madness. In the last week I squeezed in three more days in Ottawa. The Archives is open 24 hours for registered researchers. I was sleeping three to four hours a night, then caught the train back to T.O. Sat eve, hit the street for a brunch reading with Spider Robinson at the B&M Fair Sunday morning, and an interview for a TV program, *Prisoners of*

Gravity. Met my friend Valerie [Alia], just back from the Yukon, in late afternoon. We went with a bunch of people for dinner, then on to a favourite jazz bar, and out for pizza and talk. Home about three. At six I woke up feeling dizzy and light-headed and broke out in a sopping sweat that lasted about ten to fifteen minutes. Then somebody fastened a steel band around my chest and began tightening it.

Fortunately that "band of steel around the chest" metaphor was a familiar cliché. Astonished, sort of embarrassed (surely-I-was-exaggerating—?) I phoned my daughter, Ann, told her I just might be having a heart attack, started thinking about what I'd need for the hospital, heard sirens, looked out window, saw a fire truck, knew it wasn't for me.

It was, of course. Seems they always send the firemen first, because ambulance drivers don't have equipment to break in if needed. Fire truck, ambulance, Ann, all seemed to arrive on each other's heels; in retrospect, Ann could not have arrived in less than a half-hour (from being wakened to phone to clothes to car, and 5–6 miles thru downtown). Lo and behold in the hospital emergency, they said I had had a heart attack!

The odd chest pains I had been having, and the shortness of breath, were not indigestion-cum-smokers' bronchitis, they were bigod angina.

I still have some trouble believing this. I have always known I would die of cancer, and just hoped despite the smoking it would be some kind other than lung. I don't have high blood pressure or high cholesterol or a family history of heart deaths. The doctors of course know it was smoking that did it but that's partly because they haven't asked, and don't seem to want to hear, about life-style. (No, I am not trying to say smoking isn't a major cause.)

So I have cut down from about forty to fifty a day to a max of ten. When I tried to stop completely, I gained 15 lbs. in two weeks, besides getting into frightening rages and tantrums. The weight gain is serious, because about 15 lbs. more would make me diabetic. I got that high once and for-tunately was able to diet and exercise down to safety but it's waiting for me up there. I am shopping for a therapist who can help me find the magic button to turn off my infantile need for constant oral insertion.

Meantime, I have been building up a serious case of outrage about the failure to query my lifestyle, and a bunch of other medical behaviour that goes along with that. It's funny—for years, ever since reactivation of femi-nist momentum, people have been urging me to tell them about condescension/oppression I suffered as a female SF writer. All I could ever think of was one rejected wannabe making up a list of every editor I ever sold to and circulating it as a list of my lovers. (Fact is, the two editors I did sleep with never bought anything from me after. Non-literary criticism?)

But now, bigod, here is a whole medical establishment—and most of all my cardiologist—patting me on the head as a sweet little old lady who better listen to what Doctor says. Never mind that this year's heart disease buzzword is the "Alpha" personality. Alphas are middle-aged MALES, right? So: Got to locate a different doctor; working on it. Got to find a way to quit smoking completely; working on it. Got to get myself into a phys rehab program; working on it. At least, I'm in Canada, where it's all free. (And now I'm senior, even the prescriptions are free. Wheeee.)

July 18, 1991:
My memory of that whole period is skewed. Recap—

After the heart attack in October, I was told I had had a minor infarction —what they called "10 per cent"—and I was expected to be able to "get back to normal" within six months. My progress was slower than predicted, but did seem to be moving forward until spring weather began to make more activity possible. From late March I began having more "unstable angina" attacks, was in-and-out of hospital and finally in late April was given an angiogram which showed (a) a 30 per cent infarction, and (b) blockage in all coronary arteries severe enough so that my heart was only getting about 10 per cent of normal blood supply. All of which added up not to wondering why I was recovering so slowly, but rather why I was still alive.

They said IMMEDIATE BYPASS! I said bypass yes, immediate no: got to get my affairs in order (5–10 per cent fatality risk in operation, plus another 5–10 per cent chance of possibly disabling stroke or heart attack). Three weeks later another angina attack was so severe we all thought at first it was another infarction. Fortunately, no—but scary enough to make me realize it was more dangerous to wait than to have the operation, which I did on May 24.

Today is eight weeks after. First six weeks you have to be very careful because the breastbone, which they saw open, takes that long to heal. So now the incisions (second one where they take a vein from the leg) are pretty well healed and I don't have to worry about damage to the mending bone from jolts and jostles. As far as I can tell, I am this time healing as expected— only remaining post-op problem is with the breast muscles, but this is not bad enough to interfere with most activities. I'm still very slow and get easily fatigued, but that is—I think—mostly due to nine months of extremely limited activity (following about two years of diminishing activity before I knew I had a heart problem). Will probably take a year or two to rehabilitate muscles; I will start in a rehab program end of August; meantime I just keep increasing the amount of walking, and doing yogic-type stretches (non-aerobic).

Aug. 25, 1991:
Well, the objective was to finish this, get it copied, and add the wee personal notes in time to mail for delivery before the rotating postal strikes turn total.

Aug. 26, 1991:
They just did. So now I got plenty time, but no more space. I think this will almost exactly fit four pages.
So thanks, and love, J

May 21, 1992
To Kate MacLean

Dear Katie:
I'm starting this with only about twenty minutes till I have to leave but part of what I want to tell you is something I need to spell out for myself— my schedule the next few months—and when I come back tomorrow the unfinished letter will pop up on my screen.
    So—thinking of a visit, which I hope you still are—
    Between now and the end of June, I am trying to do some actual writing, and a bit of editing of old letters, toward assembling a sixty-page section to apply for an Ontario works-in-progress grant. I have shunted aside almost everything else—except physiotherapy, a cardiology checkup, and the AGM of the Writers' Union of Canada (which is in Ottawa, where I need to go for some consultation with my younger self at the National Archives anyhow) —so as to have least possible excuse for not actually putting words on paper.
    (I did do part of a piece yesterday.)
    (Or: so what else is new?)
    Once this submission sample is done—if it does indeed get done, because what else is new is in fact that I don't/can't work-binge any more; either it gets done in moderate doses or it doesn't get done—I have only one specific plan for the summer, which is to go to a conference in London, Ontario, Aug. 1–2–3, because Fritz (and Bob Bloch) will be there.
    I haven't seen Bob for about thirty years; I saw Fritz in San Francisco about three years ago. At that time he was half-blind, bent over from spine-shortening, and moderately racked with emphysema. Since then he has had a stroke—has largely recovered from its effects—his eyes are worse, etc. But he is still doing some writing, and seems to think he can manage this trip.
    (Actually nothing less than maybe-the-last-time-to-see-Fritz would take

me out of Toronto Aug. 1, which is the day we have the giant Caribana carnival-mas band-parade in Toronto.)

My plans for July and August (and indef. future) are to continue with what I'm doing now, but with less emphasis on the memoirs and more on the other three major activities: exercise, improving my knowledge of physiology (specifically, my own, and how best to keep it functioning), and making my apartment more comfortable and appealing. This last is because for the first time since I was housebound with kids/poverty, I feel the need to have a place friends can enjoy coming to—and for that matter that I can enjoy staying in whenever it is that exercise and physiology are not enough to keep me moving around. (I don't come from the kind of long-lived stock you do, nor have I worked at maintaining my bod as you have done.) I'm doing much less moving around than I used to, but at the moment that's improving.

I'm hoping to do one trip down to N.Y. and Pennsylvania over the summer —see Virginia, Chip, Merril, grandson Kevin and family (did you know he has a daughter, and I am a great-gran?), and maybe Lorna Moore—but that's contingent on the energy curve increasing—and also on when you decide to come.

The apartment is a small one-bedroom in the same general area of downtown Toronto where I lived last time you came, but my latest acquisition is a loveseat-sofa bed which makes having a visitor much more comfortable. I'm in the middle now of a major throw-out campaign, trying to pare down enough to install an Exercycle. After a lifetime of avoiding planned exercise, which I would never do just because it was good FOR me, I now have to admit it makes me FEEL so much better I have to get used to it.

(Fixing her apartment, eh? you say. Nope; I am NOT asking you to come help; just to visit.)

(Well that's not completely true. There is some help I'd like if the idea and the time suit you. So—)

Suggestion #1: Come June 24/25, planning to stay about a week, or at least over the weekend. I have to have made final decisions on the submission sample by Friday evening, the 26th. Selfishly, I'd very much value some feedback from you, but will not be startled if that is not high on your list. The main event in any case is just hang out-and-catch up time, which would start on the 27th.

Suggestion #2: Any time from June 27 thru the rest of the summer: sooner, better; if you're in the mood for it, can include Con weekend, which will be virtually cost-free, as I have had to take a room for two nights, and hope to find someone to share it, but a third person can come in for no extra cost, and there should be rides available to/from.

Note: Told Ann you were thinking of coming, and she'd like you to spend some time with them. Did I tell you she has a loving husband (Argentine, electrician) and two more small children, Julia and Daniel?

Mostly, it's just been too long. Come soon, eh?

Much love, Judy

June 18, 1992

Hey Kay!

M'god a real letter. I have become very envious of my former self, doing all this reading of old correspondence, and of course part of it is because I knew so many great people and DID so much all the time, but a good part as well has been just that the letters themselves—in both directions—were so great, and I got out of the habit years ago. Getting a letter like yours is now a rarity —and of course the only way to get 'em is to write 'em, so no time like the now, eh?

(Please note I have become a true Canadian. I say both "eh" and "zed.")

With which I went dead in the head. A lot of stuff I want to write about, but every avenue of approach seems roadblocked somewhere. No. Wrong image. It's that we don't have the substrate any more—like you worrying suddenly about whether you were boring me with your talk about your woods. Actually, I loved it probably more than I would love the woods. I would never have the patience or the energy to do the kind of job you're doing, but I can fantasize doing it; in Jamaica I learned a lot about living outdoors that I never experienced before—

Nope. That's not quite right. I always loved "outdoors," loved water, almost any kind, but especially lakes and rivers, and part of that was the surrounding woods. (I think lakes and rivers more than ocean mainly because I don't really like sand or beaches.) I loved walking in the woods, and in tall grass, campfires, cooking outdoors—almost all my "religious" experiences ("joining the universe") were outdoors. But I hated "nature walks" and came to react against the word "nature"—and more recently, the pious use of the word "natural." Did I feel my mysterious universe was being profaned somehow by the "nature" teachers? Something more than that, because I also did NOT (actively did not) want to learn biology either. I have of course regretted my ignorance in this area repeatedly, but never moved to repair it—though I have recently developed a necessary interest in physiology, and actually managed to learn spotty bits of it.

That needs some thinking about. Back to Outdoors. I think part of its excitement for me was that I was always a bit afraid of it, never felt quite "at home" in it—much the same as my basic fear of almost all animals, just not UNDERSTANDING them. I feel ashamed of these lacks and gaps, but there they still are.

Living outdoors, however, I learned first not in Jamaica but with/from Walt. Hated it, welcomed it, feared it, could handle it only because he was there.

Well, I don't know if I will ever actually walk in your woods. With luck, and application, I may be able to build up my leg muscles again enough to overcome the weakness of the joints and be able to keep my footing on uneven terrain well enough to enjoy it. But your talk about it delighted me in the same way I enjoyed watching a Jamaican friend rebuild a piece of the beach. Or—Jamaica again—my fascination watching an old-fashioned masonry job: one strong man collecting rocks from vacant land, one cracking them with a sledgehammer, the master mason chipping off edges and fitting them into a foundation for a porch; I didn't have to believe I could ever do it myself to delight in seeing it done.

22 June now.

Half of the stuff above I just wrote. And I come to this sentence, left from the earlier version, where it followed the remark about "substrate": Well, maybe if I deal with small stuff first I will fall into some seriousness along the way.

I didn't know computers got old and tired and forgetful like people. I am constantly being disillusioned about the machine interface. I have a friend here, Mike, who is my computer maven—bought my machine for me and comes (usually) when it gets temperamental, or when I try to do something I KNOW I ought to be able to do (like double space) and it won't. A few weeks ago, it lost a file; the file was an earlier version of the stuff I included for you in this letter, begun the day Asimov died. It was gone, completely gone:

ISAAC ASIMOV...

One of the commonest cruellest recognitions of advancing years: Lovers, beloveds are not forever.

Some drift away; some storm off; some gently disconnect; the rest, at last, simply die. The only way not to lose them all is to die first.

Minimally, it is clearly better to have loved and lost than never to have loved at all. The experience of the grief of final loss is evidence, if needed, that oneself is still alive.

Curious, too, and interesting to learn that there is grief, the last proof of residual love, still waiting on the deaths of otherwise long lost—one would have thought forgotten—loves.

As I write this, Isaac Asimov has just died. We were never, in the most common and narrowest use of the word, lovers, but we did love at one time: the heroic, I suppose, love of colleagues, comrades: comrades-at-arms says it best, a very special, specialized love I have heard described (by a fighting Irishman who was in all senses once a lover) as "a man I'd want at my back in a fight."

Face-to-face Ike and I sometimes amused, sometimes consoled, sometimes bedevilled each other. But back-to-back, we were on occasion a beast with eight busy limbs. We met—

I cannot quite remember. I knew him first through his stories, when I had not yet written my first science fiction, but I don't recall a Big Impact/First Contact physical meeting. It would have been 1945-6-7, somewhere close to fifty years ago when we were both members, first of the Futurian Society and then of the Hydra Club.

Those memberships and my graduation in 1948 into sf writer status made us necessary comrades. Simply being two science fiction writers, in those days, was almost enough; sf was a ghetto in the literary cosmos, mocked and despised by a smug Mainstream—a rich, seething, yeasty ghetto whose members all understood (quite correctly as it turned out) that we were the province and the provenance of the future. But even within sf, the Futurians were a nexus; dispute and debate were constant amongst us, yet we shared certain essential sensibilities and worldviews that cemented us into a sort of Young Lions' network.

Two years after my first story appeared in Astounding Science Fiction, Asimov reviewed my first novel, Shadow on the Hearth.

> Read this book on a warm sunny day, with the birds singing and the summer in full play; and, as you read, the sun will dim out, the birds will fall silent and the cold will creep in. Yet the story is only the quiet account of five days in the life of a Westchester housewife....
>
> Yet exactly this becomes an exercise in grim horror, since the story takes place during the five days after the atom bombs fall on New York City....
>
> When you have lived them, it may take a while for the sun to strike a light again and for the birds to clear their throats and find their places in the musical score. It may take a long time, and that, perhaps, is how it should be. There should be a permanent chill in every man's soul while the menace of atomic war remains.

That was June of 1950. Neither Isaac nor science fiction in general had as yet hit the big time, but he was already a fixed star within the science fiction galaxy; he had already published, in fact, all of his most memorable fiction: the robot stories, most of the Foundation series, and the unforgettable, startling, story, "Nightfall." I should have been overwhelmed by his praise, but I was only *pleased that someone who understood precisely what I meant to do had access to a major newspaper.*

The last time I saw Isaac was at a symposium I organized in Toronto.

Anyway, the damn thing wasn't on any directory, wasn't on the Windows list, wasn't halfway down the stairs—I take that back. Halfway down the stairs is where it must have been. Mike came down and got addictively more and more fascinated, hunting for it, finally pulled back, shrugged, and said, I dunno, maybe some static, nothing else wrong. Two weeks later it showed up again on the Windows list. So yes, I know the damn machines are temperamental, irrational, perverse, et al. But old and forgetful? Sheeeittt!

June 22 add: So when I came in on Friday to finish this letter, and decided to move a block of type from lower down to higher up in order to get into the rest of the stuff up there, my menu went weird, giving me only call-caps instead of words: F for Files, etc. Then the Windows list vanished completely. Then everything vanished. C-A-D did nothing, neither did Reset. I could hear the computer burping away trying to perform, but NOTHING on screen. Couldn't find Mike. My no.2 and no.3 experts were out of town. Couldn't reach Mike all weekend. Bumped into knowledgeable guy yesterday who said, first, had I checked all the plugs? I hadn't, because I got misbehaviour before silence; when I gave him more detail, he said it sounded more like the gizmo that (regulates? manages? I can't even remember the fuckin LANGUAGE!) the hard disk than like the disk itself. Reached Mike this morning, he said he'd come down this afternoon; then I came in about noon, checked all the plugs (all okay). Turned on the computer. Works. EXCEPT the Windows list, which had about twenty items, now has six. And the cursor has been, and still is, wandering when I stop to think. So go understand, huh?

I return to you now on June 18:

I am trying hard to hope you get lucky with the unemployment insurance bills, but I really want to see you. Maybe if you get extended we can have a death in the family you have to come to Toronto for? I do not recommend coming in December; aside from the weather (but due to it) with any luck I won't be here myself. Last winter was the first I had spent here in twelve years—no, the second, but the winter before, between the heart attack and the angiogram that sent me for surgery, I was hardly even aware of the weather, or much of anything else. Every now and then I would call a taxi to take me to Emergency, and in between, people would come and bring in groceries, clean up, etc. But this past winter I was supposed to be Okay, and was doing the Writer-in-Res job, which meant going to the university office twice a week, and starting physiotherapy and trying to take over caring for myself, and I discovered I was now one of the Elderly who are warned in weather forecasts not to go out at certain times. If I tried, I'd get about as far as the corner before my whole body was exhausted: simply couldn't get enough oxy into my blood.

So now I'm trying to figure out where I can go; Jamaica's out, medical services there have been IMF'd out of existence. But I don't want to be a part-time prisoner in my little apartment again.

$300 doesn't sound surprising to me. If you can get it down, that's fine, but I figured it would be somewhere around there when I made the suggestion. I have a surprising amount of money: old age stuff from Canada and U.S. adds up to almost $1,200 a month, and Public Lending Rights and the odd reading to at least another $1,000 a year, and to my astonishment there is about $50,000 in stuff accrued from the ACTRA (radio and TV) pension fund and the remains of the money I got for my papers. I've thought of this accrual in terms of interest income for some years now, but interest rates have fallen drastically now, and I expect the interest and possibly the principal to disappear (perhaps along with the pensions) when the stock market crash materializes, so I am trying to learn to spend money and get pleasures while I can and also possessions I will still have when I have no money. (I am also, like you, expecting to start earning again, but have less faith than you in WHEN my book will be finished.) This morning I bought a neat little Sony Walkman player/recorder/radio with really good sound and more micro-size buttons and functions than one would think this gadget—JUST large enough to hold a cassette—could contain. Ann is trying to persuade me to buy a cottage.

I might actually do it. I have resisted all temptations to home ownership because it has seemed to me that it is the home that owns the owner. Kept saying if I had enough to pay cash and some built-in arrangement to include someone who could handle the maintenance, I'd do it. So here's this cottage at Camp Naivelt.— This is at the far end of Brampton, a sub/ex-urban dormitory of Toronto, mostly quite unlovely, but the far end is a park, and part of the park is this relic: a camp started in 1936 by Communist (secular) Jews. Until recently, you had to be both Jewish and at least left-wing to own a place there; now they theoretically can't discriminate, and there is some mixture. Anyhow, a couple of years ago Ann and Juan got a place there, a minimal two-room-and-screen-porch shack, for $1 and a promise to repair roof and floors, etc.

Now there's a much more sophisticated place (shower, fridge, stove, furniture, storm windows!) two houses away going for $1,500, and Ann wants me to buy it—I suspect so they can shower without having to go to the shower-house. But here it is, a place I can pay cash for; now if I can pin down Ann's casual assurance that they will do any needed maintenance work …

… then I will have a place I can use about five months a year IF I get a successful cataract operation that will permit me to drive again. Meanwhile I can use it when Ann is driving in or out.

I mentioned in the last letter that she hopes you will spend some time with them when you come. I reassert this now vigorously; Emily, her eldest, who is my friend, my assistant, and cleaning woman (I can't kneel on the bad knee to do floors, or balance for high spots; can't lift more than about ten pounds without getting post-incision muscle pains), reports that Ann has been telling all the kids about you.

June 18 ends here. Now June 23.

Appointment with cardiologist this morning. He sat still for all my questions, told me which aches and pains I might just have to get used to (surgery detritus) and made suggestions about remedial ones; reduced my medications by one; pronounced heart and arteries apparently in good working shape.

So. Going by the scribbled addendum on your letter, I figure if you can come at all it will be end of July. If so, you may want to plan to stay through a second weekend, because that will be the big weekend for WOMAD, which is World of Music Art & Dance, at Harbourfront (the big waterfront park). I love it; I think you'd like it. They really do mean "world": mixture of performers from Africa, Asia, South America, and Native people, plus plain old Canadians. Everybody does one indoor paid gig and at least one outdoor freebie; unlikely combos come together, like a drum session with people from North and South America. Natives, Chinese, Indian, and African, last year. Lots of colour, excitement, and exotic foods.

Do you like Caribbean music—calypso, soca, reggae? If so, I will see if we can get a ride out to Waterloo AFTER the Caribana parade on the first of August. The Con runs thru Monday so we'd still have (more than?) enough time there.

I was going to write more about the memoirs but I have to get this out and off so that I will write more memoirs.
Much love,
Judy

July 24, 1993
To Virginia Kidd

Dear Kidd:
I will try to think this out at you, then decide whether to bother you with the actual letter.

I had lunch with Louise Dennys Thursday. It was thrilling.

Not only do I think (based on talks with people who've worked with her, as well as the quality of the list she edited at Lester & Orpen Dennys) she is probably the best editor in Canmade, and one of the best anywhere— I also (like? too weak) have been somewhat infatuated with her ever since our first meeting. (In case of doubt after all these years, no, no sexual content there.) Each time we've met, we've both expressed this attraction, and promised ourselves/each other to find time to explore friendship. Of course, her life and mine being what they are, we have never done so.

July 26
I was interrupted there by a friend of Ann's, come to carry me out to her shack (not-quite-cottage) at Camp Naivelt. Due to pollens?/citronella?/ chlorine pool? eye was nonfunctional yesterday—only a bit better today— and now you have received your letter with the second check from Italy, so will pause to say I cannot follow the deductions the way you have the statements made up. I need to know all the numbers to know which way to do it on my income tax, and so far I can't arrange them any which way to arrive at the final figure. That's for the short-story check as well as the one for *Shadow*.

So. Back to Louise, who says she is "captivated." The fact that it is the world of science fiction I'm writing about gives it an extra—exotic?—touch for her. (No. More than that. When I told her about the "Message to Mars," she was genuinely thrilled.) But the two aspects that have grabbed her are the story of becoming a writer, and the Young Woman story.

You know, I've been converted as I worked on this. All these years, when people went on about my supposed feminist role-modelling in SF I laughed and laughed, because I knew I wasn't doing anything like that. SF was ready for that change; it accepted me eagerly (as a writer—the sour stuff later was to do with being an Authority); nobody but nobody advised me to use a man's (or neutral) name; some stories were hard to sell because editors said they wanted "the woman's angle" from me. Etc. You know all this.

Now I hear over and over (most recently a show last week on A&E, apparently from the BBC) how in THE SIXTIES AND SEVENTIES women at last, through struggle, achieved the right to use their full names, write female heroes, etc. etc.—most frequently quoted authority/liberator, Joanna Russ. Bullshit. BUT—

I also hear eloquent testimony—as from MacLean and Élisabeth Vonarburg at my Tribute, and perhaps a dozen younger women—writers and readers—for instance at Readercon, that it was reading my work/anthologies in the fifties that made them realize they could write/expect to read stuff that included them in SF.

The responses I have had from non-SF women, and most recently and fluently from Louise, tell me that the exhilarating/terrifying experiences I was having in the forties and fifties were indeed twenty years ahead of their time in the Big "Real" World. They say in astonishment, How did you manage without any support network? For a while they had me convinced I never had one—but of course I did: it's just that the only FEMALE members were you and Kate (and later Barb Norville).

Where am I going with all this? I dunno. I'm just letting it take me wherever.

No. The stream of thought is wherever, but it comes out of a central theme. I want/need an editor/reader on this book who can juggle all the perspectives and keep reminding me of them:

Growing old, approaching death, accepting limitations, above all surviving the deaths of friends/lovers/network.

Offering as true a picture as distance will allow of the magical world we lived in forty or fifty years ago, a world where ideas were as important as dinner, and love could not be readily sliced up into sexual or social, agape or caritas, and where (all concomitant hostilities nonetheless) sharing was a societal norm.

A true statement about indistinguishability of learning and sexual activity in my life—and perhaps in many others' as well? This is feminist-politically incorrect these days, I know.

love, J.

Oct. 5, 1995
To Valerie Alia

Dear Valerie,

I have been about-to-write for a couple of weeks now, and kept putting it off because it's so long since I've written, I figured I should do another of my infamous catch-up letters-to-everybody first. I mean, you are not the only one I haven't written to—

Now suddenly it's less than two weeks till I leave home, so I better at least let you know I'm going to be in Vancouver for the Writers Festival. Stats: arrive Tues. evening, 17th at the Hotel Vancouver, should be checking in by six or seven o'clock; leaving noon Monday the 23rd; hosting three panels on SF & F, Wed. and Thurs. at 1 p.m., Fri. at noon; reading (briefly) from Memoirs Sun. at three. Lots of free time, obviously. With any luck, I'll get that letter-to-everybody done before I come out and save time when we see each other. Meantime, here's a chunk from a letter I finished in October '94, to give you some idea what it's been like since I moved here in February '93.

Have just come out of a stretch which included going to Winnipeg to give out an award, doing a deadline column for the Canadian trade paper *Quill & Quire*, and creating reams of material for the Friends of the (you should excuse) Merril Collection, as well as for the new Libraries Committee of the Writers' Union to try to save, not just the Merril Collection, but the whole Toronto Library system (and others elsewhere) from the ravages of the deficit-mad politicians and electronics-mad library board. (Q&Q column to do with this also.) These things coincided with conducting an SF writing workshop for Ryerson University—something I've managed to put off for two years since I first agreed to do it, and got stuck with this fall. Same time I am re-reading (and in some cases reading—stuff I missed when I couldn't see so good) the [Ursula] Le Guin oeuvre against a writer/writer interview I am to do with her in two weeks at the International Festival of Authors here.

Also, a piece I wrote last fall on invitation from the Discovery channel, probably the most important part of my serious thinking these last two years. (They didn't use it.)

Technology is neither god nor devil—not magic, just stuff you do things with. To do anything useful, it must be appropriate to its purpose, affordable, sustainable—and someone has to know how to run it and maintain it. A spaceship won't fly without a programmer (astronaut or ground-control) and enough fuel—and you can't even use a milking machine without power, a mechanic, and enough food for the cow to produce milk.

Right now the planet is running out of resources, and our governments are racing towards bankruptcy while we keep draining the Earth's substance to sell technology that is neither appropriate nor sustainable. When the Big Crash comes, we will find ourselves in a Mad Max landscape of parched earth and leftover fragments of hi-tech under the control of local warlords.

The power-base in these little tribal tyrannies will of course be muscles and guns—but also intelligence, ingenuity, and enough understanding of the leftover technology to make it appropriate and sustainable. With luck, we

Dinner at Ann's during a rare visit by Katie MacLean, Toronto, August 1992. From left: Julia Pohl-Miranda, Emily, Tobias Pohl-Weary, Ann Pohl, Daniel Pohl-Miranda, Katie, Judith.
Juan Miranda

might even have a few satellites still in orbit, so that savvy young computer hackers can maintain a scientific data base, and keep communications open between tribes until the Earth and its inhabitants can heal themselves.

So. I can get some comps, for my own programs, and some others. If there's something you'd like to attend, let me know. But mostly, I just hope for a chance to visit. Let me know your free time—write quickly, fax up thru Monday night, 16th (but check your files for address and phone below) or leave a message or call me at the hotel?
Judy

WE HAVE ALWAYS DREAMED of Heaven. This cannot be the same for you, whose consciousness as a culture began with your ancestors' flight through space.

Also—however you may have scattered and spread across your planet, you will have begun with some shared social and linguistic base. Human cultures and consciousness on Earth evolved in many languages from widely scattered and vastly varied enclaves: some broiling hot, some bitter cold; desert-dry or drenched with rain; on mountaintops, at the seaside.

But the earliest legends of each and every unique culture show that we were all, from the beginning, gazing in awe at the night skies, imagining ourselves somehow descended from those wondrous lights, looking to them for blessings, fearing their displeasure, hoping somehow, some day, to ascend once more to the brightness of the stars.

Long before there was any science of astronomy, we knew the difference between planets and stars. Pre-sciences of astrology everywhere endowed the planets with control of human life.

Great religions were shaped in the image of the constellations. We reached up; we built pyramids, towers, cathedrals, skyrockets, skyscrapers, aircraft. As I

*Originally published as an "Introduction" to an anthology, Visions of Mars, produced by The Planetary Society, 1994, and produced on CD-ROM. It included a picture of Judith Merril. The CD-ROM was sent to Mars on a Russian space shuttle.

write, it is just over forty years, two terrestrial generations, since our first space-craft broke free of Earth's gravity …

That venture—and this one, carrying messages to you who may some day inhabit the planet we call "Mars"—was made possible by a curious collaboration of science and romance.

Scientists and social/political thinkers had for centuries made use of fables, "future fiction," and imaginary voyages to preach controversial or heretical ideas. As the advancing technology of astronomy refined our knowledge of the solar system, Earth's Moon became a prime destination for imaginary voyages. Then, in 1877, Giovanni Schiaparelli observed what was mistranslated as the "canals" of Mars.

This apparent "proof" that Mars had water—and so probably air and, perhaps, life—inspired a new literary form, the tale of interplanetary adventure. The word "Mars" became synonymous with "space"—"Martian" with "extraterrestrial."

Most early space-faring stories were patterned on the sad history of Earth's partisan warfares: Martians invading Earth were literally monsters; Terrestrials invading Mars were brave pioneers, "civilizing" colonists. But the dramatic growth of astronomical knowledge in this century, plus the ever-closer prospect of actual space flight, kept pushing the writers of these romances to more serious speculations.

What technology would be needed to escape the "nursery" of Earth? What sort of life form might inhabit an alien planet? How could Terrestrials best survive in space or in the different surface conditions on another planet?

Typically, each advance in astronomy or rocketry stimulated space fiction writers to new extrapolations. Typically, the thinking of astronomers, rocket engineers, and nascent spacecraft designers was being inspired—and conditioned—by reading "science fiction."

Now the earth sciences are making us frighteningly aware of the damage done to our native planet by our philosophies of conquest and dominion.

Our stories of Mars are moving away from the old idea of the Conquest of Space. We want to revise, not replay, the history of Earth.

We have progressed from the idea of Martian-as-monster through Martian-as-mentor to Martian-as-just-other.

We are beginning to rethink our old dream of "terraforming" Mars, and speculating instead on how best to adapt ourselves to suit the planet when we can, finally, reach there.

The stories we send you here, taken together, tell a larger story.

We who have lived and worked in this confluence of science and speculation send a message of hope:

When our descendants—your ancestors—come—came—to live on your planet, we pray they came seeking not to conquer a planet, but to find consonance with it.

263

TWENTY-SIX | IMPROBABLE FUTURES*

THIS ESSAY ISN'T exactly about a person, place, or thing I have loved, but it must be included because a cloud of future prediction has been hanging over me for some time now. I have a fairly dismal view of where our race is headed, and I worry daily about my six grandchildren and two great-grandchildren.

I have even begun to feel about Canada more or less the way I felt about the United States when I had to leave that country. The only difference now is that there's no place left for me to go. Things are changing rapidly. There isn't a single place in the world that is changing in a way that makes me optimistic about our future. Fortunately, most of my grandchildren have grown up with a fair amount of survival skills, not just for living in a "civilized" society, but for basic relations with the planet.

The way I see things, civilization has come to mean industrial density, control, and high technology. For anyone who has seen the Mad Max films, that's a pretty easy way of explaining my fears: a future landscape where what we now call civilization is limited to small enclaves that are totally corporate and controlled. Those who are still alive after numerous environmental disasters, and warfare, are living in little isolated settlements. These communities are basically little baronies run by little dictators who keep slaves.

*From an interview taped six months before Judith's death and carried out by Helene Klodawsky of Imageries P.B., Montreal; the work was done for the documentary What If ... A Film about Judith Merril, which aired on Bravo! television and the Space Channel.

It won't be quite as bad as the medieval dark ages. The main reason it will be slightly better is that we have personal computers. Just like in the Mad Max movies, pockets of technology will still function as long as there is someone around who knows how to work them. Ordinary people live in a primitive fashion, with bits and pieces of technology at their disposal; one guy has an airplane and knows how to fly it, someone else has a radio that works, except nobody is broadcasting anything on the radio anymore. A laptop computer can work off the electricity in your skin. I think some of the satellites will stay in orbit, and as long as there are satellites, there will be computer communication. We should be able to keep databases a little bit better than the ones the monks kept through the dark ages.

In this decade it has become the norm for the more articulate and socially concerned artists in all fields to focus on exploring the human-machine interaction. As human beings, we have used machines since the day the first person picked up a branch to club a little animal. The objective of machines has always been to make life easier for human beings. Sometimes this holds true. However, enormous amounts of time and energy are spent figuring out how to make our machines more and more complex.

Machines are now fulfilling the role of slaves. Throughout history, many human beings have loved having slaves. Those civilizations that didn't have slaves have often been opposed to them, but those people who did have them, enjoyed them. As long as we are able to stave off the complete collapse of our society, we're going to enslave machines more and more. Those human beings who don't have access to machines will, quite literally, starve.

I don't see much alternative to this horrible future, with the iron grip that multinational corporations have on what is essentially world government. Companies are boasting record profits, and the daily news tells us that the economy is improving, yet somehow more people than ever are unemployed. This trend results in more riots, more crime, more starvation, less medical care, and less social services of all kinds. There is a tremendous distance easing itself between the "haves" and the "have-nots." It's no longer a question of discrepancies between South and North, or even what we call industrialized and undeveloped. Major inequalities occur within a single region. Things are happening in Canada at a slower pace than in some other countries, but I don't know any place in the world where the socio-political trend is moving in a different direction.

There was a time when we thought that the developing of factory automation and computer technology would be a tremendous boon for humans. When we won the forty-hour workweek, we saw the future as a time when people would be working reduced hours—maybe fifteen or twenty hours a week, total—and there would still be lots of everything to get distributed around. Now we are the future. People are not working fifteen or twenty hours a week.

Kelli MacDonald, Judith's first great-grandchild, who shares the same birthday (January 21), Philadelphia, circa 1994.
Kevin MacDonald

Some people are working much more than forty hours a week, while many others are not working at all.

Politicians avoid the problem. Corporate structures are only concerned with increasing their profits; they have a single function: the bottom line. Nobody who is on the "lucky" side wants to make changes that would be necessary to improve the situation.

This is because the essential nature of a corporation is not a human one, even though under our laws it is treated like a person. The notion that the individuals who compose a corporation might have preferences or needs is not meaningful to the corporation. If firing fifty staff people because they can be replaced with one computer is cost-efficient, that's what a corporation will do. The structure is not designed to allow for the fact that once all the companies have fired fifty people, there won't be anybody left to buy the goods. Their concern is only to produce goods at the lowest possible cost, and to sell them at the highest price.

☞

So how do you fight a giant multinational corporation? How do you fight a hundred giant multinational corporations? How do you fight a total global ideology concerned with deficits when people are going hungry? I have no idea. Until there is a total economic collapse, which I anticipate, this will not change. Among the "what if?" writers I respect, more and more are making the same kind of predictions. I don't even know that asking "what if?" will do any good any more.

We used to have a simplistic, clear-cut picture of things: there were righties and there were lefties. The lefties were those of us who were on the side of "good" and believed that stuff should be shared and that there was really, finally, for the first time in human history, more than enough for everybody. But that's not where we're at now. There is more than enough for everyone—there are stockpiles of goods locked up all over the world, just waiting to be consumed—by those who can afford to pay for it. There is no sociological or political will to make it be distributed evenly.

Things cannot continue to work indefinitely within the existing frameworks. Dialectically speaking, capitalism created socialism. But when the Soviet Union went bust everybody said, "There. This proves, beyond a doubt, that capitalism works! Hurrah!" It didn't prove anything of the sort. It proved that capitalism's antithesis did not work in that incarnation. Now we are approaching the day when the capitalist countries go bust and I fear there won't be anybody around to clap their hands, hurrah!

Judith sitting in her electronic cart on the rooftop of the Performing Arts Lodge, a couple of months before her death, 1997. Behind her is the downtown Toronto nightscape.
Simian Posen

The problem is not just economic. We cannot continue to harm the planet indiscriminately. I'm not worried about the planet itself, because I believe it has its own hydrostatic measures. Before we get into this dire strait, the planet will simply decide it can't afford this particular set of parasites anymore. It's already happening; we are seeing more natural disasters like earthquakes, storms, and landslides. They are happening partly because of specific things we humans have done, but maybe our great planet is already shrugging us off.

I don't know of anything that could make a difference, short of a major new religion based on deification of the planet itself. The last novel I tried to write was about the growth of such a religion, but the trouble is I don't believe in the religion myself, so I couldn't write it.

To my mind, such a religion would be all-encompassing, but essentially non-authoritarian. Out of necessity, there would probably be an authoritarian period at the beginning because things have moved too far already for gentle, quiet, peaceful preaching to change much. There's going to be violence. There's going to be even more violence than there is now. There's going to be at least local warfare. We're already seeing it, although it isn't exactly happening in this country. It's occurring in Eastern Europe where people, like the Serbs and Muslims, have managed to live with uneasy tolerance for years, and are suddenly raping and killing each other. It is also happening in the United States, Central America, and Africa. Because of racism, we call it tribalism when it happens in Africa and nationalism when it happens in Europe. When it happens here, we'll probably call it crime.

Appendix I

The Work of Judith Merril

Fiction

NOVELS

Shadow on the Hearth. Garden City, N.Y.: Doubleday and Family Book Club, 1950; also U.K., Italy, Mexico, Germany.

The Tomorrow People. New York: Pyramid Books, 1960, 1962; also Italy, Germany.

Gunner Cade (with C.M. Kornbluth, as "Cyril Judd"). As three installments, *Astounding Science Fiction*, March/April/May 1951. As book, New York: Simon & Schuster, 1952; New York: Ace Books, 1958; New York: Dell Publishing Co., 1959; also U.K., Italy, France.

Outpost Mars (with C.M. Kornbluth, as "Cyril Judd"). Appeared originally in three installments as "Mars Child," *Galaxy Science Fiction*, May/June/July 1952; as book, New York: Abelard Press, 1952; New York: Dell Publishing Co., 1953; also U.K., Germany.

Sin in Space (retitle of *Mars Child/Outpost Mars*). New York: Beacon Books, 1961.

SHORT STORY COLLECTIONS AND NOVELLAS

Out of Bounds. New York: Pyramid Books, 1960, 1963.

Daughters of Earth: Three Novels. Garden City, N.Y.: Doubleday, 1968; New York: Dell Publishing Co., 1970; also U.K., Germany.

The Best of Judith Merril. New York: Warner Books, 1976.

Survival Ship, and Other Stories. Toronto: Kakabeka Pub. Co., 1977.

Daughters of Earth and Other Stories. Toronto: McClelland & Stewart, 1985.

SHORT STORIES (WRITTEN UNDER THE NAME JUDITH MERRIL)

"Barrier of Dread." *Future*, July/August, 1950. Also in *SF Quarterly*, 1951; *Journey to Infinity*, ed. Martin Greenberg (New York: Gnome Press, 1951).

"Connection Completed." *Universe Science Fiction*, November 1954. Also in *Science Fantasy*, 1956; *Out of Bounds*, Merril, 1960; *Survival Ship, and Other Stories*, Merril, 1985.

"Daughters of Earth" (novella). *The Petrified Planet*, Introduction by John D. Clark, New York: Twayne Publishers, 1952. Also in *New Worlds* (London), 1966; *Daughters of Earth*, Merril, 1969; *Daughters of Earth and Other Stories*, Merril, 1985; *The Best of Judith Merril*, Merril, 1976.

"Dead Center." *Fantasy & Science Fiction*, November 1954. Also in *Fiction* (Paris), 1955; *The Best American Short Stories 1955*, ed. Martha Foley (Boston: Houghton Mifflin, 1956); *A Treasury of Great Science Fiction*, vol. 2, ed. Anthony Boucher (Garden City, N.Y.: Doubleday, 1959); *The World of Psychology*, vol. 1, ed. G.B. Levitas (New York: George Braziller, 1963); *Out of Bounds*, Merril, 1960; *The Best of Judith Merril*, Merril, 1976; *Daughters of Earth and Other Stories*, Merril, 1985.

"Death Cannot Wither" (with A.S. Budrys). *Fantasy & Science Fiction*, February 1959. Also in *Out of Bounds*, Merril, 1960; Rod Serling's *Devils and Demons*, ed. Serling (New York: Bantam Books, 1967); *The Ninth Fontana Book of Great Ghost Stories*, ed. R. Chetwynd-Hayes (London: Fontana Books, 1973).

"Death Is the Penalty." *Astounding Science Fiction*, January 1949. Also in *Beyond the End of Time*, ed. Frederik Pohl (Garden City, N.Y.: Permabooks, 1952); *Survival Ship, and Other Stories*, Merril, 1973.

"The Deep Down Dragon." *Galaxy Science Fiction*, August 1961. Also in *The Seventh Galaxy Reader*, ed. Frederik Pohl (Garden City, N.Y.: Doubleday, 1964, and London: Gollancz, 1985); *Thirteen above the Night*, ed. Conklin Groff (New York: Dell Publishing Co., 1965); *Survival Ship, and Other Stories*, Merril, 1973; *Galaxy: Thirty Years of Innovative Science Fiction*, vol. 1, ed. Frederik Pohl, Martin H. Greenberg, and Joseph D. Olander (New York: Playboy, 1980).

"Exile from Space" (novella). *Fantastic Universe*, November 1956. Also in *The Fantastic Universe Omnibus*, ed. Hans Stefan Santesson (New York: Prentice Hall, 1960); *Flying Saucers in Fact and Fiction*, ed. Santesson (New York: Lancer Books, 1968); *Survival Ship, and Other Stories*, Merril, 1973.

"The Future of Happiness" (three short-short stories). *Chatelaine*, 1979.

"Golfer's Girl." *Toronto Star Weekly*, 1949.

"Hero's Way." *Space*, 1952.

"Homecalling" (novella). *Original SF Stories*, November 1965. Also in *Impulse* (London), 1966; *Daughters of Earth*, Merril, 1969; *Daughters of Earth and Other Stories*, Merril, 1985; *Il Richiamo* (Milan: La Tartaruga Edizione, 1989).

"The Lady Was a Tramp" (first published as "Rose Sharon"). *Venture*, March 1956. Also in *Out of Bounds*, Merril, 1960; *Survival Ship, and Other Stories*, Merril, 1963; *The Venus Factor*, ed. Vic Ghidalia and Roger Elwood (New York: Macfadden-Bartell, 1972, and New York: Manor Books, 1973); *The Best of Judith Merril*, Merril, 1976; *Aliene, Amazzoni, Astronaute, Mondadori* (Milan, 1990).

"A Little Knowledge." *Science Fiction Quarterly*, 1955. Also in *Stardust SF* 3,1 (1979), ed. Forrest Fusco, Jr.

"The Lonely." *Worlds of Tomorrow*, October 1963. Also in *Survival Ship, and Other Stories*, Merril, 1973; *The Best of Judith Merril*, Merril, 1976; *Space Mail*, ed. Isaac Asimov, Martin Greenberg, and Joseph Olander (New York: Fawcett Crest, 1980); *Daughters of Earth and Other Stories*, 1985.

"Muted Hunger." *Saint Mystery Magazine*, 1961, 1962. Also in *The Saint Magazine Reader*, ed. Leslie Charteris and Hans Santesson (Garden City, N.Y.: Doubleday, 1966).

"One Death to a Customer." *Saint Mystery Magazine*, 1961, 1962. Also in *Le saint detective magazine*, 1961.

"Peeping Tom." *Startling Stories*, Spring 1954. Also in *Out of Bounds*, Merril, 1960; *Survival Ship, and Other Stories*, Merril, 1973; *The Seven Deadly Sins of Science Fiction*, ed. Isaac Asimov (New York: Fawcett Crest, 1980); *Daughters of Earth and Other Stories*, Merril, 1985.

"Pioneer Stock." *Fantastic Universe*, January 1955.

"Project Nursemaid" (novella). *Fantasy & Science Fiction*, October 1955. Also in *Six Great Short SF Novels*, ed. Groff Conklin (New York: Dell Publishing Co., 1960); (as novel) *Mondadori* (Rome, 1962); *Daughters of Earth*, Merril, 1969; *Meta Luna, Meta Marte, Urania* (Verona, 1962).

"Rain Check." *Science Fiction Adventures*, May 1954. Also in *Crime Prevention in the 30th Century*, ed. H.S. Santesson (New York: Walker & Co., 1969).

"Sea Change" (with C.M. Kornbluth, as "Cyril Judd"). *Dynamic Science Fiction*, 1953.

"The Shrine of Temptation." *Fantastic Universe*, April 1962. Also in *Gods for Tomorrow*, ed. H.S. Santesson (New York: Award Books, and London: Tandem Books, 1967); *Survival Ship, and Other Stories*, Merril, 1973; *The Best of Judith Merril*, Merril, 1976; *Daughters of Earth and Other Stories*, Merril, 1985.

"So Proudly We Hail." *Star SF Stories*, no. 1, ed. Frederik Pohl (New York: Ballantine Books, 1953). Also in *New York Post*, May 1954; *Seiun* (Japan), 1955; *Gamma*, 1965; *Survival Ship, and Other Stories*, Merril, 1973.

"Stormy Weather." *Startling Stories*, Summer 1954. Also in *The Best of Judith Merril*, Merril, 1976.

"Survival Ship." *Worlds Beyond*, January 1951. Also in *Bold*, 1953; *New Worlds*, 1955; *Tomorrow the Stars*, ed. R.A. Heinlein (Garden City, N.Y.: Doubleday, 1952); *Transformations*, ed. Daniel Roselle (New York: Fawcett Publications, 1973); *Social Education* 37,2 (1973); *Anthropology through SF*, ed. Carol Mason (New York: St. Martin's Press, 1974); *You and Science Fiction*, ed. Bernard Hollister (Skokie, Il.: National Textbook Co., 1976); *Rhetorical Considerations: Essays for Analysis*, ed. Harry Brent and William Lutz (Cambridge, Mass.: Winthrop Publishers, 1977); *Future Scapes: Explorations in Fact and Science Fiction*, ed. Robert Tompkins (Toronto: Methuen, 1977); *Responding to Reading, Level C*, ed. Robert J. Ireland (Don Mills, Ont.: Addison-Wesley, 1983); *Contexts Three*, ed. Glen Sorestad et al. (Toronto: Nelson, 1984); *Il Richiamo* (Milan: La Tartaruga Edizione, 1989).

"That Only a Mother." *Astounding Science Fiction*, June 1948. Also in *World of Wonder*, ed. Fletcher Pratt (New York: Twayne Publishers, 1951); *Children of Wonder*, ed. William Tenn (New York: Simon & Schuster, 1952) and rpt. as *The Outsiders* (Garden City, N.Y.: Permabooks, 1954); *The Damned*, ed. D. Talbot (New York: Lion Library, 1954); *First Flight*, ed. Damon Knight (New York: Lancer Books, 1963); *SF Hall of Fame*, vol. 1, ed. Robert Silverberg (Garden City, N.Y.: Doubleday, 1963); *Transformations*, ed. Daniel Roselle (New York: Fawcett Publications, 1963); *The Hitchhiker*, ed. Lorna Downman (Stockholm, Sweden: Wiksell, 1964); *Social Education* 37,2 (1973); *Introductory Psychology through Science Fiction*, ed. Harvey Katz et al. (New York: Rand McNally, 1974); *Women of Wonder*, ed. Pamela Sargent (New York: Vintage Books, 1974); *Vrouwen in Wonderland* (Amsterdam: De Arbeiderspers, 1974); *Femmes et merveilles*, ed. Pamela Sargent (Paris: Denoel, 1975); *The Best of Judith Merril*, Merril, 1976; *Mujeres y maravillas*, ed. Pamela Sargent (Barcelona: Bruguera, 1977); *Galerij der Giganted*, no. 2, ed. Robert Silverberg (Paris: Elsevier, 1977); *The Road to SF*, no.3, ed. James Gunn (New York: Mentor Books, 1979); *Isaac Asimov Presents the Great Science Fiction Stories*, no. 10, 1948, ed. Isaac Asimov and Martin Greenberg (New York: DAW Books, 1983; *Countdown to Midnight*, ed. H. Bruce Franklin (New York: DAW Books, 1984); *Daughters of Earth and Other Stories*, Merril, 1985; *Aliene, Amazzoni, Astronaute, Mondadori* (Milan, 1990); *Women of Wonder: The Classic Years* (New York: Harcourt Brace, 1995).

"Whoever You Are." *Startling Stories*, December 1952. Also in *Out of Bounds*, Merril, 1960; *Survival Ship, and Other Stories*, Merril, 1973; *The Best of Judith Merril*, Merril, 1976; *Daughters of Earth and Other Stories*, Merril, 1985.

"Wish upon a Star." *Fantasy & Science Fiction*, December 1958. Also in *Fiction* (Paris), 1959; *Survival Ship, and Other Stories*, Merril, 1973; *The Best of Judith Merril*, Merril, 1976; *Daughters of Earth and Other Stories*, Merril, 1985; *Il Richiamo* (Milan: La Tartaruga Edizione, 1989).

"A Woman of the World" (first published as "Rose Sharon"). *Venture*, January 1957.

"Woman's Work Is Never Done." *Future*, March 1951.

SHORT STORIES (WRITTEN UNDER OTHER NAMES)

As Judith Grossman:
"The Golden Fleece." *The Tower*, 1939. Also in *Bakka Magazine*, no. 6, 1977.

As Judy Zissman:
Two stories. *Crack Detective*, 1945–46.

As Eric Thorstein:
Seven stories. *Sports Leader, Western Action, Blue Ribbon Western, Double Action Western, Famous Western*, 1947–48.

As Ernest Hamilton:
Ten stories. *Sports Short Stories, Cowboy, Sports Fiction*, 1947–48.

As James McCreigh (with Frederick Pohl):
"Big Man with the Girls." *Future*, March 1953. Also in *Escape to Earth*, ed. Ivan Howard (New York: Belmont Books, 1963).

As Cyril Judd (with C.M. Kornbluth):
"Sea Change," 1953. *Dynamic Science Fiction*, 1953.

As Rose Sharon:
"The Lady Was a Tramp," 1956, "Woman of the World," 1957, both in *Venture*.

NOTES

1. Of a total of 49 short stories written by Judith Merril over her career, 28 appear in 38 trade anthologies and 11 collections designed as texts for secondary and post-secondary schools, most notably:

The Best American Short Stories 1955, ed. Martha Foley. Boston: Houghton Mifflin, 1956.

A Treasury of Great Science Fiction, ed. Anthony Boucher. Garden City, N.Y.: Doubleday, 1959.

The World of Psychology, ed. G.B. Levitas. New York: George Braziller, 1963.

The Science Fiction Hall of Fame, ed. R. Silverberg. Garden City, N.Y.: Doubleday, 1970.

Other Canadas, ed. John Robert Colombo. Toronto: McGraw-Hill Ryerson, 1979.

Women of Wonder: The Classic Years, ed. P. Sargent. New York: Harcourt Brace, 1995.

2. A total of 33 titles have been translated for publication in French, Dutch, German, Italian, Spanish, Swedish, and/or Japanese.

TRANSLATIONS OF WORKS FROM JAPANESE (BY MERRIL)

"The Sunset, 2217 A.D." (with Tetsu Yano), by Ryu Mitsuse. *Best Science Fiction for 1972*, ed. Frederik Pohl. New York: Ace Books, 1972.

"The Empty Field" (with Kinya Tsuruta), by Mono Kita. *Omega: A Collection of Original Science Fiction Stories*, ed. Roger Elwood. New York: Walker & Co., 1973, Fawcett Gold Medal, 1974.

"The Savage Mouth" (with Tetsu Yano), by Sakyo Komatsu. *Rooms of Paradise*, ed. Lee Harding. Melbourne: Quartet, 1978; New York: St. Martin's Press, 1979.

"The Road to the Sea" (with Tetsu Yano), by Takashi Ishikawa. *Proteus: Voices for the Eighties*, ed. Richard S. McEnroe. New York: Ace Books, 1981.

ANTHOLOGIES EDITED BY MERRIL

Shot in the Dark. New York: Bantam Books, 1950.

Beyond Human Ken. New York: Random House, 1952; also U.K.

Beyond the Barriers of Space and Time. New York: Random House, 1954; also U.K.

Human? New York: Lion Library, 1954.

Galaxy of Ghouls. New York: Lion Library, 1955.

England Swings SF. Garden City, N.Y.: Doubleday, 1968; New York: Ace Books, 1970; also U.K.

Tesseracts. Vancouver: Press Porcépic, 1985.

THE SF ANNUALS EDITED BY MERRIL

A 12-year series, with title and publisher changes. All 12 volumes of the series were also published in Japan, and volumes 5–9 in the U.K.

SF: The Year's Greatest Science Fiction and Fantasy. New York: Dell Originals, 1956-57-58-59; and New York: Gnome Press (as *SF*: 56/57/58/59).

The 5th [and 6th, 7th, 8th, 9th] Annual Year's Best SF. New York: Simon & Schuster, 1960-64; and New York: Dell Publishing Co., 1961-65.

The 10th [and 11th] Annual Year's Best SF. New York: Delacorte, 1965–66; and New York: Dell Publishing Co., 1966–67.

SF 12. New York: Delacorte, 1968; New York: Dell Publishing Co., 1968.

SF: The Best of the Best. New York: Delacorte, 1967; New York: Dell Publishing Co., 1967; also U.K.

Poetry *(1973-85)*

"Auction Pit." *Survival Ship, and Other Stories*, Merril, 1973; *The Best of Judith Merril*, Merril, 1976.

"In the Land of Unblind." *Fantasy & Science Fiction*, October 1974; *The Best of Judith Merril*, Merril, 1976; *Other Canadas*, ed. John Robert Colombo, Toronto: McGraw-Hill Ryerson, 1979; *Daughters of Earth and Other Stories*, Merril, 1985; *Tesseracts 3*, Vancouver: Press Porcépic, 1990.

"Space Is Sparse." *Daughters of Earth and Other Stories*, Merril, 1985.

"Woomers." Unpublished; written for reading at Harbourfront Benefit for Pages Bookstore, Toronto, 1985.

Non-Fiction

CRITICISM *(1952-97)*

More than three hundred pieces of critical writing, ranging from brief commentaries in anthologies through individual book reviews, review columns, introductions, and afterwords to annual summaries of the field and a twelve-thousand-word historical overview of speculative fiction, have appeared in critical journals, books, newspapers, and popular magazines.

CRITICISM, INTRODUCTIONS, REVIEWS, ETC.

"Summation" and story notes. Annually, in *SF: The Year's Best* anthologies, 1959–68.

"Books." From March 1963 to February 1969, regular book review feature for *Fantasy & Science Fiction*; 26 review columns.

"What Do You Mean: Science? Fiction?" A lengthy historical/critical essay, originally published in *Extrapolation* (at that time the journal of the Science Fiction Conference in the Modern Language Association), nos. 7, 8 (May/December 1956); and still widely used in university science fiction courses. Also in *SF—The Other Side of Realism: Essays on Modern Fantasy and Science Fiction*, ed. Thomas D. Clareson (Bowling Green, Ky.: Bowling Green Popular Press, 1971). The essay was also the title piece in a collection of critical writings translated for book publication in Japan. *NW-SF*, vol. 4, Japan; *SF-ni naniga dekimasuka*, ed. Asakura (Tokyo: Shobunsha, 1972).

"Guest Editorial." *Impulse*, November 1966.

"Introduction." *SF: The Best of the Best*. New York: Delacorte, 1967.

"Introduction." *Once and Future Tales from Fantasy and Science Fiction*, ed. Edward L. Ferman. Jacksonville, Il.: Harris-Wolfe, 1968.

"Introduction." *Path into the Unknown: The Best of Soviet Science Fiction*. New York: Delacorte, 1968, and New York: Dell Publishing Co., 1968.

"Introduction." *The Secret Songs*, by Fritz Leiber. London: Rupert Hart-Davis, 1968. Also Shobunsha, 1972; Meulenhoff, 1976.

"Fritz Leiber." *Fantasy & Science Fiction*, July 1969. Also in *The Best from Fantasy & Science Fiction*, ed. Edward L. Ferman (Garden City, N.Y.: Doubleday, 1974).

"Canada's Americans" (book review). *Saturday Night*, August 1971.

"SF-ni naniga dekimasuka" ("SF: What Can You Do with It?"). Collection of critical writings by Judith Merril, ed. and trans. by Hisashi Asakura. Tokyo: Shobunsha, 1972.

"900 Pages (Illustrated) of Tripe" (book review). *The Toronto Star*, 1974.

"Yesterday's Tomorrows" (book review). *The Toronto Star*, June 1974.

"Canadian Science Fiction" (annotated bibliography). *Bakka Magazine*, no. 6, 1977.

"Science Fiction Takes Off." *Weekend Magazine*, 1977.

"Readable SF" (book review). *The Globe and Mail*, June 25, 1977.

"In Memory Yet Green" (book review). *The Globe and Mail*, June 9, 1979.

"A Memoir and Appreciation." *The Science Fiction of Mark Clifton*, ed. Barry N. Malzberg and Martin H. Greenberg. Carbondale: Southern Illinois University Press, 1980.

"Women in SF" (an annotated bibliography). *Canadian Woman's Studies/Les Cahiers de la Femme*, 1981.

"Afterword." *Ark of Ice: Canadian Futurefiction*, ed. Leslie Choyce. Halifax, N.S.: Pottersfield Press, 1992.

"Emancipation Proclamation." *Gummitch and Friends*, by Fritz Leiber. Hampton Falls, N.H.: Donald M. Grant Publisher, 1992.

"Foreword." *Out of This World: Canadian Science Fiction and Fantasy Literature*, ed. Andrea Paradis. Kingston, Ont.: Quarry Press, 1995; and *Visions d'autres mondes*, Westmount, Que.: Editions Robert Davies, 1995.

OTHER NON-FICTION

"Mars—New World Waiting." *Marvel Science Fiction*, August 1951.

"The Hydra Club." *Marvel Science Fiction*, November 1951.

"Theodore Sturgeon." *Fantasy & Science Fiction*, September 1962. Also in *The Best from Fantasy & Science Fiction*, ed. Edward L. Ferman (Garden City, N.Y.: Doubleday, 1974).

"Japan: Hai!" *OSFIC*, no. 24, 1970.

"Science: Myth Tomorrow, Magic Yesterday." *Issues & Events*, February 1972.

"Basil Tomatoes à la Ipsy Wipsy." *Cooking out of This World*, ed. Anne McCaffrey. New York: Ballantine Books, 1973.

"The Three Futures of Eve." *The Canadian*, Sept. 11, 1976.

"Close Encounters of a Monstrous Kind." *Weekend Magazine*, May 6, 1978.

"Beverly Glen Copeland." *Canadian Woman's Studies/Les Cahiers de la Femme*, 1978.

"Questions Unasked, Issues Unaddressed." *Perspectives on Natural Resources—Symposium II*. Peterborough, Ont.: Sir Sandford Fleming College, 1979.

"The Future of Happiness." *Chatelaine*, January 1979. Also in *Daughters of Earth and Other Stories*, Merril, 1985.

"Jamaica: A View from the Beach." *Departures*, April 1981.

"The Crazies Are Dying." *NOW* (Toronto), Sept. 25, 1986.

"Public Disservice." *Quill & Quire*, Toronto, 1994.

"Message to Some Martians." *Visions of Mars*, CD-Rom, *Virtual Reality Laboratories*, 1994. Also in *Witness to Wilderness*, Vancouver, 1994.

Media Adaptations

DRAMATIZATIONS/ADAPTATIONS FOR PERFORMANCE

"Atomic Attack." Dramatization of *Shadow on the Hearth* for *Motorola TV Theatre*, ABC, New York, 1954.

"Survival Ship" and "The Shrine of Temptation." Adapted for reading aloud, CBC-Radio (1974) and Theatre Passe Muraille, Toronto, (1976); Caedmon Records (1978).

"Whoever You Are." Adapted with Charles Dewar; dramatized on CBC-Radio, *Ideas*, March 1974.

"Headspace." Adapted with Paul Kelman as a stage play based on "Connection Completed," "The Lady Was a Tramp," and "The Land of Unblind," for Theatre Passe Muraille, Toronto, 1978.

RADIO AND TV DOCUMENTARIES

(Scriptwriter, Interviewer, and Narrator)

CBC-Radio *Ideas*, *Kaleidoscope*, and Radio International. 25.5 hours of documentaries, 1971–75:

a ten-hour series, "Japan: Future Probable"

a five-hour series, "How to Face Doomsday without Really Dying"

fourteen individual programs of various lengths, including:

"How to Think Science Fiction," *Radio Schools*, *Kaleidoscope*, four half-hours, 1971–72

"Women of Japan," *Ideas*, one hour, 1972

"What Limits?" *Ideas*, one hour, 1973

"Growing up in Japan," *Radio Schools*, *Kaleidoscope*, five half-hours, 1973

"Science Fiction Special," Radio International, two hours, 1975

"To Make a World," *Ideas*, one hour, 1975

"Apple Bay," *Ideas*, one hour, 1975

"Space Is Sparse," CBC-Radio

readings from Elizabeth Smart's journals.

TVOntario (TVO), 108 mini-documentaries, three to seven minutes each, following broadcast episodes of *Dr. Who*, 1978–81.

CBC Arts National, readings from Emily Carr's journals, 1987.

Lectures

"Living in the Information Society." Keynote Speaker, York University Conference, Toronto, 1961.

Secondary Universe Conference (SeCon) I. Keynote Speaker, 1968.

Lecturer in Science Fiction. University of Toronto, 1970–71.

"Contemporary Mythology." McGill University, Montreal, 1972.

"Science and Myth." Sir George Williams University, Montreal, 1972.

"Privacy and Publicy." SeCon IV, 1972.

Symposium on Popular Culture. State University of New York (SUNY)-Buffalo, 1973.

Interdisciplinary Course on Extraterrestrial Life. University of Toronto, 1973, 1974.

"History of Atheism" Course. University of Toronto, 1974.

Intermedia Presentation. Erindale College, Mississauga, Ont., 1974.

Hart House Library Committee. University of Toronto, 1976.

MENSA International Congress. Banquet Speaker, Toronto, 1976; Dalhousie University Library School, Halifax, 1977.

"Living with Technology." Rensselaer Polytechnic Institute, Albany, N.Y., 1977; Ontario Institute for Studies in Education (OISE) Group for Research on Women, 1977; Festival of Women in the Arts, Centennial Community College.

Canadian Authors' Association. Conference Speaker, Toronto, 1979.

"Writers Forum." SUNY-Brockport, 1979.

Slide show on "Dream Cities." Heritage Canada Foundation Conference, Winnipeg, 1980.

"The Future of Women and Work." "Bread and Roses" Symposium, Ottawa, 1982.

"Write-On" Conference. Atkinson College, York University, Toronto, 1983.

"Feminism and Culture." Partisan Gallery, Toronto, 1983.

"Arts and the Future." Matrix/Midland Festival, Michigan, 1983.

"Women and Words" Conference. Vancouver, 1983.

"Facing Nuclear Holocaust." Temple University, Philadelphia, 1984.

"Science Fiction Treatments of Aging." American Psychological Association Conference, Toronto, 1984.

"Bio-Ethics in Science Fiction." Westminster Institute/ London Public Library, London, 1985.

"The Informal Economy." Couchiching Conference, Orillia, Ont., 1986.

Vancouver International Writers' Festival. Featured Performer, 1988.

Vancouver International Writers' Festival. Speaker, 1995.

Memberships

ORGANIZATIONS (FOUNDER, DIRECTOR)

Founder, Hydra Club, New York (science fiction professionals), 1947.

Founder, Milford Science Fiction Writers' Conference, 1956; Director, to 1960.

Organizer/Program Chair, Rochdale College Summer Festival, 1969.

Director, "Spaceship Earth" Seminar Series, Toronto, 1970.

Founder/Donor, The Merril Collection of Science Fiction, Speculation, and Fantasy (formerly The Spaced Out Library), 1970; Consultant, 1970–97.

Program Chair, SeCon IV (Fourth Annual Meeting of the Science Fiction Research Association), Toronto, 1972.

Program Organizer, "Out of This World." Reading Series, Harbourfront, Toronto, 1980.

Co-Producer, Writers' Union of Canada Science Fiction Readings at Amiga Theatre, EXPO 1986, Vancouver.

Organizer, First Annual Canadian Science Fiction Writers' Workshop, 1986.

Founder, Hydra North.

Founding Member, Science Fiction Canada.

Founding Member, Canadian Science Fiction Foundation.

Appendix II

Some of the People in
Judith Merril's Life

MILTON ACORN (1923–86)—Best known as Canada's "people's poet." A carpenter by trade, and a left-wing activist who was at various times a member of the Communist Party, the Trotskyists, and the Canadian Liberation Movement. His books of poetry include *I've Tasted My Blood*, *More Poems for People*, and *The Island Means Minago* (winner of the Governor General's Literary Award in 1975). He married poet Gwendolyn MacEwen in 1962.

BRIAN ALDISS—Prolific writer and anthologist, closely associated during the 1960s with the new wave in science fiction and the U.K. magazine *New Worlds*. His increasingly unconventional works include *The Saliva Tree*, the three "Helliconia" books, and several works of non-fiction.

VALERIA ALIA—Poet, artist, scholar, and journalist, born in the Bronx. She was the first Distinguished Professor of Canadian culture at Western Washington University, Bellingham. One of her fields of research has been the representation of Inuit people in the media; as a professor at the Centre for Research in Media and Cultural Studies, University of Sunderland, U.K., she now specializes in ways of challenging racial stereotyping in the media.

MILTON AMGOTT—Judy's lawyer and friend in New York City.

POUL ANDERSON (1926–2001)—Popular science fiction writer of over one hundred books, including *Genesis*, *The Boat of a Million Years*, *The Enemy Stars*, and *Three Hearts and Three Lions*. A former president of the *Science Fiction and Fantasy Writers of America*, he has won three Nebula Awards and seven Hugo Awards, as well as being honoured for lifetime achievement.

ISAAC ASIMOV (1920–92)—Perhaps the best-known name in science fiction. Asimov was born in Russia and brought to the United States at the age of three. He began publishing his SF stories in 1939, at the age of nineteen. He was an early member of the Futurian Society of New York, and his vast collection of works includes the "Robot" series, the "Foundation" series, the story "Nightfall" (considered by some to be the best science fiction story ever written), and much non-fiction.

MARGARET ATWOOD—Renowned Canadian novelist and poet. Atwood's books include *Alias Grace*, *A Handmaid's Tale*, *The Edible Woman*, and *Surfacing*. Her novel *The Blind Assassin* won England's Booker Prize.

HILARY BAILEY—U.K. writer of numerous science fiction stories, but perhaps best known for her mainstream fiction, which includes *All the Days of My Life*. She was associated with the New Wave movement in U.K. science fiction throughout the 1960s and into the 1970s. She was married to writer Michael Moorcock (1962–78), and is the un-credited co-author of their novel *The Black Corridor*.

IAN BALLANTINE—New York editor who went from helping to found Penguin U.S. to founding Bantam Books and then, in 1952, Ballantine Books, which became a leading and prestigious publisher of science fiction novels. Ballantine is credited with inventing the "mass-market hard-cover," including books by the likes of Shirley MacLaine, Lee Iacocca, and Chuck Yeager.

J.G. BALLARD—U.K. writer whose experience in a Japanese civilian POW camp in Shanghai 1942–45 formed the basis for his popular (non-SF) novel *Empire of the Sun*. He started publishing science fiction novels in 1956. His writing, heavily inspired by the Surrealist painters, includes the short story collection *The Terminal Beach* and the novel *Crash*.

STAFFORD BEER—Expert in management (operational research and social systems) and effective organization (cybernetics). In July 1971 he visited Chile on the invitation of President Salvador Allende to develop a new cybernetic approach to the organization and regulation of the social economy. He has written numerous articles and books, and is president of the World Organization of Systems and Cybernetics (Paris).

JAMES BLISH—U.S. science fiction writer, married to writer Virginia Kidd for sixteen years, and one of the founders of the Milford Science Fiction Writers' Conference. He is best known for his "Cities in Space" series. His "Star Trek" novels were based on the television scripts.

ANTHONY BOUCHER—The pen name of William Anthony Parker White, the founding co-editor (with J. Francis McComas) of New York's literary *Magazine of Fantasy & Science Fiction* (1949), as well as a mystery writer, critic, and anthologist. He is perhaps best-known for his story "The Quest for Saint Aquin," his stint as mysteries editor for *The New York Times*, and his yearly *Best from Fantasy & Science Fiction* anthologies.

WALTER BRADBURY—The science fiction editor at Doubleday during much of the period (1940s to 1960s) when Judy and her contemporaries were most active.

JOHN BRUNNER—British writer of SF and thrillers, whose novels *Stand on Zanzibar* and *The Shockwave Rider* are credited with paving the way for the cyber-punk movement because he discussed topics such as computer hacking and genetic engineering and described various bits of software that run by themselves as tapeworms or worms. Brunner died in 1995.

OCTAVIA BUTLER—One of the top African-American science fiction writers. Her novels and short stories combine anarchistic future societies with highly intellectual explorations of the alien perspective. Her novels include *Patternmaster*, her "Xenogenesis" trilogy—*Dawn: Xenogenesis, Adulthood Rites,* and *Imago*—and *Parable of the Sower.* In 1995 Butler was awarded a "genius grant" from the MacArthur Foundation for her unique synthesis of science fiction, mysticism, mythology, and African-American spiritualism.

HARRY CAMPBELL—Chief librarian of the Toronto Public Library system, 1956–78. Campbell was responsible for obtaining Judy's book collection (the Spaced Out Library) for the Toronto Public Library, establishing what would eventually be called the Merril Collection of Science Fiction, Speculation and Fantasy.

JOHN W. CAMPBELL (1910–71)—Science fiction writer (pseudonym Don A. Stuart) who edited the magazine *Astounding Science Fiction* (later renamed *Analog Science Fiction and Fact*) for thirty-four years. As editor of *Astounding* he was credited with "discovering" many science fiction authors, including Isaac Asimov, Robert Heinlein, Arthur C. Clarke, Poul Anderson, L. Sprague de Camp, Jack Williamson, and Ray Bradbury.

MARK CLIFTON (1906–63)—U.S. writer, long fascinated by extrasensory perception. He produced three novels and a couple of dozen stories for magazines, mostly *Astounding.* Clifton won a Hugo Award in 1955 for *They'd Rather Be Right* (with Frank Riley).

THEODORE COGSWELL—U.S. writer, perhaps best known for his short stories, although his most noted work was the novella "The Spectre General." His one novel was the historical first "Star Trek" entry, *Spock: Messiah!* co-authored with Charles Spano.

ORNETTE COLEMAN—New York jazz musician born in 1930 who played alto saxophone, trumpet, violin, and tenor saxophone. Since the late 1950s, Coleman has been teaching the world new ways of listening to music. At first, his revolutionary musical ideas concerning atonal jazz were so controversial he found it difficult to get public performance opportunities. In 1959, with the release of his debut album, "Something Else!" he ushered in a new era in jazz history.

JOHN ROBERT COLOMBO—Directly responsible for over 135 books, most of them about Canada and things Canadian, including *Canadian Quotations, Ghost Stories of Canada, Colombo's Famous Lasting Words, 1000 Questions about Canada,* and *The Penguin Book of Canadian Jokes.* He is known as Canada's Master Gatherer for his reference books and Canada's Mr. Mystery for his books relating matters of the supernatural and paranormal.

JOHN CLUTE—Born in Toronto in 1940, graduated from New York University in 1963, and moved to England in 1968. His books include *The Disinheriting Party,* the Hugo-winning *Encyclopedia of Science Fiction* (which he co-authored), and *The Encyclopedia of Fantasy* (with John Grant). With David Pringle and others he edited five "Interzone" anthologies, and with Candas Jane Dorsey he co-edited the anthology *Tesseracts 8.* A recent novel is *Appleseed.*

CHANDLER DAVIS—Since 1962 a professor of mathematics (now professor emeritus) at the University of Toronto. Davis publishes research articles on mathematics, writes science fiction, and has authored several essays, such as "The Purge," in *A Century of Mathematics in America* and *Science for Good or Ill,* a booklet in the Waging Peace Series (1990). In the late 1950s Davis was fired from the University of Michigan and served a sentence in federal prison for refusing to testify before the House Un-American Activities Committee.

The group of early science fiction writers known as the Futurian Society of New York. From left: Lester del Rey, Evelyn Harrison, Harry Harrison, Isaac Asimov, Judith, Ann Pohl (in Judith's tummy), Frederik Pohl, Poul Anderson, L. Sprague de Camp, P Schuyler Miller, New York, 1950. *Courtesy of the Merril estate*

Milford Science Fiction Writers' Conference. From left: R. Garrett, T. Thomas, unknown, Anthony Boucher, Mildred Clingerman, Judith, Ted Cogswell, James Blish, Phil Klass, Damon Knight, Robert Silverberg, unknown. Milford, Pennsylvania, circa 1958.
Courtesy of the Merril estate

GARRY DAVIS—Established a self-proclaimed World Government of World Citizens (1953) based on the notion of a borderless world and global citizenship. The organization claims that there are over 950,000 world citizens and is known for its "World Passport," which is granted to refugees as well as supporting citizens of the world. See <www.worldgovernment.org>.

SAMUEL R. (CHIP) DELANY—Publishing since 1962, and best known for the novels *Babel-17*, *Empire Star*, and *Dahlgren*. In the 1990s he published several book-length collections of non-fiction memoirs and literary criticism, including *The Motion of Light and Water: Sex and Science Fiction in the East Village*, *Silent Interviews: On Language, Race, Sex, Science Fiction and Comics*, and *Longer Views: Extended Essays*.

LOUISE DENNYS—Came to Canada from the U.K. in 1972 and worked in various capacities within the book-selling industry until 1978. At that time she joined with Malcolm Lester and Eve Orpen (Lester & Orpen) to form Lester & Orpen Dennys. Dennys concentrated on literary fiction, as exemplified by the company's international fiction list. In 1991 Dennys moved to Knopf Canada and became its publisher and the vice-president of Random House Canada.

PENNY DICKENS—Long-time executive director of The Writers' Union of Canada (TWUC).

THOMAS DISCH—Author of over a dozen novels, five story collections, seven volumes of poetry, two books of criticism, and more. Disch has been publishing since the early 1960s. His best-known SF novels are the critically acclaimed *Camp Concentration* and *334*. His book of SF criticism, *The Dreams Our Stuff Is Made Of*, won both the Hugo and Locus Awards.

CANDAS JANE DORSEY—Edmonton-born author of six books (including *Black Wine*, *Hardwired Angel*, and *Vanilla and Other Stories*), and several volumes of poetry; her collected short stories can be found in *Machine Sex and Other Stories*. A recent book is *A Paradigm of Earth*. She co-edited *Tesseracts 8* with John Clute, *Tesseracts 3* with Gerry Truscott, and the "Prairie Fire WorldCon Issue" in 1994. She is publisher of Tesseract Books (SF) and River Books (literary).

HARLAN ELLISON—Science fiction writer who has produced pulp gangland dramas, magical realism novels, and political criticism. As of 1994 he had published some thirteen hundred stories, essays, scripts, and reviews and written or edited seventy-five books.

CAROL EMSHWILLER—Magical realist and feminist best known for her books *Carmen Dog* and *The Start of the End of It All*. A recent novel is *Leaping Man Hill*, the sequel to *Ledoyt*. She teaches writing at New York University.

ED EMSHWILLER—Went into film from a background in painting and science fiction illustration, often creating cover art for pulp magazines. He married author Carol Fried (later Emshwiller) in 1949 and made his first two films in 1959.

MARIAN ENGEL (1933–85)—Toronto author of seven novels, two collections of short stories, and numerous articles and essays. She won Canada's Governor General's Award for her novel *Bear* (1976) and played a major role in the establishment of the Writers' Union of Canada.

MIGNON EBERHART (1899–1996)—Educated at Nebraska's Wesleyan University and renowned for writing novels that mix mystery and romance. She was awarded the Grand Master Award from the Mystery Writers of America in 1971. Her sleuths were usually from rather ordinary backgrounds and almost always women, in the mould of her first detective heroine, Sarah Keate.

EDWARD FERMAN—Became editor and publisher of *The Magazine of Fantasy & Science Fiction* in January 1966, following his father's resignation; he remained in the position for over twenty-five years, during which time he garnered seven Hugo Awards for best magazine or best editor. He sold the magazine in 2000 to Gordon Van Gelder.

ELLEN GODFREY—Canadian author Godfrey started Press Porcépic in Vancouver, B.C., with her husband. Since 1996 she has been writing full-time. She has published several mystery novels under her own name and "ghosted" a series of mysteries under a pseudonym.

PHYLLIS GOTLIEB—Toronto novelist and poet considered by many to be the "mother of Canadian Science Fiction." Her books include *O Master Caliban!*, *A Judgement Of Dragons*, *Son of the Morning and Other Stories*, *Emperor, Swords and Pentacles*, *The Kingdom of Cats*, and *Violent Stars*. Gotlieb's poetry has been nominated for a Governor General's Award, Canada's most prestigious literary honour.

ARNOLD HANO—Editor-in-chief of Bantam books when Judith Merril's first anthology, *Shot in the Dark*, was published. Judith was working there at the time, as a mystery editor.

DAVID G. HARTWELL—Senior editor of Tor/Forge Books, publisher of the *New York Review of Science Fiction*, chairman of the board of the World Fantasy Convention, and an administrator of the Philip K. Dick Award. He is the author of *Age of Wonders* and the editor of several anthologies, including *The Dark Descent*, *Masterpieces of Fantasy and Enchantment*, *The World Treasury of Science Fiction*, *Year's Best SF*, and *Visions of Wonder*.

ROBERT A. HEINLEIN (1907–88)—Wrote speculative fiction starting in his late twenties after he retired from the Navy. His fiction often anticipated scientific and technical advances, such as the atomic bomb and the waterbed. His novel *Stranger in a Strange Land* became a hippie handbook.

VIRGINIA KIDD—U.S. writer and, later, literary agent. She has represented a wide range of feminist science fiction writers, including Judith Merril, James Tiptree Jr., Ursula Le Guin, and Carol Emshwiller.

PHIL KLASS—Writer, under the pseudonym William Tenn, of many short stories throughout the late 1940s and early 1950s, including the chilling "Down among the Dead Men" (1954), dealing with the use of reanimated corpses as front-line troops in a savage interstellar war. Tenn's sole full-length novel, *Of Men and Monsters*, deals with an alien-occupied Earth in which humans live, mouse-like, in the walls of the aliens' dwellings.

HELENE KLODAWSKY—Quebec documentary director of several movies, including *What If... A Film about Judith Merril*, *Shoot and Cry*, *No Time to Stop: Women Immigrants*, and *Motherland*.

DAMON KNIGHT—Began writing and editing science fiction in 1941, at the age of nineteen. His novels include *A for Anything* and *Why Do Birds*. His non-fiction book, *The Futurians*, tells the story of the group of SF writers who lived in New York City during the 1940s. He is a founder of the prominent Milford Science Fiction Writers' Conference and the Science Fiction and Fantasy Writers of America association and the Nebula awards. He is married to writer Kate Wilhelm.

CYRIL KORNBLUTH—Member of the Futurians who published a number of short stories between 1940–42. In 1952 he collaborated on two science fiction novels with Judith Merril and a few years later wrote three science fiction novels and two non-SF books with Frederik Pohl. Kornbluth died prematurely at the age of thirty-five in 1958, at the height of his writing career.

DENNIS LEE—Toronto poet who helped found and served as editor for the House of Anansi Press. His overtly political collection *Civil Elegies and Other Poems* won the Governor General's Award in 1972. Lee is perhaps best-known for his children's books such as *Alligator Pie* and *Garbage Delight*.

STANISLAV LEM—Polish science fiction writer, one of the few SF writers working in a language other than English who has had the results widely available in English. He is perhaps best known for the novel *Solaris* and his series about the adventures of Ijon Tichy, intrepid explorer of satirically absurd worlds.

WILLY LEY (1906–69)—Rocket scientist and, later, science fiction writer. In pre-war Germany he was an important player in rocketry experimentation. When the Nazis established a foothold in rocketry development in the mid-1930s, Ley fled to the United States. He turned to writing in order to popularize the idea of rocketry and space travel as serious scientific subjects. He died a couple of weeks before the launch of the Apollo 11 moon flight in 1969.

JON LOMBERG—One of the world's best-known astronomical artists and a space science journalist. His work includes the cover of Carl Sagan's novel *Contact* and the most accurate painting of the Milky Way galaxy ever made. He has been associated with the search for extraterrestrial intelligence (SETI) since 1977, when he was the design director on the team that created the Voyager Interstellar Record, messages for extraterrestrials and destined to travel in interstellar space forever. He was project director for the CD-ROM *Visions of Mars*.

ROBERT "DOC" LOWNDES—U.S. science fiction writer who started writing in 1940 under various assumed names. Lowndes edited several magazines and collaborated on novels and stories with James Blish and Donald A. Wollheim during the 1940s and 1950s.

GWENDOLYN MACEWEN—Canadian author of twelve books of poetry, two novels, two collections of short fiction, drama for radio and theatre, translations and children's drama, recipient of two Governor General's Awards for Poetry (*The Shadow-Maker* and *Afterworlds*). She died in 1987, at the age of forty-six.

KATHERINE MACLEAN—One of the earlier U.S. women SF writers; best known for her short stories, many of which have been anthologized in two collections, *The Diploids* and *The Trouble with You Earth People*. Her postgraduate background in psychology and interest in telepathy greatly influenced her hard science fiction writings.

JOYCE MARSHALL—Among the most renowned translators of Quebec literature, Marshall's own writing explores the creative lives of Canadian writers Gwendolyn MacEwen, Gabrielle Roy, and Adele Wiseman. She has translated many of Roy's novels, and edited *The Selected Letters of Marie de l'Incarnation*. She is also a founding member of the Literary Translators' Association of Canada.

SCOTT MEREDITH—Founded and ran the Scott Meredith Literary Agency from 1946 to 1993. He engineered early book deals for many well-known SF writers, including Marion Zimmer Bradley, Ellery Queen, and Arthur C. Clarke.

JOHNNY MICHEL—Early member of the Futurians in New York, Michel introduced Judy to the group.

WALTER MILLER—Best-known for the novels *A Canticle for Leibowitz* and *The Darfsteller* (both of which won Hugo Awards). Miller studied engineering at university and converted to Catholicism at the age of twenty-five, after flying combat missions during World War II. He wrote profusely during the 1950s, exploring religion, war, and social issues.

MICHAEL MOORCOCK—Well known for his heroic fantasy novels, such as *Elric of Melniboné*, *Warrior of Mars*, and *Hawkmoon*, which featured the recurring character of the Eternal Champion. By the late 1960s his writing was prolific—he often produced several novels a year. He edited *New Worlds* magazine for many years, and brought many New Wave writers into the spotlight, including J.G. Ballard, Samuel R. Delany, and Thomas M. Disch.

ROBERT PRIEST—Canadian poet and songwriter. His works include *The Mad Hand* (1988), *Scream Blue Living* (1992), and *Knights of the Endless Day* (1993). Much of his work is written for children or to be performed out loud. The work for adults is often sensuous, politically engaging, and humorous.

FREDERIK POHL—A prolific writer living in Chicago who has authored dozens of science fiction and non-fiction books since he began writing at the age of seventeen. He was married to Judith Merril from 1949 to 1952. Particularly in the early years of his career, Pohl tried out the roles of critic, literary agent, teacher, and book and magazine editor before settling on writer. He later married Carol Pohl and then professor Elizabeth Anne Hull.

SPIDER ROBINSON—A science fiction writer since 1972, Robinson was born in the United States and immigrated to Canada. He is the recipient of numerous awards for his many novels, which include *Starseed*, written with his wife Jeanne Robinson, and *Callahan's Key*.

RICHARD ROHMER—Born in 1924, a former commander-in-chief of the Canadian Forces Reserve, chancellor of the University of Windsor, lawyer, and friend of the wealthy and powerful. Rohmer is a popular Canadian novelist, with his political stories regularly becoming best-sellers. His novel *Referendum* dramatizes the possible effects of Quebec separation.

JOANNA RUSS—science fiction author, perhaps best known for her novel *The Female Man*. More recent works include the novels *We Who Are About To ...*, *The Two of Them*, short story collections *The Zanzibar Cat* and *The Hidden Side of the Moon*, and essay collections *How to Write Like a Woman* and *Puritans and Perverts*.

HANS STEFAN SANTESSON—U.S. editor who headed *Fantastic Universe* magazine during the late 1950s. He edited several anthologies and later the U.S. version of *New Worlds* magazine (founded by Michael Moorcock and others in the U.K.).

LARRY SHAW—A Futurian who is now primarily known for his position as editor of *Infinite Science Fiction*, one of the most prominent science fiction magazines in the 1950s. Later he edited the science fiction line for Lancer Books, including a handful of anthologies, and then worked as editor for Dell Publishing Co.

ROBIN SKELTON—Born in England, and author of more than one hundred published works of poetry, fiction, non-fiction, art criticism, and biography. He immigrated to Canada in 1963 and became a professor at the University of Victoria. Co-founder of the *Malahat Review*, he is also a practising Wiccan Witch.

ELIZABETH SMART (1913–86)—Canadian novelist and poet, best known for the novel *By Grand Central Station I Sat Down and Wept*.

L. JEROME (JAY) STANTON—Assistant editor of John Campbell's *Astounding* in 1946 and 1947, and author of articles and reviews for the magazine. In the 1950s he was part of the Hydra Club. Stanton eventually drifted away from science fiction and made his living as a technical writer. He died in 1993.

THEODORE STURGEON (1918–85)—Sold his first story, "Heavy Insurance," in 1938 for five dollars to McClure's Syndicate for publication in newspapers. In the early years he wrote historical, mystery, and western novels, like many of his peers. Later he shifted to science fiction. Many of his short stories were adapted to television scripts, including several for Star Trek. His sensual writing led him to being both blamed and credited for bringing sex into SF.

WILL SYKORA (1913–94)—An active participant in early SF fandom in New York. Months after establishing the five-member New York City chapter of the Science Fiction League in January 1935, Sykora, along with Johnny Michel and Donald Wollheim, was expelled by League president Hugo Gernsback for criticizing his administration and non-payment of debts to authors. He was one of the people who ran the First World Science Fiction Convention held in New York in 1939, and in his role as "enforcer" he expelled the Futurians (Wollheim, Pohl, Kornbluth, and others) from the convention in the "Exclusion Act."

LORNA TOOLIS—Head librarian at Toronto's Merril Collection of Science Fiction, Speculation and Fantasy (formerly the Spaced Out Library). A personal friend of Judith Merril, she edited the anthology *Tesseracts 4* with her husband and SF writer Michael Skeet.

ÉLISABETH VONARBURG—Originally from France, moved to Quebec in 1973. She was editor of *Solaris* for eleven years and helped launch the careers of many of Quebec's best SF authors. She is also responsible for the first Québécois SF convention in 1979. She is best known for her novels *In the Mothers' Land*, *The Reluctant Voyagers*, and *The Silent City*.

BARRY WELLMAN—University of Toronto professor who studies community, communication, and computer and social networks. He founded a professional society called the International Network for Social Network Analysis. He has written many articles and is also the co-editor of three books: *Living through Networks: Using Personal Communities*, *Networks in the Global Village: Life in Contemporary Communities*, and *Social Structures: A Network Approach*.

KATE WILHELM—author of novels and short stories. Her first novel was a mystery, published in 1963, and in recent years she has returned to writing mysteries, although she is still better known for her thoughtful science fiction, including *Mrs. Bagley Goes to Mars* and *Forever Yours, Anna*. She is married to author Damon Knight.

DONALD A. WOLLHEIM (1914-90)—U.S. editor, anthologist, and writer and a 1938 founder of the Futurians. A number of novels appeared under the pseudonym of David Grinnell. He worked for Avon Books (1947–52) and Ace Books (1952–71) before founding his own publishing house, DAW Books, in 1972.

DIRK WYLIE—The pseudonym for Joseph H. Dockweiler, a member of the Futurians group who wrote several stories with Frederik Pohl and Cyril Kornbluth. He died very young, after an injury during World War II.

ROBERT ZEND (1929–85)—Experimental writer and the author of *Nicolette*, *Daymares*, *From Zero to One*, *My Friend, Jeronimo*, *Arbormundi*, and *Beyond Labels*.

SOURCES: *The Encyclopedia of Science Fiction*, ed. John Clute and Peter Nicholls; the Who's Who in the Writers' Union of Canada directory; the University of Calgary's "Canadian Poets Online" website <poets.ca>; the Science Fiction Writers of America's website <sfwa.org>; the Writers' Union of Canada's website <twuc.org>; <worldgovernment.org>; George Willick's Spacelight website <www.eyeneer.com>; <strangehorizons.com>; <fictionwise.com>; and various other websites.

Index